AUTO RECIPE 300
KENMORE
MICRO/CONVECTION
COOKING

Sears

A Benjamin **b** Company Book

Managing Editor: Virginia Schomp
Editor: Barbara Varnum
Production Assistants: Paul Pressman, Pat Drew, Susan Jablonski,
Director Consumer Education & Services: Thelma Pressman
Chief Home Economist: Thelma Pressman
Director, Recipe Testing: Betty Sullivan
Consulting Home Economists: Carol Peterson, Alice Stoltzner
Project Manager: James L. Wilson
Art & Design: Thomas C. Brecklin
Typography: A-Line, Milwaukee
Photography: Teri Sandison

USER INSTRUCTIONS

PRECAUTIONS TO AVOID POSSIBLE EXPOSURE TO EXCESSIVE MICROWAVE ENERGY

(a) DO NOT ATTEMPT to operate this oven with the door open since open-door operation can result in harmful exposure to microwave energy. It is important not to defeat or tamper with the safety interlocks.

(b) DO NOT PLACE any object between the oven front face and the door or allow soil or cleaner residue to accumulate on sealing surfaces.

(c) DO NOT OPERATE the oven if it is damaged. It is particularly important that the oven door close properly and that there is no damage to the:
>   (1) DOOR (bent)
>   (2) HINGES AND LATCHES (broken or loosened)
>   (3) DOOR SEALS AND SEALING SURFACES

(d) THE OVEN SHOULD NOT BE ADJUSTED OR REPAIRED BY ANYONE EXCEPT PROPERLY QUALIFIED SERVICE PERSONNEL.

Library of Congress Catalog Card Number: 81-65333
ISBN: 0-87502-127-1
Published by The Benjamin Company, Inc.
One Westchester Plaza
Elmsford, New York 10523
Printed in Japan
10 9 8 7 6 5 4
S Revised 10/1/84

CONTENTS

What's It All About?

You are about to enter an exciting new world of automatic cooking that combines the best of two principles into three techniques: the incredible speed of microwave, the efficiency and speed of convection, or a combination of both methods — all in a single cavity unit. In addition, there is an important plus: here, for the first time, is a micro/convection oven that has an entire cookbook preset in its computer memory. You don't have to calculate cooking time or select the proper cooking method for any of the 300 recipes in the book. The oven will automatically change from one system to another, to provide the best cooking techniques required for each recipe.

A Cooking School

We have selected both traditional and new recipes that will show off this oven to its best advantage. But before you try a recipe, please read these introductory chapters carefully. You will find a complete "cooking school" with how-to pictures and illustrations to guide you. There is nothing complicated about using this oven. All you need is a little understanding of the special possibilities it offers. Just take a few minutes to read the instructions and acquaint yourself with the principles and techniques involved in micro/convection automatic cooking.

How Does It Work?

First, let's look at convection. Convection cooking isn't new. Restaurant kitchens have enjoyed the advantages of this cooking technique for years. It is an energy-efficient cooking mode and is similar to your conventional oven in operation. Unlike conventional ovens, convection ovens have a fan that assists circulation of the heated air. This constant movement of heated air strips away the cooler air that surrounds food, again and again. To provide a hot, dry environment, you should select the convection method for items like soufflés, bread, angel food cakes, cookies, pizza, and for broiling meat and fish. No changes are required to adapt your favorite oven recipes to convection cooking. All heatproof cookware should be used in convection cooking. The notation *"Oven cooks: convec"* indicates convection-only cooking.

In microwave cooking, microwaves travel directly to the food without heating the air. Ordinary electrical current is converted into high frequency microwaves, just like radio and television waves. A stirrer-fan distributes the microwaves evenly throughout the oven. Microwaves are waves of *energy*, not heat. They will do one of three things: they will be reflected by metal surfaces; they will pass right through certain materials; or, they will be absorbed.

Glass, pottery, paper, and most plastics allow the waves to pass through. The see through panel in the oven door is made of a specially prepared material that contains a metal screen. The metal screen reflects the microwaves, yet enables you to observe the food as it cooks. The waves cannot penetrate the screen.

The moisture in food absorbs the microwaves and creates friction through the movement of the molecules. This molecular motion generates heat somewhat the way heat is generated when you rub your hands together rapidly. Cooking begins from the outside and the interior then cooks by conducted heat, in much the same way conventional cooking operates. The microwave method is the best choice for preparing sauces, vegetables, poached eggs or fish, and

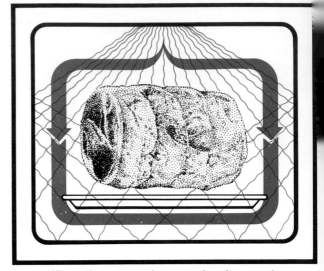

When the convection or micro/convection cooking methods are used, hot air (red) is circulated constantly. Microwaves (blue) are also used with the micro/convection method. The oven is hot when both methods are used.

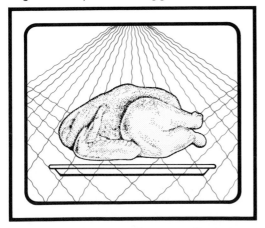

Microwaves bounce off oven walls and are absorbed by food. The oven is usually cool in microwave cooking but may be hot if another method was used recently.

for reheating, defrosting, or sautéing. No metal cookware may be used but glass, paper, and most plastics can be used. The notation *"Oven cooks: micro"* indicates microwave cooking.

In combination cooking, the convection and microwave systems contribute their best features in cooking the food. The convection system heats, browns, and dries the surface of the food for crisping. The microwave system speeds cooking and prevents dehydration. Combination cooking is best for roasting poultry, for quiches, some pies, and other food. Special considerations apply in selecting cookware; see pages 15-19. The notation *"Oven cooks: micro/convec"* indicates combination cooking.

Look What You Can Do!

Now you have an oven that can do just about everything. Here is an array of food that illustrates the results provided by the wide range of cooking techniques available with this oven. The recipes for all the dishes illustrated are in the book. You'll find that each method — microwave, convection, or micro/convection — has its own specialties. Let's take a look:

☐Angel food cake and cookies are scrumptious and use the hot, dry convection method. ☐That old-time favorite, Apple Pie, uses the micro/convection method. Microwaves cook the fruit and hot air cooks the crust to flaky perfection. ☐Convection gives Pineapple Baked Alaska its mellow goodness. ☐Candies of all kinds are easy-to-make delights provided by the microwave method. ☐Smell that bread baking! A shortcut is provided for proofing with the microwave method while convection gives just-right baking.

□Micro/convection cooking gives Roast Duck a delicious, crisp skin and it's easy, yet elegant. Oven Fried Chicken is also ready in a flash the micro/convection way and it will be perfectly crisp. □Steak is sure to become a favorite when it is cooked using the convection method. □You'll love to cook breaded or baked fish by convection for a crisp outside texture and a tender, moist inside. Reheat fish (or chicken) by convection, too, to retain that just-cooked crispness. □Bacon and scrambled eggs are cooked by the microwave method with no splatter to clean and with bacon as crisp as you like. Eggs are so fluffy and moist, there'll be no more breakfast-skipping at your house!

☐Hot appetizers can be ready as needed and are quickly cooked. Stuffed Mushrooms are stars of the microwave method and Sausage Rolls are brown and crisp, thanks to convection. ☐Now, even for the beginner, soufflé success! Spinach/Cheese Soufflé — cooked to perfection by convection. An impressive presentation for family or friends. ☐Basic White Sauce, flavored with cheese, shows off the ease and speed of microwave sauce preparation. No double boiler needed, a simple glass measure is all you need. ☐The most glamorous vegetable presentation: garden vegetable medley is full of color and nutrition, cooked by the microwave method and served in the same dish. Serve it with cheese sauce for a filling treat.

☐There's no need to turn on a big oven to heat a small pot pie, a turnover, or a pizza. Use the convection method for the hot, dry environment needed to crisp these crusts. ☐Heat soup, chili, and beverages right in the serving cup, mug, or bowl. The microwave method makes it possible. Heat a snack in just about two minutes. ☐Cut preparation time by melting butter and chocolate and softening cream cheese the microwave way.

Now that you have some idea of what this exciting oven can produce for your table, let's take a look at what you need to know to start cooking!

It is important for you to read this basic information and look at the accompanying illustrations because this oven has unique qualities. Whenever you have a question about a cooking term or method, you can refer back to this guide. It will tell you why some food cooks faster than others, provide information about timing and temperature, and tell you which cooking method is best for certain food, and what cooking utensils are appropriate to use.

You will be introduced to new cooking methods that require new terminology. You'll find references to microwave cooking, convection cooking, and micro/convection cooking. But initially, what is important is to understand the principles involved. Each recipe will tell you what method or methods are used.

You may wonder why you need all this information when 300 recipes have been preset for you. Fair question. If you follow the preset recipes exactly, you will get excellent results. But there will be times when your ingredients may vary somewhat from the preset recipe. A few ounces of difference in a cut of meat can require an adjustment in cooking time, particularly when the microwave method is used. While an adjustment in timing may also be necessary for micro/convection or convection cooking, timing is somewhat less critical with those methods. In addi-tion, the information that follows will prove useful when you want to adapt your own recipes or adjust recipes to your personal taste. In any event, study now can eliminate frustration later. Let's go to school.

ABOUT TIMING

Temperature settings and timings given for conventionally cooked recipes are meant to be guides to good cooking. This is also true for microwave, convection, or micro/convection cooking. Don't be afraid to use your instinct and judg-ment. Cooking is always a matter of observation and taste, no matter what appliance is used. However, timing for the microwave method is of particular importance because one minute can make the difference between a perfect sauce and one that is overcooked. A dish that requires one hour of cooking time in a conventional oven usually requires only one-quarter of that time when the microwave method is used. Since just one minute can make an impor-tant difference, microwave cooking requires a somewhat different ap-proach to timing. Therefore, you will find that most cookbooks give micro-wave recipes with probable minimum-maximum cooking times, such as "Cook 2 to 3 minutes." The

"Cooking Guides" or charts in this book use that same procedure. Stop cooking at the minimum time suggested and check for doneness. Then cook longer if necessary. (This procedure is not necessary for the preset recipes unless the ingredients are changed.)

The same precautions about timing apply to micro/convection cooking. However, when combination cooking is used, the microwave portion cycles on and off and therefore timing is somewhat less critical.

When using convection or micro/convection, recipes will give probable minimum/maximum cooking times such as 10 to 15 minutes. Convection cooking does not call for any more attention to timing than conventional cooking.

Cooking times for all preset recipes are precise. However, if your ingredients are changed in any way, timing will be affected and you must check as the food cooks. You may also want to adjust timing in some preset recipes to reflect your preference regarding doneness.

Why such variances in cooking times? Precise cooking times could only be provided if a way were found to guarantee that a given type of food would always be exactly the same, if the utilities would guarantee not to vary power (there are frequent changes in the voltage levels that reach our homes), and if our tastes were all alike. But the fact is that food varies in density, moisture or fat content, shape, weight, etc. And, some of us like our eggs soft-scrambled, while others prefer them firm. Even the temperature at which food is placed in the oven can affect cooking time. Therefore, the cook must be ready to adjust to these differences and be flexible. This applies even when you are using one of the 300 preset recipes. All of them have been meticulously kitchen tested by expert home economists. You will rarely find that the timing must be altered. However, as with all fine cooking, the recipes will benefit from your personal touch. (The preset timing and cooking method are presented in italics with each recipe.)

CHARACTERISTICS THAT AFFECT TIMING

Many characteristics of food, such as quantity, shape, density, and starting temperature affect timing. Understanding them will help you become an expert microwave cook.

Quantity

The larger the volume of food there is, the more time is needed to cook it. One ear of corn in the husk cooks in about 3 minutes; 3 ears may cook in 8 minutes. Therefore, if the quantity in a recipe is changed, an adjustment in timing is necessary. Many of the preset recipes have such timing changes automatically calculated for you. They are identified with this symbol ⊞ throughout the book. Consult the Use & Care Manual for details.

When changing the quantity of a microwave or micro/convection recipe on your own, follow this general rule: When doubling a recipe, increase the cooking time approximately 50 percent. When cutting a recipe in half, reduce the time by approximately 40 percent. Treat quantity adjustments for convection just as you do for conventional cooking.

Shape and Size

Thinly cut food cooks faster than thicker cuts and small pieces cook faster than large. Basic, sure, but in microwave and micro/convection cooking thick pieces are placed toward the rim of the dish to ensure even cooking. Due to the distribution pattern of the microwaves, outside areas cook faster than the center. For best results, cook pieces of similar size and shape together or place smaller and thinner pieces in the center of dish.

may require turning to promote even cooking. Otherwise, the portion of the food nearest the top of the oven could be overdone before the rest is cooked.

Density

Dense food like potatoes, roast beef, and carrots take longer to cook than porous food such as cakes, ground beef, or apples. Not such an important consideration for convection

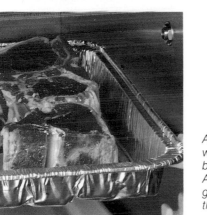

Always consider the height of the food and the cooking method when deciding which of the three positions to use. Bread is baked on the ceramic tray (above left). Pineapple Baked Alaska (page 193) is browned using the wire rack in the lower guides (above). Lamb Chops are broiled using the wire rack in the upper guides (left).

Height

To broil (convection), you want to get the food as close to the heat source as possible. When cooking microwave or micro/convection, more care is needed, especially with tall food. The microwave energy source is at the top (as is the heat coil) and some food

cooking, but it does take longer for microwave energy to penetrate the denser texture. For example, a 2-pound beef roast will take longer to cook (microwave) than a 2-pound meatloaf.

Starting Temperature

As in conventional cooking, the temperature of the food when it is placed in the oven affects cooking time. More time is needed to cook food just out of the refrigerator than food at room temperature. For example, it takes longer to heat frozen green beans than canned green beans. Also, hot water from the tap will start boiling sooner than cold. Recipes in this book assume that food is at refrigerator temperature if that is its usual storage environment.

Moisture Content

In microwave and micro/convection cooking, food with a high moisture content cooks faster than dry food because the microwave energy is more easily absorbed by the moisture in the food. For example, 1 cup of sliced zucchini will cook faster than 1 cup of carrots because of the higher water content of the zucchini.

Delicate Food

This term is used to refer to ingredients that cook so quickly by the microwave and micro/convection methods that they can overcook, causing them to toughen, separate, or curdle. This includes mayonnaise, cream cheese, eggs, cream, and dairy sour cream. Other food, such as snails, oysters, and chicken livers, may "pop." Using lower power settings (microwave) and reduced temperatures (micro/convection and convection) will prevent this. It's the same principle as reducing the heat on a gas or electric burner when food is cooking too fast. When delicate ingredients are mixed with other food, higher settings may be used. The increased volume slows down the cooking.

Sugar and Fat Content

Food high in sugar or fat heats more quickly when the microwave method is used because the energy is attracted to these areas. For example, the fruit or cheese filling of a sweet roll heats faster than the pastry itself.

Zucchini, with more moisture content, cooks faster than carrots (left). Cold food takes longer to cook than food at room temperature (center). A sweet roll heats a bit faster than a dinner roll (right).

ABOUT UTENSILS

There's no need to retire any of your favorite cookware to use this oven. Nor is it necessary to acquire anything new, although there are some unique items that can make the microwave method even more satisfying. Simply put, the cooking method or methods used will determine the type of cookware. Convection cooking needs no special comment: cookware is the same as that used in conventional ovens.

Microproof Cookware

For microwave cooking, we have created a new term, *microproof*. It means that an item is safe and recommended for microwave cooking. Since we're accustomed to the term "heatproof" for conventional cookware, it shouldn't take long for us to accept *microproof* as a just-as-familiar friend. Much heatproof cookware is also microproof. The most distinguishing feature of microproof cookware is that it is never, even partially, made of metal.

Micro/Convection Cookware

For micro/convection cooking, the general rules are fairly easy: (1) cookware must be *both* microproof *and* heatproof whenever it is to be placed on the wire rack; (2) cookware needs to be only heatproof when it is to be placed on the ceramic tray (metal is acceptable). Now, let's explore microproof cookware in more detail.

When selecting a new piece of cookware for microwave use, first check the manufacturer's directions. Also review the "Materials Checklist" on page 17 and "A Guide to Cookware" on page 19. If you are still in doubt, here is a test you can make to see if it is microproof. Place the item on the ceramic tray with a measuring cup full of water alongside. Cook (micro) on HI 45 seconds. If your dish feels hot, it is absorbing microwave energy and should not be used. If it feels barely warm, it has limited microproof capability and may be used for brief periods (warming food). If it remains cool, it is microproof. Keep in mind that metal cookware, or items trimmed with metal are not used for microwave cooking. Not only do they reflect microwaves and prevent them from reaching the food, but they can cause sparks, a static charge, known as arcing. Arcing is not harmful to you, though it will deface the oven. Oh, did you know that paper products are microproof? They are!

Selecting Containers

Containers should accommodate the food being cooked. Whenever possible use round or oval dishes, so that the microwaves are absorbed evenly into the food. Square corners in cookware receive more concentration of energy than the rest of the dish, so the food in the corners tends to overcook. Some cake and loaf recipes call for ring molds or bundt pans to facilitate more even cooking. This is because the center area in a round or oval dish generally cooks more slowly than the outside. Round cookware with a small glass inserted open end up in the

A wide variety of bundt pans, muffin pans, ring molds, cooking dishes, bacon racks, roasting racks, and glass utensils have been invented or improved in microproof form for microwave use and some are also heatproof (top left). Most paper, plastic, and woodware items are microproof (top right). Metal utensils of all kinds are used in convection cooking without reservation and can be used in micro/convection cooking only when they are placed on the ceramic tray (above right). An assortment of heatproof cookware that can be used for microwave cooking, for micro/convection cooking, or for convection cooking (above left).

center works just as well to eliminate undercooked centers. When a particular size or shape of container is specified in a recipe, it should be used. Varying the container size or shape may change cooking time. A 2-quart casserole called for in a recipe refers to a bowl-shaped cooking utensil. A 12×8-inch or a 9-inch round baking dish refers to a shallow cooking dish. In the case of puddings, sauces, and candies, large containers are specified to prevent the liquids, especially milk-based ones, from boiling over. For best results, try to use the dish cited in the recipe.

Materials Checklist

☐CHINA, POTTERY: Ideal for microwave use if no metallic trim or glaze. Fine for micro/convection and convection if heatproof.

☐GLASS: Excellent cooking material for microwave, micro/convection, and convection cooking. Since oven-proof glass is always safe, "microproof" is not mentioned when a glass or ceramic item is specified.

☐PAPER: Approved for short-term microwave cooking. Must not be foil-lined. Paper towels and waxed paper are acceptable microwave coverings. No micro/convection or convection uses approved.

☐PLASTICS: Plastics designed for microwave cooking may be used and a growing number of plastic products are available. Follow manufacturer's instructions and carefully observe maximum temperature recommendations. Plastic wraps recommended by the manufacturers make a fine cover for microwave cooking but cannot be used for micro/convection or convection cooking. (Be sure to remove the plastic wrap if a recipe calls for a shift from microwave to micro/convection or convection cooking.)

☐PLASTIC COOKING BAGS, POUCHES: Can be used for microwave cooking but slit pouches so steam can escape. Cooking bags generally approved for micro/convection and convection use. Check package or manufacturer's instructions for heatproof qualities on cooking pouches.

☐METALS: Excellent for convection. Limited use *on the ceramic tray only* for micro/convection cooking. Not suitable for microwave cooking, except as follows:

Small amounts of aluminum foil may be used to cover areas on large pieces of meat or poultry that defrost or cook more rapidly than the remainder. In microwave cooking or defrosting, this method is known as shielding.

Aluminum frozen TV dinner trays with foil covers removed can be heated microwave if the trays do not exceed ¾-inch depth. However, convection works best. Just follow the package directions for conventional ovens.

Frozen poultry containing metal clamps may be defrosted by the microwave method without removing the clamps.

Any aluminum foil or metal item must be at least 1 inch from oven walls when microwave or micro/convection cooking is in process.

☐THERMOMETERS: The temperature probe provided with the oven is used to determine internal food temperature for all cooking methods. Conventional meat thermometers may be used with convection cooking if desired. Microproof meat thermometers are available, too. A candy thermometer is helpful and, since all candy is made by the microwave method, only a microproof candy thermometer may be used in the oven.

☐STRAW AND WOOD: If no metal fasteners are present, these can be used with the microwave method only for quick warming (rolls, chips, etc.)

A Micro/Convection Note

As we've said earlier, metal does not allow microwaves to pass through and reach the food. In micro/convection cooking on the ceramic tray, metal can be used but is generally not practical because the microwaves can only be absorbed by the top of the food. There are times when that is desirable. Angel Food Cake (page 187), for example, cooks convection in a metal tube pan on the ceramic tray and is shifted to micro/convection (same metal pan, so it stays on the ceramic tray) to finish.

Ceramic Tray

The ceramic tray at the bottom of the oven will probably be your most frequently used cooking position. Most microwave cooking is done on the ceramic tray (exception, whole-meal cooking, see pages 209-218) and, therefore, no position is specified for microwave cooking. The ceramic tray is also used for micro/convection and convection cooking when specified. In micro/convection cooking, metal cookware may only be used when placed on the ceramic tray. Incidentally, microwaves pass through the ceramic tray and are reflected by the oven bottom, allowing them to cook food from the bottom as well as from the top and sides (unless a metal pan is used, of course).

Wire Rack

The removable wire rack has two positions. It can be placed in the lower guides, or in the upper guides. It is generally used to elevate food closer to the heat source in convection or micro/convection cooking and enables whole-meal preparation in microwave cooking, or whenever more than one item is cooked at the same time. Always remove the wire rack when it is not in use.

The wire rack is used in the lower guides or in the upper guides, as recipes direct. Generally, selection of wire rack position or use of ceramic tray depends upon height of food in convection or micro/convection cooking. The ceramic tray is used for most microwave cooking, except whole-meal techniques.

A GUIDE TO COOKWARE

ITEM	GOOD USE	MICRO	MICRO/ CONVEC	CONVEC
Aluminum foil products	Shielding, broiling, many cooking functions	ltd.	ltd.	ok
Boilable pouches	Heating frozen food	ok	no	no
Candy thermometers	Making candy	*	*	*
Cast aluminum, stainless steel, cast iron	Most cooking functions	no	ltd.	ok
China plates, cups	Heating	ok	no	no
Corelle®	Heating, cooking vegetables	ok	*	*
Corning Ware®	Most cooking functions	ok	ok	ok
Metal pans	Most cooking functions	no	ltd.	ok
Metal-trimmed or glazed pottery	Cooking casseroles, soup, many cooking functions	no	no	ok
Oven cooking bags	Cooking roasts, poultry	ok	ok	ok
Paper towels, plates, liners, cups, etc.	Covering, heating, or cooking (as specified)	ok	no	no
Plastic wrap	Covering	ok	no	no
Plastic cookware, dishes, roasting racks	Heating, cooking, elevating food	ok	*	*
Pottery, earthenware, clay cookers	Most cooking functions	ok	ok	ok
Pyrex®, and heat-proof glass	Most cooking functions	ok	ok	ok
Soft plastics, sherbet cartons	Reheating for very short periods	ok	no	no
Microproof meat thermometers	Determining internal temperature of food	ok	ok	ok
Waxed paper	Covering	ok	no	no
Wood products	Spoons for stirring, skewers for kabobs	ok	no	no
Straw baskets (no metal trim)	Warming bread	ok	no	no

* *Check manufacturers' recommendations. Must be microproof for microwave or micro/convection use and heatproof for convection use.*

ltd.=limited use approved. See "About Utensils" and "Materials Checklist"

ABOUT METHODS

The speed and effectiveness of microwave and micro/convection cooking are not only determined by the characteristics of the food, but also by certain techniques. You have used many of these techniques before in conventional cooking, but they do have particular applications with this oven due to the special qualities of

Arrangement

The way food is arranged in the oven and in the dish helps assure evenness in cooking and facilitates defrosting, heating, and cooking when the micro/convection methods are used. The microwaves always penetrate the outer portion of food first, so food should be arranged with

Oven Fried Chicken (page 114) is shown properly arranged for micro/convection cooking. Note oven mitt, needed for hot air micro/convection and convection environment (above). Though cooked by convection method, lamb chops can be nicely arranged for cooking. Garnish with parsley and bring to the table in the cooking dish (top left).

microwave energy. Those that are used regularly in conventional cooking will continue to be important when cooking with the convection method. Becoming familiar with these terms and methods will make your cooking easier and will help assure success.

the thicker areas near the edge of the dish and the thinner portions near the center. For example, when cooking Oven Fried Chicken (page 114 and above), the thick, meaty portions of the breasts and thighs are placed at the edge of the dish with the thin sides toward the center. The thinner, bony ends of the drumsticks are also placed toward the center. Food such as tomatoes, potatoes, and corn should be arranged in a circle, rather than in rows. Such arrangement techniques can also provide attractive cook-and-serve opportunities. Check the garden vegetable medley (page 9) and cauliflower-broccoli-carrot dish (page 145) and let your own imagination go!

Rearranging

Sometimes food that cannot be stirred must be repositioned in the dish during cooking. Be sure to use tongs and pot holders when cooking with the micro/convection or convection method because the dishes and oven will be hot. Checking food during cooking is the best way to judge whether or not rearranging is necessary.

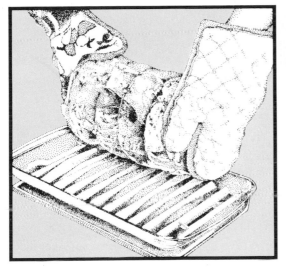

Turning Over

As in conventional cooking, some food, such as steaks, large roasts, whole poultry, ham, hamburgers, or chops, may require turning over to brown or crisp each side and to promote even cooking. Use mitts to turn large food; they provide a secure grip and juices are not lost by piercing meat with a fork. You can always wash the mitts if soiled.

Stirring

Little stirring is required when cooking in this oven. If necessary, stir from the outside to the center because the outside area heats faster than the center when microwaves are in use. Stirring blends the flavors and promotes even heating. Stir only as directed in the recipes: constant stirring is never required, frequent stirring is rare.

Some muffins and cakes need to be rotated (above left). Paper towels and plastic wrap are good microwave-method covers (above). Dishes with lids are best for micro/convection and convection methods (left).

Rotating

At times, recipes for some baked items, such as pies, cakes, or quiches, that cannot be stirred, turned over, or rearranged call for adjusting the position of the dish for more even cooking. Rotate one-quarter or one-half turn only if the baked food is not cooking or rising evenly. Most food does not need to be rotated.

Covering

Covers are used to trap steam, prevent dehydration, speed cooking time, and help food retain its natural moisture. Suitable covers for microwave cooking may differ from micro/convection and convection methods. Heat in the oven cavity will melt plastic wrap or cause paper to burn. When covering with paper towels or waxed paper, a good micro-wave cooking practice, be sure to use a double width that will enable you to tuck the paper under the bottom of the cooking dish. Otherwise, it will tend to rise off the dish due to the air movement. Plastic wrap generally adheres to the dish, of course. Paper towels are especially useful for cooking bacon because they absorb fat, yet allow the bacon to cook crisply because the paper does not trap steam. Waxed paper is best for covering poultry, fish, and any food where the retention of heat is important for even cooking but where there is no need to trap steam. Remember: paper towels and waxed paper may only be used when cooking by the microwave method. Casseroles which usually have their own lids are the best choice when covers are needed in micro/convection and convection cooking. A handy idea to keep in mind: a heatproof plate is a good substitute for a lid.

Standing Time

During standing time, heat continues to be conducted from the outside of the food to the center. After the oven is turned off, food may remain in the oven for standing time or may be placed on a heatproof surface. This procedure has long been used by professional chefs and knowledgeable cooks to retain the natural juices in turkeys, roasts, chickens, and all food that requires time to "firm up," such as custards, pies, and quiches. In roasts and poultry, juices are close to the surface after cooking. If sliced immediately, all the juice will run out. A standing time of 15 to 20 minutes gives the juices time to redistribute and the last slice can be as full of natural juice as the first. That's true with all cooking. If you are using the microwave method, standing time is even more essential. That's because there is more internal cooking activity in process with food cooked by the microwave method.

Piercing

It is always wise to break the skin or membrane of certain food, such as egg yolks, potatoes, liver, chicken giblets, eggplant, and whole squash before cooking. The skins or membranes keep moisture in and piercing will allow steam to escape. For example, pierce sausage casings in several places before cooking. A toothpick can be used for egg yolks but a fork is best for potatoes and squash. Also, pierce or slit plastic pouches with a knife.

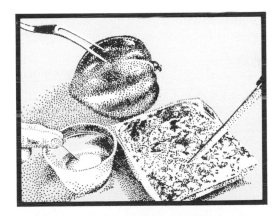

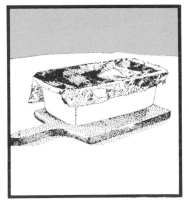

Piercing (above right). Standing time completes cooking and redistributes juices (right). Use a flat, heatproof surface during standing time (above).

Browning

Many foods do not brown as much in microwave cooking as they do in conventional cooking. In convection cooking, however, browning is usually superior to conventional methods with the constantly moving hot air promoting more even browning. That's why this oven was designed: to combine the two systems, creating a unique new environment for food to cook better than ever. But don't be fooled: some browning does occur with the microwave method alone. Usually, food does not crisp, although the high fat content in bacon enables it to crisp and brown in minutes. However, when browning or crispness is the goal, the micro/convection or convection method is the choice.

You've probably heard of a "browning dish" and may have one if you are a second-generation microwave cook. Although it may be used in microwave cooking on the ceramic tray, according to the browning dish manufacturer's instructions, it's not a necessary item for this oven. All browning dish functions are accomplished with the convection cooking ability of the oven.

Adjusting for High Altitudes

As in conventional cooking, microwave cooking at high altitudes requires adjustments in cooking time for leavened products like breads and cakes. Other foods may require a slightly longer cooking time to become tender, since water boils at a lower temperature. Usually, for every 3 minutes of microwave cooking time you add 1 minute for the higher altitude. Therefore, a recipe calling for 3 minutes needs 4 minutes and a recipe requiring 6 minutes needs 8 minutes. The wisest procedure is to start with the time given in the recipe and then check for doneness. Adding time is easy, but overcooking can be a real problem. Here again your judgment is vital.

Your micro/convection oven gives you the ability to select from many power settings with the microwave method and from a range of temperatures with the convection method. These settings give you flexibility and control, just as in conventional cooking. Selection of the appropriate power settings and temperatures is automatic, as is the timing, for the 300 preset recipes. For your own recipes and for items identified in the *Cooking Guides* (see recipe chapters), you set the power and/or temperature. For the microwave method, in addition to HI, there are 99 settings. The control panel lists the main settings and gives them familiar cooking terms. You may find, however, that other settings work best for you. You may want to warm certain foods on 13 or 15, for example.

The oven automatically pairs microwave power with a convection temperature of 350°F for micro/convection cooking. The microwave power can't be altered with this method but you can change the oven temperature, if a higher or lower temperature is best for the food being cooked.

Oven temperature is adjustable in ten-degree increments from 200°F to 450°F. In convection cooking, you select the oven temperature just as you do in conventional cooking. You can also preheat the oven when necessary.

The Guide below will help you select the cooking method for most food. The most satisfactory results will be achieved when you use the cooking method listed as "Best." Equal and alternate methods are listed as "Good." If a method is not recommended, "No" is indicated.

Touch Pad

The touch pads on the oven control panel need only to be touched to be activated. A beep tone assures that the setting is being entered.

GUIDE TO COOKING METHODS

FOOD	MICRO	MICRO/ CONVEC	CONVEC
Appetizers	Good	Good	Good
Bread, baking	No	Good	Best
rising	Best	No	No
Cakes, batter	Good	Good	Best
angel food	No	No	Best
Candies	Best	No	No
Casseroles	Good	Best	Good
Cookies, drop	No	Good	Best
bar	Good	Best	Good
Defrosting	Best	No	No
Eggs	Best	Good	Good
Fruit	Best	Good	Good
Hot drinks	Best	No	No

FOOD	MICRO	MICRO/ CONVEC	CONVEC
Meat, broiling	No	Good	Best
roasting	Good	Best	Good
Pies, 1-crust	Good	Best	Good
2-crust	No	Best	Good
Poultry	Good	Best	Good
Quiches	Good	Best	Good
Reheating	Best	Good	Good
Sauces	Best	No	No
Seafood, poaching	Best	Good	No
broiling	No	Good	Best
Soufflés	No	No	Best
Soup	Best	Good	No
Vegetables	Best	Good	No

Temperature Probe

When inserted into the food, the temperature probe enables you to cook food to a preselected internal temperature. When the desired temperature is reached, the oven automatically holds food warm up to 1½ hours. Instead of setting the oven to a certain number of minutes, you set the probe at the exact temperature you want the food to reach prior to standing time to attain desired doneness. The oven must also be set at the power level and/or oven temperature at which the food is to be cooked. Probe temperature, power setting and oven temperature are automatically determined for the preset recipes that use the probe. The probe provides accuracy in cooking almost any food, from instant coffee and sauces to beef casseroles and roast chicken. You can even watch the display window as the food reaches the selected temperature.

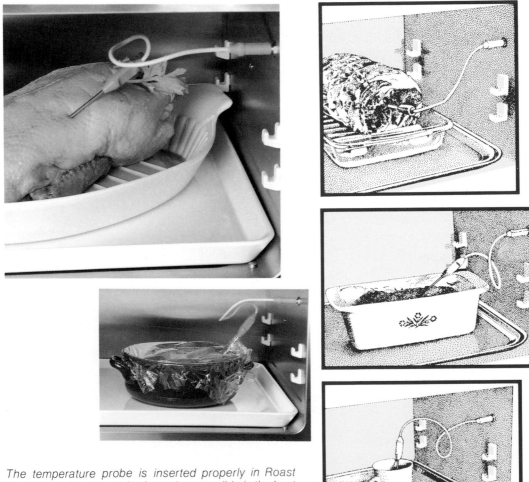

The temperature probe is inserted properly in Roast Duck (top). As close to horizontal as possible is the best probe placement in roasts (top right). No more guessing for meatloaf or hot drinks (above right and right). In microwave cooking, plastic wrap covering is not pierced by probe (above).

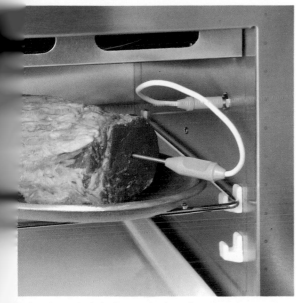

A beef tenderloin is cooked, using the temperature probe, on the wire rack in the upper guides (nearest heat source) by convection for true broiled flavor.

rises about 5°F to 15°F. For example, after 10 minutes of standing time, the temperature of rare beef will reach 135°F; well done lamb will reach its proper serving temperature of 170°F to 180°F. The temperature of beverages, however, drops in 10 minutes from 150°F to 136°F.

Guide to the Temperature Probe*
Suggested Temperature Probe Settings

120°	Rare Beef, Fully Cooked Ham
130°	Medium Beef
140°	Fish Steaks and Fillets, Well Done Beef
150°	Vegetables, Hot Drinks, Soups, Casseroles
155°	Veal
165°	Well Done Lamb, Well Done Pork
170°	Poultry Parts
180°	Well Done Whole Poultry
200°	Cake Frosting

Refer to individual Cooking Guides (see Index) for specific instructions.

The probe must be carefully and properly inserted in the food for the best results. The probe tip should be in the center of the dish, cup, or casserole or in the thickest portion of the meat. Do not allow the probe to touch bone, fat, or any metal foil being used as a shield. After using the probe, remove it from the oven. Use warm, soapy water to wash the part that contacted the food. Rinse and dry. Do not immerse the probe in water or wash it in a dishwasher.

The "Guide to the Temperature Probe" provides a range from 120°F to 200°F. Follow the directions in the recipes for placement of the probe and covering of the dish, if specified, and consult the "Tips for Probe Use" for step-by-step directions.

Standing time is essential for most food to reach its optimum serving temperature. Because of the nature of microwave energy, during standing time the temperature of most food

Tips for Probe Use

1. Place food in container, as recipe directs.
2. Place temperature probe in the food with the first inch of probe secured in the center of the food. Probe should not touch bone or a fat pocket. Probe should be inserted from the side or the front, not from the top of the food, except when inserting into casseroles, a cup of soup, etc. Try to insert probe as close to a horizontal position as possible.
3. Plug probe into receptacle on side wall of oven cavity.
4. Make sure the end of the temperature probe, inserted in the food, does not touch the cooking container, or sides of oven.
5. Touch "Clear."

6. Touch "Oven Temp/Preheat." Or, touch "Micro Control" if cooking by the microwave method.
7. Touch "4-0-0" for 400°F (or the correct numbers for oven temperature desired). If the temperature is 350°F, this step is eliminated because that temperature is set automatically.

   If cooking by the microwave method, touch "8-0" for 80 or correct number for power setting desired. HI is automatically set unless changed.
8. Touch "Convec Temp," or "Micro/ Temp" to select the cooking method.
9. Touch "1-2-0" for 120°F (or correct numbers for internal food temperature desired).
10. Touch "Start."
11. Steps 5 through 10 are not necessary for any of the 300 preset recipes that use the probe.
12. Never operate the oven with the temperature probe in the cavity unless the probe is plugged in and inserted into food.

Reheating

One of the major assets of the microwave oven is its efficiency in reheating cooked food. Not only does most food reheat quickly, but it also retains moisture and its just-cooked flavor when properly arranged and covered. Reheat food in serving dishes or on paper plates and save extra clean-up time. Follow these tips to help get excellent results:

☐ Use 80 except when otherwise specified. You can use the temperature probe for reheating casseroles, beverages, and other food. Set "Micro Temp" control at 150°F to 160°F.

☐ To arrange a combination of food on a plate, place dense food, like meat, at the edges and more porous food, like bread, toward the center.

☐ Dense food, such as mashed potatoes and casseroles, reheats better if a depression is made in the center, or if the food is shaped in a ring.

☐ To retain moisture during reheating, cover food with plastic wrap or a microproof lid.

☐ As a general guide to reheating a plate of food, start with 1½ to 2 minutes, then check for doneness. If the plate on which the food is cooked feels warm, the food is probably heated through. Its warmth has heated the plate.

Food Drying

Your micro/convection oven includes a special dehydration feature that enables you to dry apples, mushrooms, flowers, and other items expertly. The "Dehydrate Time" touch pad is used. For full information and instructions, see your Use & Care Manual.

Now it's time for some practical experience using your Kenmore Auto Recipe 300 Micro/Convection Oven. First, a quick hot drink, then we will bake some Hot Dog Wrap Ups without using the preset method to familiarize you with convection cooking. A micro/convection Baked Apple is next and, finally, you'll experience the special convenience of the automatic, preset recipes with a first course soup. Ready? Let's go!

Lesson One

Uses the microwave method because it's best to heat liquids.

Take your favorite mug or cup, making sure it has no gold or silver trim. (If you are not certain your mug is microproof, test it as directed on page 15.) Follow these step-by-step directions:

1. Fill mug with water and place on the ceramic tray, in the center of the oven. Close the oven door.

CLEAR

2. Touch the "Clear" pad to clear any previous programming.

MICRO TIME

3. Touch the "Micro Time" pad, then touch pads 2-0-0. Your oven is now programmed to cook (micro) on HI for 2 minutes. It was not necessary to touch "Micro Control" because your oven is automatically on HI when the microwave method is used unless programmed to another setting.

START

4. Now touch the "Start" pad.
5. The timer will beep when 2 minutes are up. The oven turns off automatically. Open the door.
6. Remove the mug. The handle will be cool enough to hold and the cup warm from the heated water.
7. Stir in instant coffee, tea, or soup . . . enjoy!

Lesson Two

Convection provides the hot, dry environment for Hot Dog Wrap Ups.

1. Position wire rack in lower guides of oven.

2. Touch "Clear" pad; touch "oven Temp/Preheat" pad; touch 3-8-0. The oven is programmed to preheat to 380°F.

3. Touch "Start".

4. Prepare recipe for Hot Dog Wrap Ups, arranging 8 on a cookie sheet and 8 on a plate. Cover plate well with plastic wrap and refrigerate for later use.

5. When beep tone begins, oven has reached 380°F. Place cookie sheet on wire rack, close door.

6. Touch "Oven Temp/Preheat" pad; touch "Convec Time" pad; touch 1-5-0-0. Oven is programmed to cook by the convection method at 380°F for 15 minutes.

7. Touch "Start".

8. When the programmed time ends, the beep tone is heard and the oven turns off automatically.

Hot Dog Wrap Ups is also one of your preset automatic recipes. *See page 41 and go automatic the next time.*

Lesson Three

A micro/convection treat, a Baked Apple. Microwaves cook the fruit and the hot air helps caramelize the topping.

1 large apple
3 tablespoons water
2 teaspoons brown sugar
1 teaspoon chopped walnuts
$^{1}/_{4}$ teaspoon cinnamon

2. Touch "Clear" pad; touch "Micro/Convec Time" pad; touch 6-0-0. Touch "Start." Oven is programmed to cook by the micro/convection method at 350°F for 6 minutes. Because the 350°F oven temperature is automatic with micro/convection cooking unless a different temperature is entered, we did not have to program the oven temperature for this recipe.

3. When the 6 minutes are up, the beep tone is heard, and the oven shuts off automatically. Such a nice after-school treat.

1. Remove stem from apple and cut small circle around top in criss-cross fashion. Carefully remove small portion of pulp. Place apple in microproof/heatproof small dish. Add water. Place sugar and walnuts in center of apple and sprinkle with cinnamon.

Surprise! Don't your Hot Dog Wrap Ups, Baked Apple, and Hot Tea with Lemon make a nice just you lunch?

Lesson Four
First Course Soup

Why not surprise the family with a first course of homemade soup as your first microwave recipe tonight? It's really easy, thanks to the convenience of the preset feature with your Kenmore Auto Recipe 300 oven. We've selected Cream of Corn Soup, Recipe No. 22 (page 51).

Cream of Corn Soup

1   can (17 ounces) cream-style corn
1   can (13¾ ounces) chicken broth
²/₃ cup water
¹/₄ cup thinly sliced zucchini
2   tablespoons water
1   tablespoon cornstarch
2   large eggs, lightly beaten
1   green onion, finely chopped

1. Combine corn, broth, ²/₃ cup water, and zucchini in 2-quart microproof casserole or soup tureen. Cover and place in oven.

2. Touch "Clear" pad; touch "Recipe #" pad; then touch pads 2 and 2. Oven is ready to cook.

3. Touch "Start". (Oven will cook on HI for 13 minutes.)

PAUS

4. At the end of first cooking sequence, timer will beep and "Pause" will appear in display window. Combine 2 tablespoons water and cornstarch; stir until cornstarch is dissolved. Open door and add cornstarch to soup; blend well. Do not cover.

START

5. Close door. Touch "Start" pad. (Oven will cook on HI for 5 minutes.)
6. Pour eggs into hot soup in thin stream, stirring briskly. Garnish with green onion — voila! — serve to smiles all around.

There is so much more that you can do in this oven than ever before possible in a single-cavity unit. Because you have such flexibility, you may be concerned about proper selection of the cooking method to use — microwave, micro/convection, or convection — when you are cooking on your own. It's truly not difficult. When you are ready to convert one of your own favorite recipes to this oven, look through the cookbook for a similar one — you should get some ideas on how to proceed. Also, the beginning of each chapter has hints on recipe converting to help you along. Here are a few guidelines:

☐ Candies, always difficult to prepare in conventional cooking because of the need for double boilers, the mess of scorched pans, constant stirring, and other time-consuming techniques, are now easy to make. Ingredient adjustments are not needed and the microwave method is best.

☐ Chicken recipes will benefit from micro/convection cooking when converted. If the exterior must be very crisp, preheating the oven will enable micro/convection cooking to provide superior results over any other method.

☐ Prepare most casseroles and stews exactly as you would con-

ventionally and use the micro/convection method. If using cheese on top of your casserole, it might be wise to add the cheese just before the end of the cooking time.

☐ As a general rule, you can assume that most microwave recipes are cooked in about one-quarter to one-third of the conventional recipe time. Check for doneness after one-quarter of the time before continuing to cook.

Now let's try converting a conventional recipe to the micro/convection method. Suppose you have a favorite recipe for Chicken Cacciatore that you would like to prepare in this oven. The closest recipe in this book turns out to be Chicken Marengo, Recipe No. 129 on page 114. Let's see how to go about converting.

Chicken Cacciatore
Conventional Style
4 to 6 servings

$^{1}/_{4}$ cup butter or margarine
1 medium onion, chopped
1 medium green pepper, thinly
    sliced
1 can (28 ounces) whole tomatoes
$^{1}/_{4}$ cup all-purpose flour
1 bay leaf
1 tablespoon parsley flakes
$^{1}/_{2}$ teaspoon salt
1 clove garlic, minced
$^{1}/_{2}$ teaspoon oregano
1 teaspoon paprika
$^{1}/_{4}$ teaspoon basil
1 cup dry red wine
1 frying chicken (about 3 pounds),
    cut up

Preheat oven to 350°F. Melt butter in medium skillet over medium heat. Add onion and green pepper and cook, stirring occasionally, until onion is transparent. Add tomatoes and flour and stir until smooth. Add all remaining ingredients, except chicken. Cover and cook until sauce is slightly thickened, about 5 minutes, stirring every minute. Arrange chicken in a baking dish and pour sauce over top. Cover and bake about 45 minutes or until chicken is tender.

Reviewing the Chicken Cacciatore recipe will help point out some of the differences between conventional cooking and this unit. Notice that the amount of butter needed in the traditional skillet is much greater than what is needed for the first steps by the microwave method with this oven. The skillet needs to be well lubricated so the food does not stick and burn from the direct heat essential in stove-top cooking. More wine is needed in the conventional version to prevent evaporation during the longer cooking time. Here's the converted recipe:

Chicken Cacciatore
Micro/convection Style
4 to 6 servings

1 medium onion, chopped
1 medium green pepper, thinly
    sliced
1 tablespoon butter or margarine
1 can (28 ounces) whole tomatoes
$^{1}/_{4}$ cup all-purpose flour
1 bay leaf
1 clove garlic, minced
1 tablespoon parsley flakes
1 teaspoon paprika
$^{1}/_{2}$ teaspoon salt
$^{1}/_{2}$ teaspoon oregano
$^{1}/_{4}$ teaspoon basil
$^{1}/_{2}$ cup dry red wine
1 frying chicken (about 3 pounds),
    cut up

Combine onion, green pepper, and butter in 3-quart glass or ceramic casserole. Cover and cook (micro) on HI 4 to 5 minutes, or until onion is transparent. Add tomatoes and flour and stir until smooth. Blend in all remaining ingredients except chicken. Cover and cook (micro) on HI 5 minutes. Add chicken, covering pieces completely with sauce. Cover dish, set on ceramic tray and cook (micro/convec) at 350°F 25 to 30 minutes, or until chicken is tender.

Cooking Casseroles

Micro/convection cooking is particularly good for preparing casseroles. Vegetables keep their bright fresh color and crisp texture and meat is tender and flavorful. Generally economical, too, the casserole is growing in popularity for family meals and is perfectly in order for entertaining. Here are some hints:

☐ Most casseroles can be made ahead of time, refrigerated or frozen, then reheated later by the microwave method.

☐ Store leftover casserole portions in disposable single-serving containers for easy reheating and quick lunches when needed.

☐ Casseroles usually are cooked covered. Uncover to melt cheese topping or to provide top browning during the final minutes of cooking.

☐ Sauté any vegetables in the casserole dish first with microwave energy, then add other ingredients and change to micro/convection.

About Lower Calories

You can use less fat when cooking with the microwave or micro/convection methods. And, of course, broiling the convection way is the naturally low-calorie way to cook. In general, you can reduce calories in many recipes by:

Using bouillon or water instead of butter when sautéing or softening vegetables.

Substituting fresh vegetables for pasta or other starchy food.

Removing the skin from chicken or turkey before cooking.

Using milk instead of cream or half-and-half for quiches.

Substituting skim milk for whole milk.

Substituting skim milk cheeses like low-fat cottage, ricotta, or mozzarella for creamy, high-butterfat cheeses.

Natural juices from food mixed with herbs can be substituted for cream or butter-based sauces.

Substitute fruit cooked in its natural juices for those cooked with added sugar.

Using Preset Recipes

The flexibility of this oven is truly amazing. There's just no end to what it can do for you and you can be creative in your approach to it. For example, there's no reason why you cannot use a preset recipe's functions for a totally-new recipe of your own creation! That's why you'll find the oven's functions included in italics within each recipe. You can use that information to decide which preset recipe might cook your new dish best.

You can also combine preset recipes by setting two, or more, recipe numbers in sequence to cook your new recipe. In fact, some of the preset recipes employ that technique to extend the usefulness of your oven. *(See Recipe Number 4, Sausage Rolls, for an example of this technique.)*

Preheating

Convection and micro/convection cooking sometimes calls for preheating the oven, just as you do a conventional oven. When the desired temperature is reached, a beep tone is heard intermittently to remind you that the oven is ready. The tone stops when the oven door is opened or when the "Stop" pad is touched. ("Pause" appears in the display window if you touch the "Stop" pad or open the door when one of the 300 preset recipes is being used.)

By the Way . . .

To get the greatest pleasure out of your oven, keep in mind that certain food is best prepared by cooking methods that do not use the closed environment of the oven. Sure, you *can* prepare pancakes or French toast in the oven, but why? Certain things still belong on that range top that hasn't changed much since the days when it was heated with a wood fire. We don't advise using the oven for the following:

☐ Eggs cooked in the shell, because the light membrane surrounding the yolk collects energy, which then causes a steam build-up that could explode the egg. Don't experiment. It's a mess to clean up!

☐ Deep-fat frying, because the confined environment of the oven is not suited to the handling of the food or oil and is not safe.

☐ Pancakes, because no crust forms. (But the oven is great for reheating pancakes, waffles, and similar items.)

☐ Home canning, because it is impossible to judge exact boiling temperatures inside jar and you cannot be sure that the temperature and length of cooking are sufficient to prevent contamination of the food.

☐ Heating bottles with small necks, like those for syrups and toppings, because they are apt to break from the pressure build-up.

☐ Large items, such as a 25-pound turkey, are also not recommended for preparation in this unit. The food would be to close to the microwave and heat sources and the top would overcook before the rest was done.

Finally, about popcorn:

Do not attempt to pop corn in a paper bag, since the corn may dehydrate and overheat, causing the paper bag to catch on fire. Due to the many variables, such as the age of the corn and its moisture content, popping corn in the microwave oven is not recommended. Microwave popping devices are available. While safe to use, they usually do not give results equal to those of conventional popping methods. If the microwave device is used, *carefully follow the instructions provided with the product.*

A Good Beginning

Appetizers can be the most creative food of today's entertaining. They can be hot or cold, simple or fancy, light or hearty depending upon the occasion. There are no rules, so you can let your imagination soar. Until now *hot* appetizers were the most troublesome and time-consuming for the host or hostess. But that's no longer true with the microwave oven. Parties are much easier and more enjoyable because the microwave eliminates all that last-minute hassle and lengthy cooking over a hot stove. You can assemble most appetizers and nibbles in advance, and at the right moment, just coolly "heat 'n serve!" This chapter presents many recipes for entertaining your guests, but you'll also be tempted to prepare delicious snacks and munchies just for the family. There's no doubt about it — appetizers cooked in the microwave oven are fun to make, fun to serve, and fun to eat.

Stuffed Mushrooms (page 45) and Rumaki (page 45), are ready-to-cook (above). The micro/convection method cooks Sausage Rolls (page 41) to perfection (above right). To freshen corn chips and other snacks, just pop the serving bowl or basket in the oven on HI, 15 seconds; let stand 3 minutes (right).

Converting Your Own Recipes

For most appetizers, the cool convenience of the microwave method will probably be your first choice. You can use your prettiest platters (micro-proof) or paper plates for informal times. Use micro/convection for items that require a browned outside or top and will also profit from speedier cooking of the inside. The convection method is best for appetizers that are pastry-based and need a flaky crust. Appetizers generally don't need any ingredient changes to fit either of this oven's cooking methods. Do be sure to match the cooking dish to the method you plan to use. Find a similar recipe in this chapter or refer to pages 15 through 19 for a review of recommended cookware. Here are some helpful tips:

- ☐ For a crisper bottom crust on items cooked on the wire rack by the micro/convection method, line the bottom of a glass baking dish with aluminum foil. The technique is illustrated with Sausage Rolls in the photo on page 37.
- ☐ Because of its very delicate nature, a sour cream dip should be covered and heated with the temperature probe to 90°F on 50 (simmer).
- ☐ Toppings for canapés can be made ahead, but do not place on bread or crackers until just before heating to assure a crisp base.
- ☐ Cover appetizers or dips only when the recipe specifies doing so. Use fitted glass lids, waxed paper, plastic wrap, or paper toweling.
- ☐ You can heat two batches of the same or similar appetizers at one time by using both oven levels, the wire rack in the upper guides and the bottom glass tray. Watch closely; those on top may cook more quickly than those on bottom.
- ☐ The temperature probe set at 130°F on 70 provides an excellent alternative for heating hot dips containing seafood, cheese, or food to be served in a chafing dish or fondue pot.

COOKING GUIDE — CONVENIENCE APPETIZERS*

Food	Programming Method	Setting	First Stage	Second Stage	Probe Method	Special Notes
Dips, cream, ½ cup	micro	10 (warm)	1½ - 2½ min.		90°	Cover with plastic wrap.
Eggrolls, 6 oz. (12)	convec	follow package directions				Upper guides. Preheat.
Meat spread, 4 oz. can	micro	80 (reheat)	30-45 sec.			Use microproof bowl.
Sausages, 5 oz. can	micro	80 (reheat)	1½ - 2 min.			Use microproof casserole. Cover.
Tacos, mini, 5½ oz.	convec	400°	6 - 9 min.			Upper guides. Preheat. Use cookie sheet or foil tray.
Swiss fondue, 10 oz.	micro	80 (reheat)	5 - 6 min.		150°	Slit pouch. Set on microproof plate.

* Due to the tremendous variety in convenience food products available, times given here should be used only as guidelines. We suggest you cook food for the shortest recommended time and then check for doneness. Be sure to check the package for microwave and oven (convec) instructions.

Recipe No. | 01 |

Sombrero Dip

Preset Cooking Time: 24 minutes

- 1 pound lean ground beef
- 1 large onion, chopped
- ½ cup catsup
- 1 tablespoon chili powder
- 1 teaspoon garlic salt
- 1 teaspoon cumin
- 1 teaspoon oregano
- 3 drops hot pepper sauce
- 1 can (24 ounces) kidney beans, undrained
- ½ cup shredded Cheddar cheese
  Green pepper slices

Combine beef and onion in 2-quart microproof bowl. Cover with plastic wrap. Place in oven. Set recipe number 01. Touch START. (Oven cooks: micro, HI, 5 minutes.)

At Pause, stir through several times. Cover. Touch START. (Oven cooks: micro, HI, 3 minutes.)

At Pause, pour off any fat. Add catsup, chili powder, garlic, cumin, oregano, and hot pepper sauce and blend well. Pureé beans in food processor or blender. Stir into beef. Cover. Place in oven. Touch START. (Oven cooks: micro, HI, 8 minutes.)

At Pause, stir. Cover. Touch START. (Oven cooks: micro, HI, 8 minutes.) Stir through several times. Turn into serving dish. Sprinkle with cheese and garnish with green pepper. Serve hot with crackers or chips.

about 5 cups

Recipe No. | 02 | ⊞

Fresh Vegetable Dip

Preset Cooking Time: 5 minutes

- 1 package (10 ounces) frozen chopped spinach
- 1 cup dairy sour cream
- ½ cup chopped fresh parsley
- ½ cup chopped green onions
- ½ cup mayonnaise
- 1 teaspoon fines herbes seasoning
- ½ teaspoon dillweed

Set unopened spinach on microproof plate. Place in oven. Set recipe number 02. Touch START. (Oven cooks: micro, HI, 5 minutes.) Drain well; squeeze dry. Transfer to bowl. Add all remaining ingredients and blend thoroughly. Season with salt and pepper. Cover and refrigerate overnight. Serve with fresh vegetables, crackers, or chips.

about 3½ cups

Recipe No. | 03 |

Miniature Hot Dog Treats

Preset Cooking Time: 11 minutes

- 2 frankfurters
- 1 package (8 ounces) butterflake roll dough

Position wire rack in lower guides of oven. Set recipe number 03. Touch START. (Oven preheats: convec, 380°F.) Cut each frankfurter into 6 equal pieces. Separate dough into 12 equal pieces. Arrange dough on baking sheet. Push frankfurter slices firmly into center of each piece of dough.

At 380°F, place baking sheet in oven on wire rack. Touch START. (Oven cooks: convec, 380°F, 11 minutes.) Serve hot.

12 canapés

⊞ Recipe can be increased. See "Quantity", page 12.

Recipe No. | 04 |

Sausage Rolls

Preset Cooking Time: 15 minutes

1   medium onion, chopped
1   tablespoon vegetable oil
½   pound lean bulk sausage,
     crumbled
1   tablespoon tomato sauce or
     catsup
1   teaspoon fresh lemon juice
1   package (8 ounces) crescent
     roll dough
1   egg yolk, beaten

Combine onion and oil in 1-quart glass measure or microproof bowl. Place in oven. Set recipe number 13. Touch START. *(Oven cooks: micro, HI, 4 minutes.)*

At Pause, stir. Add sausage to bowl. Place in oven. Touch START. *(Oven cooks: micro, HI, 3 minutes.)* Drain off fat. Stir in tomato sauce and lemon juice. Set aside.

Position wire rack in upper guides of oven. Set recipe number 04. Touch START. *(Oven preheats: convec, 400°F.)* Meanwhile, line bottom of 9 × 13-inch glass baking dish with aluminum foil; grease foil. Cut pastry into 4 rectangles. Divide sausage mixture into fourths. Spread sausage mixture down center of dough. Brush edge of pastry with beaten egg. Fold pastry over, enclosing sausage completely. Brush with egg yolk. Cut each length into 1-inch pieces. Arrange in prepared dish.

At 400°F, place dish in oven on wire rack. Touch START. *(Oven cooks: micro/convec, 400°F, 8 minutes.)* Serve hot.

16 appetizers

This is one of several recipes that use the preset functions of another recipe for part of the cooking sequence. Set recipe number 13 first. At the end of that sequence, set recipe number 04.

← *Sombrero Dip (page 39), Sausage Rolls Hot dog Wrap Ups*

Recipe No. | 05 |

Crab Meat Puffs

Preset Cooking Time: 10 minutes

2   egg whites
½   cup mayonnaise
1   can (6½ ounces) crabmeat,
     rinsed, drained, and flaked
½   teaspoon salt
¼   teaspoon paprika
¼   teaspoon dried tarragon
50 cheese or rye crackers

Position wire rack in upper guides of oven. Set recipe number 05. Touch START. *(Oven preheats: convec, 380°F.)* Meanwhile, beat egg whites until stiff. Fold in all remaining ingredients except crackers. Spread crab mixture over crackers. Arrange half of canapés on baking sheet.

At 380°F, place baking sheet in oven on wire rack. Touch START. *(Oven cooks: convec, 380°F, 5 minutes.)*

At Pause, remove from oven. Arrange remaining canapés on baking sheet. Place in oven. Touch START. *(Oven cooks: convec, 380°F, 5 minutes.)* Serve immediately.

about 50 appetizers

Recipe No. | 06 |

Hot Dog Wrap Ups

Preset Cooking Time: 15 minutes

1   package (8 ounces) crescent
     roll dough
16 cocktail-size frankfurters

Position wire rack in upper guides of oven. Set recipe number 06. Touch START. *(Oven preheats: convec, 380°F.)* Meanwhile, divide dough into 8 wedges. Cut each wedge lengthwise through tip, making 16 equal triangles. Place frankfurter at widest part of dough and roll up, ending with point at top. Repeat with remaining dough and frankfurters. Transfer to baking sheet. At 380°F, place baking sheet in oven on wire rack. Touch START. *(Oven cooks: convec, 380°F, 15 minutes.)* Serve hot with mustard.

16 canapés

Recipe No. 07

Cheddar Cheese Canapés

Preset Cooking Time: 30 seconds

- ½ cup (2 ounces) grated Cheddar cheese
- 2 tablespoons light cream
- 1 tablespoon grated Parmesan cheese
- 1 tablespoon sesame seed
- ⅛ teaspoon Worcestershire sauce
- ⅛ teaspoon hot pepper sauce
- 12 crisp crackers or toast rounds
  Chopped parsley

Combine Cheddar cheese, cream, Parmesan cheese, sesame seed, Worcestershire, and hot pepper sauce; blend until smooth. Spread about 1 teaspoon mixture on each cracker. Arrange canapés on microproof plate. Place in oven. Set recipe number 07. Touch START. *(Oven cooks: micro, 70, 30 seconds.)*

Garnish with parsley and serve warm.

12 canapés

Recipe No. 08

Crab Supremes

Preset Cooking Time: 1½ minutes

- 1 can (6½ to 7 ounces) crab meat, drained
- ½ cup finely minced celery
- ½ cup mayonnaise
- 4 teaspoons sweet pickle relish
- 2 teaspoons prepared mustard
- 2 green onions, thinly sliced
- 24 crisp crackers or toast rounds

Place crab meat in bowl; pick over and remove cartilage. Flake with fork. Add celery, mayonnaise, relish, mustard, and onions; blend well. Spoon about 1 tablespoon mixture onto each cracker. Arrange 12 canapés on microproof plate. Place in oven. Cover with waxed paper. Set recipe number 08. Touch START. *(Oven cooks: micro, 70, 45 seconds.)*

At Pause, remove from oven. Arrange remaining 12 canapés on microproof plate. Place in oven. Cover. Touch START. *(Oven cooks: micro, 70, 45 seconds.)*

Serve warm.

24 canapés

Recipe No. 09

Curry Dipper

Preset Cooking Time: 2 minutes

- 1 can (10¾ ounces) cream of mushroom soup, undiluted
- 1½ tablespoons curry powder
- 1 teaspoon lemon juice
- 1 clove garlic, minced

Combine all ingredients in 4-cup glass measure; blend well. Place in oven. Set recipe number 09. Touch START. *(Oven cooks: micro, HI, 2 minutes.)*

Serve hot with Tiny Meatballs (page 44), cubed sirloin, shrimp, or scallops.

1¼ cups

*Shrimp (Guide, page 125) makes an especially →
attractive appetizer when combined with
marinated artichokes and fresh dill. Tiny Meatballs (page 44), and Nachos (page 44) complete
this party table that also includes a bowl of
toasted pecans, freshened before serving by
cooking, micro, HI, 45 seconds.*

Recipe No. [10]

Tiny Meatballs

Preset Cooking Time: 12 minutes

- 1 pound lean ground beef
- ½ pound ground pork
- 1 cup dry bread crumbs
- 1 cup milk
- 1 small onion, finely minced
- 1 large egg, lightly beaten
- 2 teaspoons soy sauce
- 1 teaspoon salt
- ¼ teaspoon pepper
- ¼ teaspoon allspice

Combine all ingredients; blend well. Shape into 1-inch balls. Arrange half of the meatballs in single layer on microwave roasting rack. Place in oven. Set recipe number 10. Touch START. *(Oven cooks: micro, 90, 6 minutes.)*

At Pause, remove meatballs from oven and place in chafing dish to keep warm. Arrange remaining meatballs on rack as above. Place in oven. Touch START. *(Oven cooks: micro, 90, 6 minutes.)*

Add to chafing dish. Use toothpicks to spear meatballs. Serve hot with Curry Dipper (page 42.)

60 meatballs

Meatballs can be prepared in advance and reheated on HI 2 to 3 minutes.

Recipe No. [11]

Nachos

Preset Cooking Time: 2 minutes

- 1 can (3⅛ ounces) jalapeño bean dip
- 1 bag (8 ounces) tortilla chips
- 1½ cups (6 ounces) grated Cheddar cheese
- 1 can (2¼ ounces) sliced jalapeño peppers

Spread bean dip lightly on chips. Top with cheese and peppers. Arrange 10 chips on microproof plate. Place in oven. Set recipe number 11. Touch START. *(Oven cooks: micro, 70, 40 seconds.)*

At Pause, remove from oven. Arrange 10 more chips on microproof plate. Place in oven. Touch START. *(Oven cooks: micro, 70, 40 seconds.)*

At Pause, repeat with remaining 10 chips. Touch START. *(Oven cooks: micro, 70, 40 seconds.)*

Serve warm.

30 canapés

Recipe No. [12]

Cold Eggplant Appetizer

Preset Cooking Time: 9 minutes

- 1 eggplant (1 pound)
- 1 small onion, minced
- ½ medium green pepper, seeded and minced
- 1 clove garlic, minced
- 1 teaspoon lemon juice
- ½ teaspoon salt
- ⅛ teaspoon pepper
- 1 cup plain yogurt

Wash eggplant and pierce skin in several places. Place on microwave roasting rack. Place in oven. Set recipe number 12. Touch START. *(Oven cooks: micro, HI, 7 minutes.)*

At Pause, remove from oven; set aside. Combine onion, green pepper, garlic, and lemon juice in small microproof bowl. Place in oven. Touch START. *(Oven cooks: micro, HI, 2 minutes.)*

Cut eggplant in half lengthwise. Scoop pulp into serving bowl. Add onion mixture, salt, and pepper; blend well. Stir in yogurt. Cover and chill thoroughly before serving. Serve with pumpernickel bread, party rye, or crackers.

2 cups

Cold Eggplant Appetizer is a wonderful low-calorie topping for cut-up raw vegetables.

Recipe No. ☐ 13 ☐

Rumaki

Preset Cooking Time: 7 minutes
(repeat twice)

- ½ pound chicken livers, rinsed and drained
- ¼ cup soy sauce
- ¼ teaspoon garlic powder
- 12 thin slices bacon, cut into thirds
- 1 can (8 ounces) sliced water chestnuts, drained

Cut chicken livers into thirty-six 1-inch pieces; discard membranes; set aside. Combine soy sauce and garlic powder; blend well. Dip 1 piece liver in soy sauce mixture. Place on 1 piece bacon. Top with 1 slice water chestnut. Roll up and fasten with toothpick; repeat with remaining liver pieces. Place 12 rumaki in circle on microwave roasting rack. Place in oven. Cover with paper towel. Set recipe number 13. Touch START. *(Oven cooks: micro, HI, 4 minutes.)*

At Pause, turn over. Cover. Touch START. *(Oven cooks: micro, HI, 3 minutes.)*

Repeat procedure for remaining rumaki, cooking 12 at a time. Set recipe number for each batch.

36 appetizers

Recipe No. ☐ 14 ☐

Cheese Fondue

Preset Cooking Time: 8 minutes

- 4 cups (16 ounces) shredded Swiss cheese
- ¼ cup all-purpose flour
- ¼ teaspoon salt
- ¼ teaspoon nutmeg
  Pinch pepper
- 2 cups dry white wine
- 2 tablespoons kirsch
- 1 loaf French bread, cut into cubes

Combine cheese, flour, salt, nutmeg, and pepper in 1½-quart microproof casserole and stir gently to coat cheese with flour. Blend in wine. Cover. Place in oven. Set recipe number 14. Touch START. *(Oven cooks: micro, 50, 2 minutes.)*

At Pause, stir. Recover. Touch STAR *(Oven cooks: micro, 50, 2 minutes.)*

At Pause, stir. Recover. Touch START. *(Oven cooks: micro, 50, 2 minutes.)*

At Pause, stir. Cover. Touch START. *(Oven cooks: micro, 50, 2 minutes.)* Stir through several times to finish melting cheese. Mix in kirsch. Serve immediately with cubes of French bread for dipping. If fondue cools, cook (micro) on 50, 1 to 2 minutes.

6 to 8 servings

Recipe No. ☐ 15 ☐

Stuffed Mushrooms

Preset Cooking Time: 4 minutes

- 24 medium mushrooms, stems removed
- 2 green onions, finely chopped
- ½ cup (2 ounces) shredded Cheddar cheese
- ⅓ cup dry bread crumbs
- ¼ cup butter or margarine, melted
- ½ teaspoon salt
- ½ teaspoon Italian seasoning
- ¼ teaspoon garlic powder
- ⅛ teaspoon pepper
- ½ teaspoon Worcestershire sauce

Chop mushroom stems finely; set caps aside. Combine chopped stems, onions, and cheese; blend well. Add bread crumbs, butter, seasonings, and Worcestershire; blend well. Spoon mixture into caps, mounding slightly in center. Arrange on 10-inch round microproof plate. Place in oven. Set recipe number 15. Touch START. *(Oven cooks: micro, HI, 4 minutes.)*

24 appetizers

The Lunch Counter

Soups, sandwiches, some surprises, and salads will make the family happy at lunch time or anytime. And, for the cook, there's more preparation ease than ever before. Microwave, micro/convection, and convection methods all contribute special and soon-to-be-favorite recipes. You'll especially like soups! Try Country Vegetable Soup (page 52) with a splendid assortment of vegetables or our approach to the traditional favorite, Chicken in the Pot (page 51). Japanese Cauliflower Soup (page 52) will please fans of that vegetable and just might convert those who "wouldn't touch it."

Perhaps the nicest contribution of the oven is its ability to reheat single portions of soup by the microwave method right in the serving cup, mug, or bowl.

Ahhh, sandwiches! Why stick with the same old thing when you can liven-up appetites so easily? Meal-in-One Sandwich (page 60) is enough for a small crowd while Bacon-Tomato-Cheese Grill (page 61) is just-for-you. Deep Dish Pizza (page 61), something like a big open-faced sandwich, also finds a home in this chapter along with other surprises. Try them all with a nice hot beverage!

 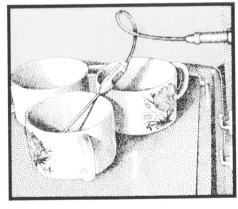

If you are a fan of French Onion Soup with a baked cheese topping, the convection method is the easy answer. Position wire rack in the upper guides and preheat to 450°F. Place soup bowls in oven as shown (above left) and cook, convec, at 450°F 5 minutes, or until cheese is melted and brown. The temperature probe can be used when heating 1 to 4 cups of soup. Arrange cups in a circle and insert probe in one cup. Cook, micro, 80 to 150°F (above right).

← *Country Vegetable Soup (page 52)*

Converting Your Own Soup and Hot Beverage Recipes

Up to now, you've probably looked solely to the stove-top in order to cook soup or heat a beverage. Well, soup adapts so well to this oven and hot beverage preparation is so easy that you might not look to the stove for them ever again! To convert soup, find a recipe in this book similar in density and volume to the conventional soup you want to try. Most soup is cooked by the microwave method but you will want to use micro/convec as well for navy bean, split pea, and others (Old World Lentil Soup, below, is a good guide for those). Here are some tips to remember:

☐ Be careful with milk-based liquids or quantities larger than 2 quarts. They can boil over quickly. Always select a large enough microproof or microproof *and* heatproof container. Fill individual cups no more than two-thirds full.
☐ Soup is cooked covered. Use microproof and heatproof lids or a plate for micro/convection; use those or plastic wrap for microwave.
☐ Cooking time varies with the volume of liquid and density of food in soup. Remember that the shorter cooking times mean less evaporation of liquid. You may want to reduce liquid just a bit when converting.

Recipe No. ☐ 16 ☐

Old World Lentil Soup

Preset Cooking Time: 1 hour

- ¾ cup dried lentils, rinsed and drained
- 5 cups water
- ½ pound Polish sausage, cut into ½-inch slices
- 1 cup chopped onions
- ½ cup chopped celery
- 1 medium tomato, peeled, seeded, and chopped
- 1 clove garlic, minced
- ¼ teaspoon pepper
- ¼ teaspoon salt
- 1 bay leaf

Combine lentils and water in 3-quart casserole and let soak 45 minutes. Add remaining ingredients and mix well. Cover. Place in oven on ceramic tray. Set recipe number 16. Touch START. *(Oven cooks: micro/convec, 320°F, 60 minutes.)* Discard bay leaf. Serve hot.

4 to 6 servings

Recipe No. ☐ 17 ☐

Chili Con Queso Soup

Preset Cooking Time: 18 minutes

- 3 tablespoons butter or margarine
- 1 large onion, minced
- 1 can (28 ounces) peeled tomatoes, drained and cut into pieces, liquid reserved
- 1 can (4 ounces) diced green chilies
- 1 jar (2 ounces) pimientos, diced
  Salt and pepper to taste
- ½ pound Cheddar cheese, shredded
- ¼ pound Monterey Jack Cheese, shredded

Combine butter and onion in 2-quart microproof bowl or soup tureen. Cover with plastic wrap. Place in oven. Set recipe number 17. Touch START. *(Oven cooks: micro, HI, 4 minutes.)*

At Pause, stir through once. Touch START. *(Oven cooks: micro, HI, 3 minutes.)*

At Pause, add tomatoes and liquid, chilies, pimientos, salt, and pepper and blend well. Cover. Touch START. *(Oven cooks: micro, HI, 10 minutes.)*

At Pause, stir in cheeses. Touch START. *(Oven cooks: micro, HI, 1 minute.)* Serve hot.

4 to 6 servings

Japanese Cauliflower Soup (page 52), Tuna Turnovers (page 60)

Recipe No. 18

Canadian Pea Soup

Preset Cooking Time: 1 hour 10 minutes

     5 cups water
     1 package (6 ounces) split pea
        soup mix
     1 potato, peeled and finely chopped
     1 carrot, finely chopped
     1 large onion, chopped
  1½ cup chopped celery
     2 parsley sprigs
     1 clove garlic, minced
     1 bay leaf
     2 teaspoons chicken bouillon
        granules

Combine all ingredients in 3-quart microproof casserole or bowl and blend well. Cover. Place in oven. Set recipe number 18. Touch START. *(Oven cooks: micro, HI, 10 minutes.)*

At Pause, stir. Touch START. *(Oven cooks: micro, HI, 10 minutes.)*

At Pause, stir through several times. Cover. Touch START. *(Oven cooks: micro, 50, 25 minutes.)*

At Pause, stir through several times. Cover. Touch START. *(Oven cooks: micro, 50, 25 minutes.)* Let stand 15 minutes. Discard bay leaf. Add hot water to thin, if desired.

4 to 6 servings

Recipe No. 19

English Beef Rib Broth

Preset Cooking Time: 1 hour 30 minutes

     1 pound beef short ribs
     1 package (6 ounces) dry vegetable
        soup mix with mushrooms
     1 teaspoon salt
     1 teaspoon basil, crumbled
     3 small potatoes, peeled and diced
     2 large carrots, peeled and diced
     1 medium parsnip, peeled and diced
     1 large celery stalk, diced,
        leaves reserved
     1 bay leaf
     7 cups boiling water

Rinse ribs well under hot running water and drain. Arrange in 5-quart glass or ceramic casserole. Add all remaining ingredients, setting celery leaves on top. Cover. Place in oven on ceramic tray. Set recipe number 19. Touch START. *(Oven cooks: micro/convec, 350°F, 60 minutes; stands: 0, 30 minutes.)* Discard bay leaf. Reheat briefly before serving, if necessary.

6 servings

If oven is needed for other cooking during standing time, remove casserole from oven. Touch CLEAR. Set new instructions.

Recipe No. 20

Canned Soup

Preset Cooking Time: About 5 minutes

     1 can (10¾ ounces) soup,
        undiluted

Pour soup into 1½- to 2-quart microproof casserole. Add milk or water as directed on can; blend well. Place in oven. Insert temperature probe. Set recipe number 20. Touch START. *(Oven cooks: micro, 80, 1 to 2½ minutes to 120°F.)*

At Pause, stir. Touch START. *(Oven cooks: micro, 80, to 150°F; holds warm: 1.)*

2 servings

Recipe No. [21]

Chicken in the Pot

Preset Cooking Time: 1 hour 15 minutes

Boiling water
1 chicken (4 pounds), cut up,
   giblets except liver and
   kidney reserved
5 to 6 cups hot water
4 large carrots, cut into chunks
3 medium stalks celery, cut into
   chunks, tops reserved
1 medium onion, cut into quarters
1 small parsnip, peeled and cut
   into chunks
1 tablespoon chicken bouillon
   granules
⅛ teaspoon pepper
Minced parsley

Pour boiling water over chicken to rinse; drain well. Arrange chicken and giblets in 4-quart microproof casserole. Add remaining ingredients except parsley; add more hot water to cover chicken if necessary. Cover and place in oven. Set recipe number 21. Touch START. (*Oven cooks: micro, HI, 1 hour; stands: 0, 15 minutes.*)

Discard celery tops. Divide parsley among individual soup bowls. Ladle soup over parsley.

4 to 6 servings

The boiling water rinse reduces fat and helps eliminate foam. If desired, soup can be strained after cooking and broth served separately. Arrange chicken and vegetables on serving platter, and sprinkle with parsley.

Recipe No. [22] ⊞

Cream of Corn Soup

Preset Cooking Time: 18 minutes

1 can (17 ounces) cream-style corn
1 can (13¾ ounces) chicken
   broth
⅔ cup water
¼ cup thinly sliced zucchini
2 tablespoons water
1 tablespoon cornstarch
2 large eggs, lightly beaten
1 green onion, finely chopped

Combine corn, broth, ⅔ cup water, and zucchini in 2-quart microproof casserole or soup tureen. Cover and place in oven. Set recipe number 22. Touch START. (*Oven cooks: micro, HI, 13 minutes.*)

At Pause, combine 2 tablespoons water and cornstarch; stir until cornstarch is dissolved. Add to soup; blend well. Do not cover. Touch START. (*Oven cooks: micro, HI, 5 minutes.*)

Pour eggs into soup in thin stream, stirring briskly. Garnish with onion and serve immediately.

4 servings

⊞ *Recipe can be increased. See "Quantity", page 12.*

Recipe No. ☐ 23 ☐

Country Vegetable Soup

Preset Cooking Time: 50 minutes

- 4 cups beef broth
- 2 medium potatoes, peeled and cut into ½-inch cubes
- 2 medium carrots, thinly sliced
- 2 small onions, chopped
- 1 can (12 ounces) whole-kernel corn, drained, or 1½ cups fresh corn
- 1 cup shredded cabbage
- 1 can (16 ounces) stewed tomatoes
- 1 teaspoon salt
- ½ teaspoon thyme
- ⅛ teaspoon pepper
- 1 bay leaf
- ⅓ cup chopped parsley

Combine all ingredients except parsley in 4-quart microproof casserole. Cover and place in oven. Set recipe number 23. Touch START. *(Oven cooks: micro, HI, 20 minutes.)*

At Pause, stir. Cover. Touch START. *(Oven cooks: micro, 50, 25 minutes; stands: 0, 5 minutes.)*

Discard bay leaf. Divide parsley among 6 individual soup bowls, and ladle soup over parsley. Serve with crackers or hard rolls.

6 servings

Recipe No. ☐ 24 ☐

Japanese Cauliflower Soup

Preset Cooking Time: 28 minutes

- 3 tablespoons butter or margarine
- ¼ cup all-purpose flour
- ⅛ teaspoon ground nutmeg
- 4 cups chicken broth
- 1 head cauliflower (2½ pounds), broken into florets
- ¼ cup heavy cream or undiluted evaporated milk
- 1 egg yolk
  Minced parsley

Place butter in 2-quart microproof casserole or soup tureen. Place in oven. Set recipe number 24. Touch START. *(Oven cooks: micro, HI, 2 minutes.)*

At Pause, add flour and nutmeg; stir until smooth. Blend in broth. Cover. Touch START. *(Oven cooks: micro, HI, 7 minutes.)*

At Pause, add cauliflower; blend well. Cover. Touch START. *(Oven cooks: micro, HI, 15 minutes.)*

At Pause, remove soup from oven; let stand 10 minutes. Transfer soup in batches to blender or food processor container; cover and purée. Return to casserole. Cover and place in oven. Touch START. *(Oven cooks: micro, HI, 4 minutes.)*

Combine cream and egg yolk; blend well. Add small amount warm soup to egg yolk mixture; blend well; gradually blend into soup. Sprinkle with parsley and serve immediately.

4 servings

Recipe No. | 25 |

Hearty Cheese and Frank Soup

Preset Cooking Time: 23 minutes

- ½ cup sliced celery
- 1 medium carrot, thinly sliced
- ¼ cup chopped onion
- ¼ cup butter or margarine
- 2 tablespoons all-purpose flour
- 2 cans (13¾ ounces each) chicken broth
- ½ pound frankfurters, sliced
- 2 cups (8 ounces) shredded Cheddar cheese
- 1½ cups milk or half-and-half

Combine celery, carrot, onion, and butter in 3-quart microproof casserole or soup tureen. Cover and place in oven. Set recipe number 25. Touch START. (Oven cooks: micro, HI, 4 minutes.)

At Pause, stir. Cover. Touch START. (Oven cooks: micro, HI, 4 minutes.)

At Pause, add flour; stir until smooth. Stir in broth and frankfurters. Cover. Touch START. (Oven cooks: micro, HI, 10 minutes.)

At Pause, add cheese; stir until melted. Stir in milk. Cover. Touch START. (Oven cooks: micro, 50, 5 minutes.)

6 servings

Recipe No. | 26 |

Instant Soups, Soup Mixes

Preset Cooking Time: about 2 minutes

- 1 envelope (1¼ ounces) instant soup mix
- ⅔ cup water

Combine soup mix and water in 8-ounce microproof mug or cup; blend well. Place in oven. Insert temperature probe. Cover with waxed paper. Set recipe number 26. Touch START. (Oven cooks: micro, HI, to 150°F; holds warm: 1.)

1 serving

Recipe No. | 27 |

Quick Green Pea Soup

Preset Cooking Time: 11 minutes

- 1 can (2 ounces) mushroom stems and pieces
- 1 tablespoon butter or margarine
- 2 cans (11½ ounces each) green pea soup, undiluted
- 1 cup grated carrots
- ½ teaspoon salt

Drain mushroom liquid into 2-cup measure. Add water to equal 2 cups liquid; set aside. Place butter in 2-quart microproof casserole or soup tureen. Place in oven. Set recipe number 27. Touch START. (Oven cooks: micro, 60, 1 minute.)

At Pause, add mushrooms, soup, and mushroom-water mixture; stir with fork until blended. Add carrots and salt; blend well. Cover with waxed paper. Touch START. (Oven cooks: micro, 80, 10 minutes.)

Serve hot with croutons or crackers.

4 to 6 servings

Recipe No. 28

New England Clam Chowder

Preset Cooking Time: 19 minutes

- ¼ cup butter, melted
- ¼ cup all-purpose flour
- 2 cans (7½ ounces each) minced clams
- 2 slices bacon, diced
- 2 medium potatoes, peeled and cut into ½-inch cubes
- 1 medium onion, chopped
- 3 cups milk
- ½ teaspoon salt
- ⅛ teaspoon white pepper

Combine butter and flour; blend well; set aside. Drain clam liquid into 2-cup measure; add water to equal 2 cups liquid; set aside. Place bacon in 3-quart microproof casserole or soup tureen. Place in oven. Set recipe number 28. Touch START. *(Oven cooks: micro, HI, 3 minutes.)*

At Pause, add potatoes and onion. Cover. Touch START. *(Oven cooks: micro, 90, 10 minutes.)*

At Pause, add flour mixture; blend well. Stir in clam-water mixture, clams, milk, salt, and pepper. Cover. Touch START. *(Oven cooks: micro, HI, 1 minute.)*

At Pause, stir. Cover. Touch START. *(Oven cooks: micro, HI, 5 minutes.)*

4 to 6 servings

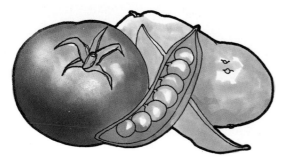

Recipe No. 29 ⊞

Cream of Mushroom Soup

Preset Cooking Time: 7 minutes

- 3 cups chopped mushrooms
- 2½ cups chicken broth
- ½ teaspoon onion powder
- ¼ teaspoon salt
- ⅛ teaspoon garlic powder
- ⅛ teaspoon white pepper
- 1 cup heavy cream

Combine mushrooms, broth, and seasonings in 2-quart microproof casserole or soup tureen. Place in oven. Set recipe number 29. Touch START. *(Oven cooks: micro, HI, 5 minutes.)*

At Pause, blend in cream. Touch START. *(Oven cooks: micro, 60, 2 minutes.)*

6 servings

Recipe No. 30

Tomato Soup Piquante

Preset Cooking Time: 20 minutes

- ½ cup finely chopped celery
- 1 tablespoon butter or margarine
- 1 quart tomato juice
- 1 can (10½ ounces) beef consommé, undiluted
- 1 tablespoon dry sherry
- 1 teaspoon sugar
- ½ teaspoon thyme
- ½ teaspoon celery salt
- ⅛ teaspoon hot pepper sauce
- 4 to 6 slices lemon

Combine celery and butter in 2-quart microproof casserole or soup tureen. Place in oven. Set recipe number 30. Touch START. *(Oven cooks: micro, HI, 5 minutes.)*

At Pause, add remaining ingredients except lemon. Cover. Touch START. *(Oven cooks: micro, 80, 12 minutes; stands: 0, 3 minutes.)*

Garnish with lemon slices before serving.

4 to 6 servings

Recipe No. 31

Cappuccino

Preset Cooking Time: 3½ minutes

  2 cups milk
  ¼ cup semisweet chocolate pieces
  2 teaspoons sugar
  2 teaspoons instant coffee powder
  ½ cup brandy
    Whipped cream

Combine milk, chocolate, sugar, and coffee in 4-cup glass measure. Place in oven. Set recipe number 31. Touch START. *(Oven cooks: micro, HI, 2 minutes.)*

At Pause, stir. Touch START. *(Oven cooks: micro, HI, 1½ minutes.)*

Stir until sugar is dissolved. Divide among 4 mugs. Stir 2 tablespoons brandy into each mug. Top each with dollop of whipped cream before serving. Sprinkle with cinnamon or nutmeg, if desired.

4 servings

Recipe No. 32 ⊞

Irish Coffee

Preset Cooking Time: 2 minutes

  3 tablespoons Irish whiskey
  1 tablespoon instant coffee powder
  2 teaspoons sugar
    Whipped cream

Pour whiskey into 8-ounce microproof mug or cup. Add coffee and sugar. Add water to fill three-fourths full; blend well. Place in oven. Set recipe number 32. Touch START. *(Oven cooks: micro, HI, 2 minutes.)*

Stir until sugar is dissolved. Top with dollop of whipped cream. Do not stir. Coffee should be sipped through the layer of cream.

1 serving

Recipe No. 33 ⊞

Spicy Apple Drink

Preset Cooking Time: 10 minutes

  1 quart apple cider
  ¼ cup firmly-packed brown sugar
  2 sticks cinnamon
  8 whole cloves
  ½ medium lemon, thinly sliced
    Pinch mace
    Pinch nutmeg
  1 medium orange, thinly sliced

Combine cider, brown sugar, cinnamon, cloves, lemon, mace, and nutmeg in 2-quart glass measure; stir until brown sugar is dissolved. Place in oven. Set recipe number 33. Touch START. *(Oven cooks: micro, HI, 10 minutes.)*

Strain into 4 mugs. Garnish with orange slices before serving.

4 servings

Recipe No. 34 ⊞

Hot Buttered Rum

Preset Cooking Time: 1½ minutes

  ¼ cup rum
  2 teaspoons brown sugar
  1½ teaspoons unsalted butter
    Dash nutmeg
  1 stick cinnamon

Combine rum and brown sugar in tall microproof mug or cup. Add water to fill two-thirds full. Place in oven. Set recipe number 34. Touch START. *(Oven cooks: micro, HI, 1½ minutes.)*

Add butter and stir until melted. Sprinkle with nutmeg. Insert cinnamon stick as stirrer.

1 serving

⊞ *Recipe can be increased. See "Quantity", page 12.*

Recipe No. [35] ⊞

Hot Cranberry Punch

Preset Cooking Time: 11 minutes

    3 cups cranberry juice
    1 cup apple juice
    ½ cup orange juice
    3 tablespoons lemon juice
    3 tablespoons sugar
       Whole cloves
    1 stick cinnamon
    1 orange, sliced

Combine juices, sugar, 4 cloves, and cinnamon in 2-quart microproof casserole. Cover and place in oven. Set recipe number 35. Touch START. *(Oven cooks: micro, HI, 11 minutes.)*

Stir until sugar is dissolved. Strain into warmed punch bowl. Stick cloves into orange slices and float slices on punch as garnish.

8 servings

Recipe No. [36]

Hot Devilish Daiquiri

Preset Cooking Time: 6½ minutes

    ½ cup light rum
    1½ cups hot water
    1 can (6 ounces) frozen lemonade
       concentrate
    1 can (6 ounces) frozen limeade
       concentrate
    ¼ cup sugar
    2 sticks cinnamon
    8 whole cloves

Pour rum into 1-cup glass measure; set aside. Combine remaining ingredients in 2-quart microproof casserole; blend well. Place in oven. Set recipe number 36. Touch START. *(Oven cooks: micro, HI, 6 minutes.)*

At Pause, remove from oven; set aside. Place rum in oven. Touch START. *(Oven cooks: micro, HI, 30 seconds.)*

Remove rum from oven. Ignite and pour flaming rum over hot juice mixture. Ladle into punch cups and serve. Garnish with lemon slice and whole clove, if desired.

8 to 10 servings

Recipe No. [37] ⊞

Russian Tea Mix

Preset Cooking Time: 2 minutes

    1 jar (9 ounces) powdered orange
       breakfast drink
    1 package (3 ounces) lemonade mix
    1½ cups instant unsweetened tea
    ⅓ cup sugar
    1 teaspoon cinnamon
    1 teaspoon ground cloves
    ¾ teaspoon ginger
    ¼ teaspoon nutmeg
    1 cup water or cider

Combine all ingredients. Store in covered jar or container until ready to use. To make 1 serving, place 1 to 2 teaspoons mix in 8-ounce microproof mug or cup. Add water or cider; blend well. Place in oven. Set recipe number 37. Touch START. *(Oven cooks: micro, HI, 2 minutes.)* Stir before serving.

64 servings (about 3 cups mix)

For a lower-calorie drink, omit the sugar. If you'd like to serve your guests the regular drink but fix a low-calorie one for yourself, place 1 cup water, 1½ teaspoons instant unsweetened tea, ½ teaspoon grated orange peel, and 1 whole clove in microproof mug. Cook on HI 1½ minutes. If desired, artificial sweetener equal to 2 teaspoons sugar, or to taste, can be added after mixture is heated. Stir with cinnamon stick.

⊞ *Recipe can be increased. See "Quantity", page 12.*

West Coast Cocoa (page 58), →
Cappuccino (page 55),
Hot Devilish Daiquiri

Recipe No. [38] ⊞

Tomato Warmer

Preset Cooking Time: 6 minutes

- 2½ cups tomato juice
- 1 can (10½ ounces) beef broth
- ¼ cup lemon juice
- 1 teaspoon prepared horseradish
- 1 teaspoon parsley flakes
- ½ teaspoon celery salt
- ¼ cup dry sherry (optional)

Combine all ingredients except sherry in 4-cup glass measure. Place in oven. Set recipe number 38. Touch START. (Oven cooks: micro, HI, 6 minutes.)

Pour into 6 mugs. Stir 2 teaspoons sherry into each mug before serving.

6 servings

Recipe No. [39] ⊞

West Coast Cocoa

Preset Cooking Time: 7 minutes

- ⅓ cup unsweetened cocoa powder
- ¼ cup sugar
- 3 cups milk
- 2 teaspoons grated orange peel
- ¼ teaspoon almond extract
- 4 sticks cinnamon

Combine cocoa and sugar in 4-cup glass measure. Add ½ cup milk; blend to make smooth paste. Stir in remaining 2½ cups milk, orange peel, and almond extract; stir until sugar is dissolved. Place in oven. Set recipe number 39. Touch START. (Oven cooks: micro, 70, 7 minutes.)

Pour into 4 mugs. Insert cinnamon sticks as stirrers.

4 servings

Recipe No. [40]

Hot Milk

Preset Cooking Time: about 3 minutes

- 1 cup (8 ounces) milk

Pour milk into microproof mug or cup. Place in oven. Insert temperature probe. Set recipe number 40. Touch START. (Oven cooks: micro, 70, to 140°F; holds warm: 1.)

1 serving

This is an ideal way to heat milk for hot chocolate or any milk-based beverage.

⊞ *Recipe can be increased. See "Quantity", page 12.*

Recipe No. 41

Hot Water

Preset Cooking Time: about 1¾ minutes

1 cup (8 ounces) water

Pour water into microproof mug or cup. Place in oven. Insert temperature probe. Set recipe number 41. Touch START. *(Oven cooks: micro, HI, to 150°F.)*

1 serving

Recipe No. 42 ⊞

Hot Water for Instant Beverages

Preset Cooking Time: 1½ minutes

1 cup (8 ounces) water

Pour water into microproof mug or cup. Place in oven. Set recipe number 42. Touch START. *(Oven cooks: micro, HI, 1½ minutes.)*

1 serving

This is an ideal way to heat water for tea, instant coffee, bouillon, etc.

Converting Your Own Sandwich Recipes

With the renewed interest in bread baking, as well as the whole grain and wonderful French and Italian breads available commercially, the enormous variety of sandwich combinations you can create will tickle your imagination. They are easy to heat in your oven and will leave you well nourished. Unless you want a very crisp bread texture or a grilled effect, you will enjoy doing most sandwiches by the microwave method. Use micro/convection and be sure to preheat the oven if you want a crunch in the bread. It is also helpful to place the sandwich directly on the wire rack whenever you can. Use the convection method with the wire rack in the upper guides for all kinds of grilled sandwiches. You can warm meat sandwiches, filled only with several thin slices of meat per sandwich. Cook, micro, on HI as follows:

1 sandwich: 45 to 50 seconds
2 sandwiches: 1 to 1½ minutes
4 sandwiches: 2 to 2½ minutes

☐ The best breads to use for warmed sandwiches are day-old, full-bodied breads such as rye and whole wheat, and breads rich in eggs and shortening.
☐ When using the microwave method, heat sandwiches on paper napkins, paper towels, or paper plates to absorb the steam and prevent sogginess. Wrap with a paper towel to prevent splattering. Remove wrapping immediately after warming.
☐ Several thin slices of meat heat more quickly and taste better than one thick slice. The slower-cooking thick slice often causes bread to overcook before meat is hot.
☐ Moist fillings, such as that in a Sloppy Joe or a barbecued beef sandwich, should generally be heated separately from the rolls, to prevent sogginess.
☐ For 12-inch frozen pizza, position wire rack in lower guides of oven and preheat to 380°F. Cook, convec, at 380°F 15 to 20 minutes or until brown and crisp.

Recipe No. 43

Tuna Turnovers
Preset Cooking Time: 20 minutes

- 2 hard-cooked eggs
- 1 can (6½ ounces) tuna, drained
- ¼ cup chopped celery
- ¼ cup thinly sliced green onion
- ½ cup mayonnaise
  Salt and pepper to taste
- 1 package (8 ounces) crescent
  roll dough
- 1 cup shredded Cheddar cheese
- 1 egg, beaten

Position wire rack in lower guides of oven. Set recipe number 43. Touch START. *(Oven preheats: convec, 350°F.)* Meanwhile, line glass or ceramic baking dish with aluminum foil. Mash eggs coarsely in mixing bowl. Add tuna, celery, onion, mayonnaise, salt, and pepper and blend well. Unroll dough and separate into 4 rectangles, smoothing perforated lines together. Sprinkle ¼ cup cheese over half of each rectangle. Divide tuna mixture evenly over cheese. Fold dough over tuna mixture, crimping edges to seal. Transfer to dish. Brush turnovers with beaten egg.

At 350°F, place dish in oven. *(Oven cooks: convec, 350°F, 20 minutes.)*

4 servings

If additional browning is desired, cook, convec, at 350°F, 1 to 3 minutes.

Recipe No. 44

Meal-in-One Sandwich
Preset Cooking Time: 4 minutes

- 1 loaf (1 pound) French bread
- 1 to 2 tablespoons mustard
- 2 to 4 tablespoons mayonnaise
- 2 jars (6 ounces each) marinated
  artichoke hearts, drained,
  liquid reserved
- 1 small onion, thinly sliced
  into rings
- 1 large tomato, thinly sliced
- 1 pound sliced meat
- ½ pound sliced Monterey Jack
  or mozzarella cheese

Position wire rack in lower guides of oven. Set recipe number 44. Touch START. *(Oven preheats: convec, 450°F.)* Slice bread in half lengthwise. Spread one half with mustard and the other half with mayonnaise. Break up artichoke hearts and arrange on both halves. Overlap onion rings on bottom half; top with tomato slices. Alternate half of meat on both sides of bread. Spoon some of the artichoke liquid over meat. Top with half of cheese. Add another layer of meat and cheese to both halves.

At 450°F, place halves in oven directly on wire rack. Touch START. *(Oven cooks: micro/convec, 450°F, 4 minutes.)* Remove from oven and close into sandwich. Slice and serve.

6 to 8 servings

Salami, corned beef, ham, turkey, roast beef, or bologna. Choose your favorite or combine them all for this king-size sandwich.

Recipe No. | 45 |

Bacon-Tomato-Cheese Grill

Preset Cooking Time: 8 minutes

    1 tablespoon butter or margarine
    2 slices bread
    2 slices Cheddar cheese
    4 slices bacon, cooked
    1 slice tomato, ½-inch thick

Position wire rack in upper guides of oven. Set recipe number 45. Touch START. *(Oven preheats: convec, 450°F.)* Butter both slices of bread on one side only. Place 1 slice of bread, buttered side down, on baking sheet or aluminum foil tray. Top with 1 slice cheese, then bacon, tomato, and remaining cheese. Top with remaining bread, buttered side up.

At 450°F, place in oven. Touch START. *(Oven cooks: convec, 450°F, 4 minutes.)*

At Pause, turn sandwich over. Touch START. *(Oven cooks: convec, 450°F, 4 minutes.)* Serve immediately.

1 serving

Recipe No. | 46 |

Broiled Hamburgers (medium)

Preset Cooking Time: 8 minutes

    1 pound lean ground beef
    2 tablespoons minced onion
    1 large clove garlic, minced
    ¼ teaspoon salt
    ⅛ teaspoon pepper

Position wire rack in upper guides of oven. Set recipe number 46. Touch START. *(Oven preheats: convec, 450°F.)* Combine all ingredients in medium bowl and mix lightly. Shape into 4 patties. Place on aluminum broiling pan or on sizzle platter.

At 450°F, place in oven. Touch START. *(Oven cooks: convec, 450°F, 4 minutes.)*

At Pause, turn hamburgers over. Touch START. *(Oven cooks: convec, 450°F, 4 minutes.)* Serve immediately.

4 servings

Recipe No. | 47 |

Deep Dish Pizza

Preset Cooking Time: 25½ minutes

    1 loaf (1 pound) frozen white
        bread dough, thawed
    1 can (8 ounces) tomato sauce
    1 large clove garlic, minced
    ½ teaspoon sugar
    ½ teaspoon oregano
    ¼ teaspoon salt
    ⅛ teaspoon pepper
    ¾ cup shredded Monterey Jack
        cheese
    ¾ cup shredded mozzarella cheese
    ¼ cup grated Parmesan cheese

Roll dough out into 12-inch circle. Transfer to deep-dish pizza pan. Cover with towel. Let stand in warm draft-free area. Combine tomato sauce, garlic, sugar, oregano, salt, and pepper in 1-quart glass measure. Cover with plastic wrap. Place in oven. Set recipe number 31. Touch START. *(Oven cooks: micro, HI, 2 minutes.)*

At Pause, stir. Touch START. *(Oven cooks: micro, HI, 1½ minutes.)*

Set sauce aside. Position wire rack in lower guides of oven. Set recipe number 47. Touch START. *(Oven preheats: convec, 350°F.)*

At 350°F, set crust on wire rack. Touch START. *(Oven cooks: convec, 350°F, 10 minutes.)*

At Pause, cover with sauce, spreading evenly. Top with cheeses and your choice of other toppings. Place in oven. Touch START. *(Oven cooks: convec, 350°F, 12 minutes.)* Cut into wedges and serve immediately.

6 to 8 servings

This is one of several recipes that use the preset functions of another recipe for part of the cooking sequence. Set recipe number 31 first. At the end of that sequence, set recipe number 47.

Recipe No. | 48 |

Pita Pizza

Preset Cooking Time: 7½ minutes

- 6 pita (pocket) breads
- 3 cups Italian-style tomato sauce
- 1 cup shredded Cheddar cheese
  Minced parsley

Split pitas in half, as for English muffins. Set 4 halves, split side up, on large microproof plate. Spoon ¼ cup sauce over each half and sprinkle with cheese. Repeat with remaining halves on separate microproof plates. Place in oven. Set recipe number 48. Touch START. *(Oven cooks: micro, HI, 2½ minutes.)*

At Pause, place second plate in oven. Touch START. *(Oven cooks: micro, HI, 2½ minutes.)*

At Pause, place third plate in oven. Touch START. *(Oven cooks: micro, HI, 2½ minutes.)* Sprinkle with parsley before serving.

12 servings

Recipe No. | 49 |

Beef Tacos

Preset Cooking Time: 7 minutes

- 1 pound lean ground beef
- 1 small onion, chopped
- 1 envelope (1¼ ounces) taco seasoning mix
- 10 taco shells
- 1½ cups (6 ounces) shredded Cheddar cheese, divided
- 2 cups shredded lettuce
- 2 medium tomatoes, chopped
- 1 avocado, peeled and diced
  Dairy sour cream (optional)
  Hot pepper sauce (optional)

Crumble beef into 2-quart microproof casserole. Add onion. Place in oven. Set recipe number 49. Touch START. *(Oven cooks: micro, HI, 2 minutes.)*

At Pause, stir to break up beef. Touch START. *(Oven cooks: micro, HI, 3 minutes.)*

At Pause, remove from oven. Stir beef; drain. Stir in seasoning mix. Stand taco shells in large, shallow, microproof baking dish. Divide beef mixture among shells. Top each with about 1 tablespoon cheese. Place in oven. Touch START. *(Oven cooks: micro, HI, 2 minutes.)*

Remove tacos from oven. Top each with lettuce, tomatoes, remaining cheese, and avocado. Pass sour cream and hot pepper sauce separately.

10 tacos

Diced radishes, cucumber, or green onions also make delicious toppings.

Recipe No. | 50 |

Italian Meatball Sandwich

Preset Cooking Time: 9 minutes

- 1 pound lean ground beef
- 1 cup cooked rice
- 1 small onion, finely chopped
- 2 large eggs, lightly beaten
- 1 tablespoon Italian seasoning
- 1 jar (15 ounces) spaghetti sauce
- 1 loaf (1 pound) French or Italian bread, cut in half lengthwise
  Grated Parmesan cheese

Combine beef, rice, onion, eggs, and seasoning; blend well. Shape into 8 balls. Arrange meatballs in circle on microwave roasting rack. Place in oven. Set recipe number 50. Touch START. *(Oven cooks: micro, HI, 3 minutes.)*

At Pause, turn over. Touch START. *(Oven cooks: micro, HI, 2 minutes.)*

At Pause, remove meatballs from oven. Place in microproof casserole. Top with sauce. Cover and place in oven. Touch START. *(Oven cooks: micro, HI, 4 minutes.)*

Spoon meatballs and sauce onto bottom half of loaf. Sprinkle generously with cheese. Cover with top of loaf, slice in half, and serve hot.

← Reuben Sandwich (page 64)

2 sandwiches

Recipe No. | 51 | ⊞

Coney Island Hot Dog

Preset Cooking Time: 1¼ minutes

- 1 jumbo hot dog (3 ounces)
- 1 hot dog bun, split
  Prepared mustard
- 2 tablespoons drained sauerkraut
  Pickle relish, chili, grated
    cheese, chopped onion
    (optional)

Score opposite sides of hot dog in several places. Place on microproof plate. Place in oven. Set recipe number 51. Touch START. *(Oven cooks: micro, HI, 1 minute.)*

At Pause, remove from oven. Place hot dog in bun. Place in oven. Touch START. *(Oven cooks: micro, HI, 15 seconds.)*

Top with mustard, sauerkraut, and selected garnish.

1 serving

Recipe No. | 52

Reuben Sandwich

Preset Cooking Time: 8 minutes

- 4 slices rye or pumpernickel bread
  Butter or margarine
- 6 ounces corned beef, thinly
    sliced
- ½ cup drained sauerkraut
- 2 heaping tablespoons Thousand
    Island dressing
- 2 slices Swiss cheese

Position wire rack in upper guides of oven. Set recipe number 52. Touch START. *(Oven preheats: convec, 450°F.)* Lightly butter one side of each slice of bread. Place 2 slices bread, buttered side down, on baking sheet or aluminum foil tray. Layer remaining ingredients evenly over tops. Cover with remaining slices of toast, buttered side up.

At 450°F, place in oven. Touch START. *(Oven cooks: convec, 450°F, 4 minutes.)*

At Pause, turn sandwiches over. Touch START. *(Oven cooks: convec, 450°F, 4 minutes.)* Serve immediately.

2 servings

Recipe No. | 53

Hot Tuna Buns

Preset Cooking Time: 2 minutes

- 1 can (6½ to 7 ounces) tuna,
    drained and flaked
- 1 cup chopped celery
- ¼ cup mayonnaise
- 2 tablespoons catsup
- 1 teaspoon lemon juice
    Salt and pepper to taste
- 4 hamburger buns, split

Combine tuna, celery, mayonnaise, catsup, and lemon juice. Season with salt and pepper. Spoon mixture onto bottom halves of buns; cover with tops of buns. Place 2 sandwiches on microwave roasting rack. Place in oven. Set recipe number 53. Touch START. *(Oven cooks: micro, 80, 1 minute.)*

At Pause, remove sandwiches from oven. Place remaining 2 sandwiches on rack in oven. Touch START. *(Oven cooks: micro, 80, 1 minute.)*

4 sandwiches

Recipe No. | 54

Hot Ham and Swiss

Preset Cooking Time: about 3 minutes

- 2 slices rye bread
  Butter or margarine
  Mayonnaise
- 2 thin slices boiled ham
- 1 slice Swiss cheese

Spread bread with butter and mayonnaise. Place ham and cheese between bread slices. Place on microwave roasting rack. Place in oven. Insert temperature probe at least 1 inch into center of sandwich. Set recipe number 54. Touch START. *(Oven cooks: micro, HI, to 110°F; stands: 0, 2 minutes.)*

1 sandwich

⊞ *Recipe can be increased. See "Quantity", page 12.*

Sausage and Pepper Heroes (page 66) →
Coney Island Hot Dog

Recipe No. [55]

Bacon Cheesewiches

Preset Cooking Time: 4 minutes

- ½ cup (2 ounces) grated Cheddar cheese
- 1 tablespoon mayonnaise
- 2 teaspoons catsup
- 1 large egg, hard-cooked and chopped
- 2 slices bacon
- 2 hamburger buns, split

Combine cheese, mayonnaise, catsup, and egg; blend well; set aside. Place bacon on paper towel-lined microproof plate. Place in oven. Cover with paper towel. Set recipe number 55. Touch START. (Oven cooks: micro, HI, 2½ minutes.)

At Pause, remove from oven. Break each slice in half; set aside. Spread half of the cheese mixture on bottom half of each bun. Place on microwave roasting rack. Place in oven. Touch START. (Oven cooks: micro, 50, 1 minute.)

At Pause, place 2 halves bacon on each sandwich. Cover with tops of buns. Touch START. (Oven cooks: micro, 50, 30 seconds.)

2 sandwiches

Recipe No. [56]

Barbecued Beef-on-a-Bun

Preset Cooking Time: 19 minutes

- 1 pound top round steak
- ¼ cup butter or margarine
- 1½ tablespoons cornstarch
- ¼ cup beef broth
- ¼ cup lemon juice
- ½ cup chili sauce
- 1 tablespoon brown sugar
- 1 tablespoon instant minced onion
- 1 tablespoon Worcestershire sauce
- 1 teaspoon prepared horseradish
- ½ teaspoon salt
- ¼ teaspoon paprika
- ¼ teaspoon hot pepper sauce
- 1 small clove garlic, minced
- 6 heated buns

Cut steak across grain into very thin strips; set aside. Place butter in 2½-quart

microproof casserole. Place in oven. Set recipe number 56. Touch START. (Oven cooks: micro, HI, 1 minute .)

At Pause, add steak; stir to coat. Cover. Touch START. (Oven cooks: micro, 50, 5 minutes.)

At Pause, stir. Cover. Touch START. (Oven cooks: micro, 50, 3 minutes.)

At Pause, dissolve cornstarch in broth and lemon juice. Add to steak. Add remaining ingredients except buns; blend well. Cover. Touch START. (Oven cooks: micro, 50, 10 minutes.)

Let stand 2 minutes before serving on buns.

6 sandwiches

It's hard to imagine a sandwich that is not improved by warming the buns first. Cook 6 buns on 20 for 2 to 3 minutes; 4 buns take 1 to 1½ minutes.

Recipe No. [57]

Sausage and Pepper Heroes

Preset Cooking Time: 6½ minutes

- 4 Italian sausages
- ½ cup barbecue sauce
- 1 medium green pepper, seeded and cut into strips
- 4 hero rolls

Score sausages on opposite sides in several places. Place on microwave roasting rack. Place in oven. Cover with paper towel. Set recipe number 57. Touch START. (Oven cooks: micro, HI, 3 minutes.)

At Pause, remove from oven; set aside. Combine barbecue sauce and green pepper in 2-cup glass measure. Place in oven. Touch START. (Oven cooks: micro, HI, 2 minutes.)

At Pause, remove from oven. Split rolls in half without cutting all the way through. Place 1 sausage in each roll. Top each with sauce. Wipe rack clean with paper towel. Arrange rolls on rack. Place in oven. Touch START. (Oven cooks: micro, 50, 1½ minutes.)

4 sandwiches

The Baker's Secret

Press your face against the "window" of this scrumptious array of breads, sweet rolls, muffins, and coffee cakes. Imagine the aroma of yesterday that they can bring to your kitchen! The baker's secret? Convection ovens were first employed by commercial bread bakers to circulate the heated air and provide even browning. How natural it is, then, that the convection method performs at its best with baked goods in your new oven. If you are new to baking, so much the better — you're lucky to begin now with the advantage of commercial baking technology. You will find, of course, that the microwave and micro/convection methods make their own contributions to your success, too.

There are many breads and rolls here, including a fancy Braided Bread (page 69), the basic Homemade White Bread (page 72), and Cinnamon Loaf (page 70). Shortcut baking is also provided with rising and baking instructions for Bread-from-the-Freezer (page 69). Next comes an array of muffins and quick-breads to delight even the fussiest family. Buttermilk fans have their choice of Buttermilk Bran Muffins (page 69) or Buttermilk Corn Bread (page 70). If you want smiles all-around the table, why not wake the gang up to a piping-hot Sour Cream Coffeecake (page 76). Go ahead! Your oven knows the way.

One of the aids to fine baking that the microwave method provides is a shortcut approach to the dough-rising process. Nearly-fill a 1-cup glass measure with water and place in the oven. Cook, micro, HI, 3 minutes. Place loaf pan in oven with glass measure as illustrated (above left). Cook, micro 10, 5 minutes. Turn dough over and continue to cook, micro, 10, for another 5 minutes. The procedure is preset for you in the Bread-from-the-Freezer recipe (page 69). Custard cups arranged in a circle may be used to make muffins using an alternate microwave-only method. Cook, micro, HI, 2½ minutes, six at a time until all batter has been used (above right).

Converting Your Recipes

The convection method is the starting point for conversion of your own bread, coffeecake or muffin recipes. Remember that except for the increased efficiency of the fan-circulated hot air, this method is identical to your conventional oven.

There are, however, several times when the micro/convection method is appropriate, Oatmeal Muffins (page 75) is an example. The microwaves assist the cooking process. But the best clue, again, will be a recipe here that is similar to the one you want to try. Tips:

☐ Frozen bread dough is remarkably versatile. Don't hesitate to substitute it for homemade dough, and vice versa.

☐ When baking with the microwave or micro/convection method, fill cake pans and muffin pans only one-half full to allow for the increased rising those methods produce.

☐ Heat bread slices on paper napkins or paper towels to absorb excess moisture. Cook, micro, 80, 10 seconds for 1 to 3 slices.

GUIDE TO CONVENIENCE BREADS*

Food	Programming Method	Setting	First Stage	Second Stage	Special Notes
Butterflake rolls, refrigerated, 8 oz.	convec	350°	10 - 12 min.		Lower guides. Preheat. 6-cup metal muffin pan.
Buttermilk biscuits, refrigerated, 8 oz.	convec	380°	10 - 13 min.		Lower guides. Preheat. Cookie sheet or foil tray.
Caramel rolls, refrigerated, 11 oz.	convec	follow package directions			Lower guides. Preheat. Cookie sheet or foil tray.
Cinnamon rolls, refrigerated, 9½ oz.	convec	370°	8 - 10 min.		Lower guides. Preheat. Cookie sheet or foil tray.
Cornbread mix, 15 oz.	convec	400°	10 min. turn	change to micro/convec 400° 10 min.	On ceramic tray. Preheat. 8-inch square baking dish.
Crescent rolls, refrigerated, 8 oz.	convec	380°	10 - 13 min.		Lower guides. Preheat. Cookie sheet or foil tray.
English muffins, waffles, frozen, (2)	micro	HI (max. power)	30 - 45 sec.		Place on paper towels.
Hamburger buns, hot dog rolls, frozen, 1 lb.	micro	30 (defrost)	1 - 2 min.	1 - 2 min.	Original container, paper plate or towels. On microproof rack.
Muffin mix	micro or convec	follow package directions			Lower guides. Preheat.
Nut bread mix	micro or convec	follow package directions			Lower guides. Preheat.
Sweet rolls, muffins, (4)	micro	80 (reheat)	18 - 20 seconds		Place on paper plate or towels. Add 15 seconds if frozen.

* Due to the tremendous variety in convenience food products available, times given here should be used only as guidelines. We suggest you cook food for the shortest recommended time and then check for doneness. Be sure to check the package for microwave and oven (convec) instructions.

Recipe No. [58]

Braided Bread

Preset Cooking Time: 30 minutes

Dough for Homemade White Bread
(page 72)
1 egg yolk, beaten
Poppy seeds, sesame seeds, or
uncooked oatmeal flakes

Prepare dough and let rise as directed. Generously grease baking dish. Set aside. Divide dough into thirds. Stretch each into cylinder about 9 inches long. Attach strips at one end and braid. Transfer to prepared baking dish. Cover with towel. Let stand in warm, draft-free area until doubled.

Position wire rack in lower guides of oven. Set recipe number 58. Touch START. *(Oven preheats: convec, 350°F.)* Brush top of loaf with egg yolk and sprinkle with topping.

At 350°F, place in oven on wire rack. Touch START. *(Oven cooks: convec, 350°F, 30 minutes.)* Turn loaf out onto wire rack and let cool before slicing.

1 loaf

Recipe No. [59]

Bread-from-the Freezer

Preset Cooking Time: 43 minutes

1 loaf (1 pound) frozen bread
dough
1 cup water
1 egg, beaten
Poppy seeds, sesame seeds,
uncooked oatmeal flakes
dehydrated onion flakes
(optional)

Place frozen dough in 8×5-inch microproof loaf pan or in microproof dish. Nearly fill 1-cup glass measure with water. Place in oven. Set recipe number 59. Touch START. *(Oven cooks: micro HI, 3 minutes.)*

At Pause, place loaf pan in oven (leave water in oven). Touch START. *(Oven cooks: micro, 10, 5 minutes.)*

At Pause, turn dough over in pan. Touch START. *(Oven cooks: micro, 10, 5 minutes.)*

Let dough stand in pan until at least doubled, 45 to 60 minutes. Dough may now be worked, if desired, and shaped into rolls or fitted into pizza pan. To bake loaf: generously grease 8×5-inch metal loaf pan. Turn dough into pan. Cover with towel. Let

stand in warm, draft-free area until doubled.

Set recipe number 62. Touch START. *(Oven preheats: convec, 350°F.)* Brush top of loaf with egg. Sprinkle with topping, if desired.

At 350°F, set pan on ceramic tray. Place in oven. Touch START. *(Oven cooks: convec, 350°F, 30 minutes.)* Transfer to wire rack and let cool before slicing.

1 loaf

This is one of several recipes that use the preset functions of another recipe for part of the cooking sequence. Set recipe number 59 first. At the end of that sequence, set recipe number 62.

Recipe No. [60]

Buttermilk Bran Muffins

Preset Cooking Time: 8 minutes

2 cups whole wheat flour
1½ cups whole unprocessed bran
or bran bud cereal
2 tablespoons sugar
1½ teaspoons baking soda
¼ teaspoon salt
2 cups buttermilk
½ cup molasses
1 egg, beaten
3 tablespoons butter or margarine,
melted
1 cup chopped nuts

Position wire rack in lower guides of oven. Set recipe number 60. Touch START. *(Oven preheats: convec, 370°F.)* Meanwhile, prepare microproof muffin pan (one that manufacturer specifies is also heatproof) with paper liners. Mix flour, cereal, sugar, baking soda, and salt in medium bowl. Blend buttermilk, molasses, egg, and butter in large bowl. Add dry ingredients and mix thoroughly. Fold in nuts. Fill liners three-quarters full.

At 370°F, place in oven. Touch START. *(Oven cooks: micro/convec, 370°F, 4 minutes.)*

At Pause, remove from oven. Prepare second batch with remaining batter. Place pan in oven. Touch START. *(Oven cooks: micro/convec, 370°F, 4 minutes.)*

16 to 20 muffins

Recipe No. | 61 |

Buttermilk Corn Bread

Preset Cooking Time: 35 minutes

- 1½ cups fine cornmeal
- ½ cup all-purpose flour
- 3 teaspoons baking powder
- 1 tablespoon sugar
- 1 teaspoon salt
- 1 cup buttermilk
- 2 eggs, lightly beaten
- ¼ cup butter or margarine, melted
- 1 can (7 ounces) corn kernels with green peppers and pimiento, drained

Set recipe number 61. Touch START. *(Oven preheats: convec, 420°F.)* Meanwhile, grease 8-inch square metal baking pan. Set aside. Mix cornmeal, flour, baking powder, sugar, and salt in medium bowl. Blend buttermilk, eggs, and butter in another bowl. Add to cornmeal mixture and blend thoroughly. Stir in corn. Pour into prepared pan.

At 420°F, place in oven. Touch START. *(Oven cooks: convec, 420°F, 30 minutes.)*

At Pause, rotate dish one-half turn. Touch START. *(Oven cooks: convec, 420°F, 5 minutes.)* Cut into squares and serve warm or at room temperature.

8 servings

Recipe No. | 62 |

Cinnamon Loaf

Preset Cooking Time: 30 minutes

- Dough for Homemade White Bread (page 72)
- ¼ cup butter or margarine, melted, divided
- ½ cup firmly-packed light brown sugar
- ¼ cup cinnamon

Prepare dough as directed. Grease 8×5-inch metal loaf pan; set aside. Roll dough out into 8×12-inch rectangle. Brush with all but 2 teaspoons melted butter. Sprinkle brown sugar and cinnamon evenly over top. Carefully roll up into cylinder; shape into loaf. Transfer to prepared pan. Cover with towel and let stand in warm, draft-free area until doubled.

Set recipe number 62. Touch START. *(Oven preheats: convec, 350°F.)* Brush top of loaf with remaining melted butter.

At 350°F, place in oven. Touch START. *(Oven cooks: convec, 350°F, 30 minutes.)* Transfer to wire rack. Serve warm.

1 loaf

Recipe No. | 63 |

Garlic Bread

Preset Cooking Time: 6 minutes

- 1 loaf (1 pound) French or sourdough bread
- ½ cup mayonnaise
- ¼ cup grated Parmesan cheese
- 3 cloves garlic, minced or 1 teaspoon garlic powder
- Paprika

Position wire rack in lower guides of oven. Set recipe number 63. Touch START. *(Oven preheats: convec, 450°F.)* Set foil or aluminum pan underneath rack to catch drippings. Slice bread in half lengthwise. Set halves, cut side up, on work surface. Combine mayonnaise, cheese, and garlic in small bowl and blend well. Spread mixture generously over each half of loaf. Sprinkle lightly with paprika.

At 450°F, place bread in oven directly on wire rack. Touch START. *(Oven cooks: convec, 450°F, 6 minutes.)* Serve immediately.

8 servings

Yes, that's right, this delicious garlic bread uses mayonnaise! The more traditional way is to substitute ¼ cup butter or margarine for the mayonnaise.

Onion Board (page 72), →
Quick Crescent Rolls (page 74),
Buttermilk Corn Bread

Recipe No. | 64 |

Homemade White Bread

Preset Cooking Time: 35 minutes

- 1 package active dry yeast
- ¼ cup warm water (105° to 115°F)
- 1 cup warm water (105° to 115°F)
- 1 cup warm milk (105° to 115°F)
- 3 tablespoons sugar
- 3 tablespoons solid vegetable shortening, melted
- 1 tablespoon salt
- 5 to 6 cups all-purpose flour
- 1 egg yolk mixed with 1 teaspoon water

Lightly grease large bowl and two 9 × 5-inch metal loaf pans; set aside. Dissolve yeast in ¼ cup warm water in another large bowl. Let stand until foamy, about 10 minutes. Add 1 cup warm water, milk, sugar, shortening, and salt, and mix well. Blend in 4 cups flour, then gradually add enough remaining flour to make dough easy to handle. Turn dough out onto lightly floured surface and knead until smooth and elastic. Transfer to greased bowl, turning to coat all surfaces. Cover and let stand in warm, draft-free area about 1 hour, or until doubled in bulk.

Punch dough down; divide in half. Roll each half out on lightly floured surface into 9 × 14-inch rectangle. Roll up along short end, pinching to seal. Transfer to prepared metal loaf pans. Cover each with towel. Let stand in warm, draft-free area 1 to 1½ hours, or until doubled.

Position wire rack in lower guides of oven. Set recipe number 64. Touch START. *(Oven preheats: convec, 350°F.)*

At Pause, brush each loaf with some of egg mixture. Set pans in center of rack. Touch START. *(Oven cooks: convec, 350°F, 35 minutes.)*

Turn loaves out onto wire rack and let cool before slicing.

2 loaves

For an easy and foolproof method of rising, nearly fill 1-cup glass measure with water and cook on HI about 3 minutes, or until boiling. Leave in oven and set dough alongside.

Recipe No. | 65 |

Onion Board

Preset Cooking Time: 28 minutes

- ¾ cup dehydrated onion flakes
- ¾ cup water
- 1 loaf (1 pound) frozen white bread dough
- 1 egg yolk, lightly beaten
- 1 teaspoon poppy seeds (optional)

Combine onions and water in small bowl. Set aside. Thaw dough and let rise according to directions for Bread-from-the-Freezer (page 69). Roll dough into 12-inch circle. Transfer to aluminum deep-dish pizza pan. Cover with towel and let stand in warm, draft-free area 1 hour.

Position wire rack in lower guides of oven. Set recipe number 65. Touch START. *(Oven preheats: convec, 370°F.)* Meanwhile, drain onions well. Spread evenly over dough, leaving 1-inch border around edge. Brush border and any other exposed dough with egg yolk. Sprinkle with poppy seeds.

At 370°F, place pan in oven on wire rack. Touch START. *(Oven cooks: convec, 370°F, 10 minutes.)*

At Pause, rotate dish one-half turn. Touch START. *(Oven cooks: convec, 370°F, 8 minutes; stands: 0, 10 minutes.)* Cut into wedges and serve. For additional crisping, let stand on rack in cool area several hours.

6 to 8 servings

For real New York bakery Onion Board, spread onion mixture over dough before letting dough rise. Let rise just slightly; flatten, then bake as directed above.

Chocolate Soufflé (page 192), Braided Bread (page 69), Homemade White Bread →

Recipe No. | 66 |

Onion-Cheese Loaf

Preset Cooking Time: 30 minutes

Dough for Homemade White
Bread (page 72)
½ cup dehydrated onion flakes
½ cup warm water
1 cup (4 ounces) shredded Cheddar
cheese
2 tablespoons poppy seeds, divided
1 tablespoon butter or margarine,
melted

Prepare dough as directed. Generously grease 8 × 5-inch metal loaf pan. Combine onions and warm water in 1-cup measure. Let stand 5 minutes to soften; drain well. Set aside 1½ tablespoons onion. Transfer remainder to small bowl. Add cheese and 1 tablespoon poppy seeds and mix well. Roll dough into 6 × 12-inch rectangle. Sprinkle with cheese mixture. Roll up into cylinder. Shape into loaf and seal edges. Transfer to prepared metal loaf pan. Cover with towel. Let stand in warm, draft-free area until doubled.

Set recipe number 66. Touch START. *(Oven preheats: convec, 350°F.)* Brush top of loaf with melted butter. Sprinkle with remaining onion and poppy seed.

At 350°F, place in oven. Touch START. *(Oven cooks: convec, 350°F, 30 minutes.)* Turn out onto rack and let cool before slicing.

1 loaf

Recipe No. | 67 |

Pumpkin Nut Ring

Preset Cooking Time: 16 minutes

1 cup canned pumpkin
1 cup sugar
½ cup buttermilk
⅓ cup vegetable oil
2 eggs, well beaten
1⅔ cups all-purpose flour
1 cup chopped walnuts
2 teaspoons pumpkin pie spice
1 teaspoon baking soda
½ teaspoon salt

Set recipe number 67. Touch START. *(Oven preheats: convec, 350°F.)* Generously grease 6-cup glass or ceramic ring mold.

Combine pumpkin, sugar, buttermilk, oil, and eggs in large bowl and mix thoroughly. Blend flour, nuts, spice, baking soda, and salt in another bowl. Add to pumpkin mixture and blend well. Pour into prepared mold.

At 350°F, place in oven on ceramic tray. Touch START. *(Oven cooks: micro/convec, 350°F, 8 minutes.)*

At Pause, rotate dish one-half turn. Touch START. *(Oven cooks: micro/convec, 350°F, 8 minutes.)* Let cool slightly before removing from mold.

8 to 10 servings

Recipe No. | 68 |

Quick Crescent Rolls

Preset Cooking Time: 15 minutes

1 loaf (1 pound) frozen bread
dough
1 egg yolk

Thaw dough and let rise as directed for Bread-from-the-Freezer (page 69). Roll dough into 8 × 12-inch rectangle. Cut into 6 equal pieces. Cut each piece into 2 triangles. Beginning with wide end, roll each triangle, ending with point on top. Transfer to baking sheet. Cover with towel. Let stand in warm, draft-free area until doubled. Gently brush tops with egg yolk.

Position wire rack in lower guides of oven. Set recipe number 68. Touch START. *(Oven preheats: convec, 350°F.)*

At 350°F, place rolls in oven. Touch START. *(Oven cooks: convec, 350°F, 15 minutes.)* Serve warm.

12 rolls

For cloverleaf rolls: Divide dough into 36 pieces and form each piece into ball. Place 3 in each cup of muffin pan. Cover with towel. Let stand in warm, draft-free area until doubled. Gently brush tops with egg yolk. Sprinkle with poppy seeds, if desired. Set recipe number 68 and continue as above.

For cinnamon rolls: Roll dough into 8 × 12-inch rectangle. Brush with 2 tablespoons

elted butter. Combine 2 teaspoons cin-
amon, ½ cup sugar, and ¼ cup raisins.
prinkle over dough, reserving 2 table-
poons. Beginning with long side, roll dough
p tightly jelly-roll fashion. Cut into 12 slices.
lace in lightly buttered 9-inch pie plate.
Brush with 1 tablespoon melted butter and
prinkle with remaining cinnamon mixture.
Cover with towel. Let stand in warm, draft-
ree area until doubled. Set recipe number
68 and continue as above.

Recipe No. 69

Quick Date Nut Bread

Preset Cooking Time: 25 minutes

- 2½ cups all-purpose flour
- 1 cup firmly-packed brown sugar
- 1 tablespoon baking powder
- ½ teaspoon salt
- 1¼ cups milk
- 3 tablespoons butter or margarine, melted
- 1 egg, beaten
- ¾ cup chopped dates
- ¾ cup chopped walnuts

Position wire rack in lower guides of the oven. Set recipe number 69. Touch START. (Oven preheats: convec, 320°F.) Meanwhile, grease and flour 9×5-inch glass or ceramic loaf pan, shaking out excess flour. Combine 2½ cups flour, sugar, baking powder, and salt in 2-quart bowl. Add milk, butter, and egg and mix well. Fold in dates and walnuts. Pour into prepared pan.

At 320°F, place in oven. Touch START. (Oven cooks: micro/convec, 320°F, 10 minutes.)

At Pause, rotate pan one-half turn. Touch START. (Oven cooks: micro/convec, 320°F, 15 minutes.) Let stand 5 minutes. Invert onto wire rack and let cool completely before slicing.

1 loaf

Recipe No. 70

Oatmeal Muffins

Preset Cooking Time: 12 minutes

- 3 tablespoons chopped nuts
- 2 tablespoons brown sugar
  Dash nutmeg
- ⅔ cup firmly packed brown sugar
- ½ cup vegetable oil
- ½ cup buttermilk or sour milk
- 2 large eggs, beaten
- 1 cup all-purpose flour
- ⅔ cup rolled oats
- 1 teaspoon baking powder
- ½ teaspoon baking soda
- ½ teaspoon salt

Combine nuts, 2 tablespoons brown sugar, and nutmeg; set aside. Combine ⅔ cup brown sugar, oil, buttermilk, and eggs and blend well. Add remaining ingredients except nut mixture and stir just until moistened.

Set recipe number 70. Touch START. (Oven preheats: convec, 370°F.) Spoon one-third of batter into 6 paper-lined microproof and heatproof muffin cups, filling cups half full. Sprinkle with one-third of nut mixture.

At 370°F, place in oven on ceramic tray. Touch START. (Oven cooks: micro/convec, 370°F, 4 minutes.)

At Pause, remove from oven. Turn out of molds and cool on rack. Prepare 6 additional muffin cups. Place in oven on ceramic tray. Touch START. (Oven cooks: micro/convec, 370°F, 4 minutes.)

At Pause, remove from oven. Turn out of molds and cool on rack. Prepare final 6 muffin cups. Place in oven on ceramic tray. Touch START. (Oven cooks: micro/convec, 370°F, 4 minutes.)

18 muffins

Recipe No. | 71 |

Sour Cream Coffeecake

Preset Cooking Time: 18 minutes

   ½ cup chopped nuts
   ⅓ cup firmly-packed brown sugar
   2 tablespoons all-purpose flour
   2 tablespoons butter or margarine
   ¼ teaspoon cinnamon
   ⅛ teaspoon salt
   ½ cup butter or margarine,
        softened
   ½ cup sugar
   2 large eggs
   ½ teaspoon vanilla
 1½ cups all-purpose flour
   ½ teaspoon baking soda
   ½ teaspoon baking powder
   ½ cup dairy sour cream

Set recipe number 71. Touch START. *(Oven preheats: convec, 350°F.)* Meanwhile, combine nuts, brown sugar, 2 tablespoons flour, 2 tablespoons butter, cinnamon, and salt and mix until crumbly; set aside. Cream ½ cup butter and sugar with electric mixer until light and fluffy. Add eggs and vanilla and blend well. Sift 1½ cups flour, baking soda, and baking powder into another bowl. Alternately beat flour mixture and sour cream into creamed mixture. Spread half of the batter in 8-inch round microproof baking dish. Sprinkle with half of the nut mixture. Carefully spread remaining batter on top. Sprinkle with remaining nut mixture.

At 350°F, place in oven on ceramic tray. Touch START. *(Oven cooks: micro/convec, 350°F, 6 minutes.)*

At Pause, rotate dish one-half turn. Touch START. *(Oven cooks: micro/convec, 350°F, 7 minutes; stands: 0, 5 minutes.)* Serve warm.

9 servings

Recipe No. | 72 |

Zucchini-Nut Bread

Preset Cooking Time: 26 minutes

   1 cup sugar, divided
   2 teaspoons cinnamon
   1 cup grated zucchini
   2 large eggs
   ½ cup vegetable oil
   ½ cup plain yogurt
   1 teaspoon vanilla
 1¾ cups all-purpose flour
   ⅔ cup chopped walnuts
   1 teaspoon baking soda
   1 teaspoon salt

Position wire rack in lower guides of oven. Set recipe number 72. Touch START. *(Oven preheats: convec, 350°F.)* Lightly grease 6-cup microproof and heatproof ring mold. Combine 2 teaspoons sugar and cinnamon. Sprinkle into mold, shaking to spread evenly; discard excess. Set mold aside. Combine remaining sugar, zucchini, eggs, oil, yogurt, and vanilla and blend well. Add remaining ingredients and mix well. Pour into prepared mold.

At 350°F, place in oven on wire rack. Touch START. *(Oven cooks: micro/convec, 350°F, 8 minutes.)*

At Pause, rotate one-half turn. Touch START. *(Oven cooks: micro/convec, 350°F, 8 minutes; stands: 0, 10 minutes.)* Turn out onto rack. Cool completely before slicing.

12 to 18 servings

The perfect method for cooking meat is here: micro/convection cooking. While the outside of the roast is seared and browned by the constantly-moving hot-air (convection), the inside is being cooked quickly by the microwaves. Whether it's that elegant anniversary dinner of Prime Rib (page 86) with yorkshire pudding or the simplicity of Chuck Roast in a Bag (page 85), you'll rate as best-cook-on-the-block with family and friends. How are you able to provide "exactly as they like it" doneness for everyone? It's simple: once you cut the rare slices you need from the roast, you can slip other slices back in the oven and cook them just a bit longer, using the microwave method. Everybody's happy and you're a genius!

The convection method will be your first choice for steaks and chops. When you place the wire rack in the upper guides and preheat to 450°F, you have the perfect broiling environment. The fan-assisted hot air movement promotes crispness of the fat without drying out the meat. You can expect a line-up at your door when you prepare Vegetable Stuffed Flank Steak (page 85), Lamb Chops with Mint Glaze (page 99), and other recipes. Finally, look to the microwave method for superb stews, stir-fry dishes, etc.

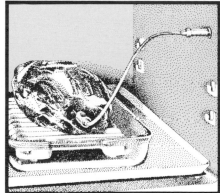

The convection method enables the use of disposable broiling pans or other metal utensils. Vegetable Stuffed Flank Steak (page 85) is broiled using the upper guides position for the wire rack (above). The temperature probe is a true worry saver for roasting meat, such as Pork Loin Roast (page 82). Note horizontal probe position (above right). Meatloaf (page 88) has a surprise inside and uses micro/convection, lower guides (right).

Converting Your Recipes

The Guides on the following pages provide detailed instructions for the defrosting and cooking of the most popular cuts of meat. If you don't find your particular favorite listed, you are sure to find a quite similar one to use as a guide. You can also refer to the individual recipes and will likely find one to use in adapting your favorite recipe.

For steaks, chops, and patties, you will have more surface browning if you preheat the oven to 450°F and cook at that temperature whenever you choose to use micro/convection or convection. Since such items vary greatly in thickness, fat content, and weight, cooking times can only be regarded as estimates. If you determine, using the Guide, that 9 minutes is recommended (ground beef patties, medium, for example), check doneness at 7 minutes.

You should be aware that a boned roast will require less cooking time than one with a bone. Be careful, too, in positioning the temperature probe, if you choose the Probe Method from the Guide. A large amount of fat running through the roast will cause an inaccurate reading of internal temperature if the probe is touching the fat. All roasts should be turned over during the cooking time to provide even browning, distribute juices, and assure even doneness.

As you cook, remember that *all meat profits from standing time of 10 to 15 minutes* after the programmed cooking time has ended. Tips:

☐ Special microwave roasting racks are available to elevate meat from its drippings during cooking with that method. Many are also heatproof but be sure to check manufacturer's instructions before using with micro/convection or convection methods.

☐ Recipe times here presume meat is at refrigerator temperature. If your meal requires lengthy preparation, during which the meat may reach room temperature, reduce cooking times.

☐ Baste, marinate, or season meat just as you would for conventional cooking.

☐ Optional method: use a tight cover and cook, micro, on 40 or 50 for the less tender cuts of meat such as chuck, bottom round, brisket, and stewing meat cooked in liquid.

☐ Check dishes that use relatively long cooking times to be sure liquid has not evaporated. Add liquid as necessary.

☐ Most ground beef recipes call for lean meat. If you are using regular ground beef, drain fat before adding sauce ingredients.

☐ Large cuts not usually cooked on the charcoal grill, such as ham, leg of lamb, pork roast, turkey, and whole chicken, may be partially cooked in the oven and finished on the grill for a lovely charcoal flavor. It's also a great time saver for spareribs.

Using the Defrosting Guide

1. All defrosting uses the microwave method.
2. You may begin defrosting meat within its original paper or plastic wrappings.
3. As soon as possible, remove wrappings and place meat in microproof dish.
4. Defrost in the oven only as long as necessary. Standing time completes thawing. Separate chops, bacon slices, and frank-

furters into pieces as soon as possible. If separated pieces are not thawed, distribute evenly in oven and continue defrosting.

5. Slightly increase the time for weights larger than on the chart. Do not double.
6. If you do not plan immediate cooking, follow guide for only one-half of recommended time. Place meat in refrigerator until needed.

DEFROSTING GUIDE — MEAT

Meat	Amount	Micro Control	Time (in minutes per pound)	Standing Time (minutes)	Special Notes
Beef					
Ground beef	1 lb.	30 (defrost)	5 - 6	5	Turn over once. Remove thawed portions with fork. Return remainder. Freeze in doughnut shape. Depress center when freezing. Defrost on plate.
	2 lbs.	30 (defrost)	5 - 6	5	
	1/4-lb. patty	30 (defrost)	1 per patty	2	
Pot roast, chuck	under 4 lbs.	30 (defrost)	3 - 5	10	Turn over once.
	over 4 lbs.	70 (roast)	3 - 5	10	Turn over once.
Rib roast, rolled	3 to 4 lbs.	30 (defrost)	6 - 8	30 - 45	Turn over once.
	6 to 8 lbs.	70 (roast)	6 - 8	90	Turn over twice.
Rib roast, bone in		70 (roast)	5 - 6	45 - 90	Turn over twice.
Rump roast	3 to 4 lbs.	30 (defrost)	3 - 5	30	Turn over once.
	6 to 7 lbs.	70 (roast)	3 - 5	45	Turn over twice.
Round steak		30 (defrost)	4 - 5	5 - 10	Turn over once.
Flank steak		30 (defrost)	4 - 5	5 - 10	Turn over once.
Sirloin steak	1/2" thick	30 (defrost)	4 - 5	5 - 10	Turn over once.
Tenderloin steak	2 to 3 lbs.	30 (defrost)	4 - 5	8 - 10	Turn over once.
Stew beef	2 lbs.	30 (defrost)	3 - 5	8 - 10	Turn over once. Separate.
Lamb					
Cubed for stew		30 (defrost)	7 - 8	5	Turn over once. Separate.
Ground lamb	under 4 lbs.	30 (defrost)	3 - 5	30 - 45	Turn over once.
	over 4 lbs.	70 (roast)	3 - 5	30 - 45	Turn over twice.
Chops	1" thick	30 (defrost)	5 - 8	15	Turn over twice.
Leg	5 - 8 lbs.	30 (defrost)	4 - 5	15 - 20	Turn over twice.
Pork					
Chops	1/2" thick	30 (defrost)	4 - 6	5 - 10	Separate chops halfway through defrosting time.
	1" thick	30 (defrost)	5 - 7	10	
Spareribs, country-style ribs		30 (defrost)	5 - 7	10	Turn over once.
Roast	under 4 lbs.	30 (defrost)	4 - 5	30 - 45	Turn over once.
	over 4 lbs.	70 (roast)	4 - 5	30 - 45	Turn over twice.
Bacon	1 lb.	30 (defrost)	2 - 3	3 - 5	Defrost until strips separate.
Sausage, bulk	1 lb.	30 (defrost)	2 - 3	3 - 5	Turn over once. Remove thawed portions with fork. Return remainder.
Sausage links	1 lb.	30 (defrost)	3 - 5	4 - 6	Turn over once. Defrost until pieces can be separated.
Hot dogs		30 (defrost)	5 - 6	5	

DEFROSTING GUIDE — MEAT

Meat	Amount	Micro Control	Time (in minutes per pound)	Standing Time (minutes)	Special Notes
Veal					
Roast	3 to 4 lbs.	30 (defrost)	5 - 7	30	Turn over once.
	6 to 7 lbs.	70 (roast)	5 - 7	90	Turn over twice.
Chops	1/2" thick	30 (defrost)	4 - 6	20	Turn over once. Separate chops and continue defrosting.
Variety Meat					
Liver		30 (defrost)	5 - 6	10	Turn over once.
Tongue		30 (defrost)	7 - 8	10	Turn over once.

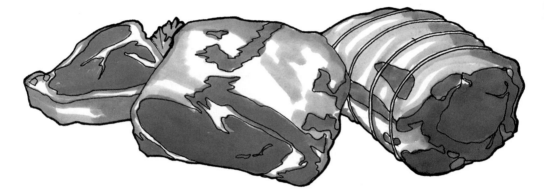

Using the Cooking Guides

1. All meat should be completely thawed before cooking.
2. Place meat fat side down on a roasting rack set in a baking dish that is safe for the cooking method planned. Rack and dish must be microproof for the microwave method; microproof and heatproof for the micro/convection method; heatproof for convection.
3. Use the Probe Method for the most accurate cooking of larger meat. Place temperature probe as horizontally as possible in the densest area, avoiding fat pockets or bone.
4. Unless otherwise noted, times given for steaks and patties will give medium doneness.
5. Ground meat to be used in casseroles should be cooked briefly first. Crumble it into microproof dish and cook (micro) with a double length of paper towel covering and tucked under the dish. Drain fat and add to casserole.
6. During standing time, the internal temperature of roasts will rise to serving temperature. Allow 10 to 15 minutes standing time because it is essential to complete cooking.
7. Place wire rack in lower or upper guides according to amount of browning desired and height of meat. Most roasts are cooked on the ceramic tray.
8. Cutlets and chops that are breaded are cooked at the same time and method as shown in the Guide for unbreaded.

COOKING GUIDE — MEAT

Food	Programming Method	Setting	First Stage	Second Stage	Probe Method	Special Notes
Beef						
Ground beef, bulk	micro	HI (max. power)	2½ min. per lb.	2½ min. per lb.		Crumble in dish. Cook covered.
Ground beef patties, 1 - 4, 4 oz. each	convec	450°	Rare: 5 min. Med: 6 min. Well: 6 min.	4 - 5 min. 5 min. 6 - 7 min.		Upper guides. Preheat. Use broiling pan or aluminum tray.
Meatloaf, ½ - 1¾ lbs.	micro/convec	400°	25 min.		160°	Preheat. Let stand 5 - 10 minutes.
Beef rib roast, boneless	micro/convec	330°	6 min. per lb. turn over	6 min. per lb.	Rare: 120° Med: 130°	On ceramic tray in glass dish with trivet.
Beef rib roast, bone-in, 5 lb.	micro/convec	350°	8 min. per lb. fat-side down turn over	8 min. per lb.	Rare: 120° Med: 130° Well: 140°	On ceramic tray. In glass or ceramic dish.
Beef round, rump, or chuck, boneless, 3 lbs.	micro/convec	330°	7 min. per lb. turn over	7 min. per lb.	Med: 130° Well: 140°	On ceramic tray. Casserole with tight cover or cooking bag.
Beef brisket, boneless, corned beef, flat cut, 2 - 3 lbs.	micro/convec	320°	20 - 30 min. per lb. check liquid add if necessary	15 - 30 min. per lb.		On ceramic tray. 4-quart covered casserole. Cover with water. Let stand 20 - 30 minutes.
Top round steak, 2 - 3 lbs.	micro/convec	350°	8 - 12 min. per lb. turn over check liquid	8 - 15 min. per lb.		Casserole with tight cover or browning bag. Needs liquid. On ceramic tray.
Sirloin steak, ¾" thick	convec	450°	Rare: 7 min. Med: 7 min. Well: 8 min. turn over	6 min. 7 - 8 min. 8 - 9 min		Upper guides. Preheat. Metal pan or foil tray.
Minute steak, cube steak, 4 - 6 oz.	convec	450°	4 min. turn over	4 - 5 min.		Upper guides. Preheat. Metal pan or foil tray.
Tenderloin steak, 4 - 8 oz. 1-inch thick	convec	450°	Rare: 6 min. Med: 6 min. Well: 7 min. turn over	5 min. 6 min. 7 min.		Upper guides. Preheat. Metal pan or foil tray.
Rib eye or strip steak, 1-inch thick	convec	450°	Rare: 6 min. Med: 7 min. Well: 8 min. turn over	7 min. 8 min. 9 min.		Upper guides. Preheat. Metal pan or foil tray.
Lamb						
Ground lamb patties, 4 4 oz. each	convec	450°	Rare: 5 min. Med: 5 min. Well: 6 min. turn over	4 - 5 min. 5 - 6 min. 6 - 7 min.		Upper guides. Preheat. Metal pan or foil tray.
Lamb chops ¾" thick	convec	450°	Rare: 4 min. Med: 5 min. Well: 7 min.	3 - 4 min. 4 - 5 min. 4 - 5 min.		Upper guides. Preheat. Metal pan or foil tray.
Lamb leg or shoulder roast, bone in, 6½ lbs.	micro/convec	330°	3 min. per lb. fat side down turn over	5 - 5½ min. per lb.	Rare: 145° Med: 155° Well: 165°	On ceramic tray in glass or ceramic dish with trivet.
Lamb roast, boneless 3 - 4 lbs.	micro/convec	330°	4 min. per lb. fat side down turn over	4 - 4½	150°	On ceramic tray. In glass or ceramic dish with trivet. Preheat.
Veal						
Shoulder or rump roast, boneless, 3 - 3½ lbs.	micro/convec	330°	3 - 5 min. per lb. turn over	8 - 10	155°	On ceramic tray. Glass or ceramic dish with trivet. Preheat.
Veal cutlets or loin chops ½" thick	convec	450°	4 min. turn over	3 - 4		Upper guides. Preheat. Metal pan or foil tray.

COOKING GUIDE — MEAT

Food	Programming Method	Setting	First Stage	Second Stage	Probe Method	Special Notes
Pork						
Pork chops, ½ - ¾" thick	convec	450°	Med: 7 min. Well: 9 min. turn over	7 min. 8 min.		Upper guides. Preheat. Metal pan or foil tray.
Spareribs, 3 - 4 lbs.	micro/convec	350°	15 - 20 min. per lb.	2 - 3 min. per lb. turn over 2 - 3 min. per lb.		Lower guides. Start in 3 - 4 quart casserole and finish in 9 × 13 baking dish. Needs liquid.
Pork shoulder roast, boneless, 3 - 5 lbs.	micro/convec	320°	6 - 7 min. per lb. turn over	6 - 7 min. per lb.	165°	On ceramic tray. Glass or ceramic baking dish.
Pork loin, center cut, 4 - 5 lbs.	micro/convec	320°	8 - 10 min. per lb. turn over	8 - 10 min. per lb.	165°	On ceramic tray. Glass or ceramic baking dish.
Ham, boneless precooked	micro	70 (roast)	5 - 7 min. per lb. turn over	5 - 7 min. per lb.	120°	11 × 7 microproof baking dish with microproof roasting rack.
Ham slice, center cut, precooked.	convec	450°	4 - 5 min. turn over	5 - 6 min.		Upper guides. Preheat. Metal pan or foil tray
Ham, canned 3 lbs. 5 lbs.	micro	70 (roast)	5 - 6 min. per lb. turn over 4 - 5 min. per lb.	5 - 6 min. per lb.	120° 120°	11 × 7 microproof baking dish with microproof roasting rack.
Sausage patties, ½ - ¾" thick	convec	450°	7 min. turn over	7 - 9 min.		Upper guides. Preheat. Metal pan or foil tray
Sausage bulk, 1 lb.	micro	HI (max. power)	3 min. per lb. stir	1 - 2 min. per lb.		Crumble in 1½-quart dish, covered.
Pork sausage links, ½ - 1 lb.	convec	450°	5 min. turn	7 - 9 min.		Upper guides. Preheat. Metal pan or foil tray
Polish sausage, knockwurst, ring bologna	micro	80 (reheat)	2 - 2½ min. per lb. rearrange	2 - 2½ min. per lb.		Pierce casing. Cook in casserole
Hot dogs-1 2 4	micro	80 (reheat)	25 - 30 sec. 25 - 40 sec. 50 - 55 sec.			Shallow dish or wrapped in paper napkin.
Bacon-1 slice 2 slices 4 slices 8 slices	micro	HI (max. power)	45 sec. - 1 min. 2 - 2½ min. 3 - 4 min. 5 - 6 min.			On dish or bacon rack covered with paper towel with edges tucked under rack or dish.

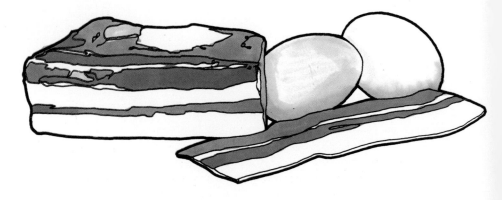

COOKING/DEFROSTING GUIDE — CONVENIENCE MEAT*

d	Programming Method	Setting	Time (in minutes)	Probe Method	Special Notes
ecued beef, stews, hash 16 oz. can	micro	80 (reheat)	3 to 5	150°	Remove from package. Place in microproof plate or casserole Cover. Stir halfway through cooking time.
es, frozen 8 oz.	follow package directions				Lower guides.
-size TV dinners, 20 oz.	follow package directions				Lower guides.
ed peppers, bage rolls, chow n, etc., 16-32 oz.	micro	80 (reheat)	5 to 9	150°	or follow package directions.
dinners ⁄2-14 oz.	follow package directions				Lower guides.
al pie ible crust. oz.	convec	follow package directions for oven (convec) cooking			Lower guides. Preheat.

ue to the tremendous variety in convenience food products available, times given here should be used only s guidelines. We suggest you cook food for the shortest recommended time and then check for doneness. Be ure to check the package for microwave and oven (convec) instructions.

Special Tips about Bacon

☐ Cook bacon on a paper-lined plate, and cover with paper towels to prevent splatters and absorb drippings.

☐ To reserve drippings, cook bacon on a meat rack in a baking dish or on a microwave bacon rack. Bacon can also be cooked, in slices or cut up, in a casserole and removed, if necessary, with a slotted spoon.

☐ For bacon that is soft rather than crisp, cook at the minimum timing.

☐ Bacon varies in quality. The thickness and amount of sugar and salt used in curing will affect browning and timing. Cook thicker slices a bit longer than the chart indicates. You will also find that sweeter bacon cooks more quickly.

☐ Sugar in bacon causes brown spots to appear on the paper towels. If the bacon tends to stick a bit to the towel, it is due to an extra high amount of sugar.

Recipe No. | 73 |

Filet of Beef Tenderloin (rare)

Preset Cooking Time: about 30 minutes

 1 2- to 3-pound beef tenderloin,
    trimmed
 ½ envelope onion soup mix or
    ½ teaspoon garlic powder
 ½ pound mushrooms, chopped
    or sliced

Position wire rack in upper guides of oven. Set meat in shallow glass or ceramic baking dish and sprinkle with soup mix. Insert temperature probe in thickest portion of meat. Place meat in oven on wire rack. Plug in probe. Set recipe number 73. Touch START. *(Oven preheats: convec, 450°F.)*

At 450°F, arrange mushrooms over and around roast. Touch START. *(Oven cooks: convec, 450°F, to 90°F.)*

At Pause, turn meat over and baste with mushrooms and drippings, being careful not to remove probe. Touch START. *(Oven cooks: convec, 450°F, to 120°F; stands: 0, 5 minutes.)*

4 to 6 servings

Recipe No. | 74 |

Filet of Beef Tenderloin (medium)

Preset Cooking Time: about 35 minutes

 1 2- to 3-pound beef tenderloin,
    trimmed
 ½ envelope onion soup mix or
    ½ teaspoon garlic powder
 ½ pound mushrooms, chopped
    or sliced

Position wire rack in upper guides of oven. Set meat in shallow glass or ceramic baking dish and sprinkle with soup mix. Insert temperature probe in thickest portion of meat. Place meat in oven on wire rack. Plug in probe. Set recipe number 74. Touch START. *(Oven preheats: convec, 450°F.)*

At 450°F, arrange mushrooms over and around roast. Touch START. *(Oven cooks: convec, 450°F, to 90°F.)*

At Pause, turn meat over and baste with mushrooms and drippings, being careful not to remove probe. Touch START. *(Oven cooks: convec, 450°F, to 130°F; stands: 0, 5 minutes.)*

4 to 6 servings

Recipe No. ☐ 75 ☐

Vegetable Stuffed Flank Steak

Preset Cooking Time: 21½ minutes

    1   1½-pound flank steak
   ¼   cup chopped celery
   ¼   cup chopped green onion
    2   cloves garlic, minced
    2   teaspoons chopped parsley
    1   tablespoon butter or margarine
    1   cup seasoned croutons, crushed
    2   tablespoons dry white wine
    1   tablespoon soy sauce
        Pinch of pepper

Score both sides of steak using tip of sharp knife; set aside. Combine celery, onion, garlic, and parsley in small microproof bowl. Add butter. Cover with plastic wrap. Place in oven. Set recipe number 34. Touch START. *(Oven cooks: micro, HI, 1½ minutes.)* Remove vegetable mixture from oven. Stir.

Position wire rack in lower guides of oven. Set recipe number 75. Touch START. *(Oven preheats: convec, 350°F.)* Add crushed croutons to vegetable mixture and blend well. Spread stuffing over meat, leaving 1-inch border on all sides. Carefully roll meat up lengthwise; tie in 3 places. Arrange seam-side down in ceramic or glass baking dish. Combine wine, soy sauce, and pepper and brush over meat.

At 350°F, place in oven on wire rack. Touch START. *(Oven cooks: micro/convec, 350°F, 10 minutes.)*

At Pause, brush meat with wine mixture. Turn meat over and brush again. Touch START. *(Oven cooks: micro/convec, 350°F, 10 minutes.)* Brush with remaining wine mixture. Let stand 3 to 5 minutes before serving.

4 to 6 servings

For an extra-special stuffing, place ½ pound bulk pork sausage in microproof bowl. Cook, micro, on HI 3 minutes. Add ½ cup crushed saltine crackers, ½ cup chopped tart apple, ¼ cup chopped celery, 1 tablespoon minced onion, ¼ teaspoon salt, and ¼ teaspoon paprika. Spread over flank steak. Set recipe number 75. Proceed as above.

Recipe No. ☐ 76 ☐

Chuck Roast in a Bag

Preset Cooking Time: 1 hour 30 minutes

    3   tablespoons all-purpose
        flour
    1   tablespoon brown sugar
   ½   teaspoon salt
   ½   teaspoon dry mustard
   ¼   teaspoon pepper
   ¾   cup catsup
   ½   cup water
    2   tablespoons Worcestershire
        sauce
    1   tablespoon vinegar
    1   4-pound chuck roast
        center cut
    4   medium potatoes, peeled and
        halved
    2   large carrots, peeled and cut
        into 2-inch chunks
    1   green pepper, sliced into
        thin strips
    1   large onion, quartered

Combine flour, sugar, salt, mustard, and pepper in small bowl. Stir in catsup, water, Worcestershire, and vinegar. Cut a 1-inch strip from open end of cooking bag. Place roast in bag. Set bag in 9 × 13-inch glass or ceramic baking dish. Spoon catsup mixture over meat. Add potatoes and carrots. Close bag with strip cut from open end of bag. Place in oven on ceramic tray. Set recipe number 76. Touch START. *(Oven cooks: micro/convec, 350°F, 45 minutes.)*

At Pause, add green pepper and onion to bag. Check liquid around meat and add small amount of water if mixture seems too dry. Touch START. *(Oven cooks: micro/convec, 350°F, 30 minutes; stands: 0, 15 minutes.)*

4 to 6 servings

Recipe No. | 77 |

Spicy Beef Short Ribs

Preset Cooking Time: 1 hour 40 minutes

  3 pounds beef short ribs,
       trimmed
  8 to 10 cups hot water
  1 large onion, thickly sliced
       into rings
  1 teaspoon salt
  6 celery tops with leaves
       Barbecue Sauce (page 173)

Rinse ribs with hot water and drain well. Arrange in 4-quart glass or ceramic baking dish. Top with onion and sprinkle with salt. Arrange celery over onions. Add enough hot water to completely cover mixture. Cover and place in oven on ceramic tray. Set recipe number 77. Touch START. *(Oven cooks: micro/convec, 350°F, 55 minutes.)*

At Pause, drain ribs, discarding onion and celery. Pour sauce over ribs, turning to coat evenly. Cover. Place in oven. Touch START. *(Oven cooks: micro/convec, 350°F, 15 minutes.)*

At Pause, turn ribs over; cover. Touch START. *(Oven cooks: micro/convec, 350°F, 25 minutes.)*

At Pause, turn ribs over and baste. Leave uncovered. Touch START. *(Oven cooks: micro/convec, 350°F, 5 minutes.)* Serve immediately with rice, if desired.

4 servings

Recipe No. | 78 |

Prime Rib (rare)

Preset Cooking Time: about 45 minutes

  1 5-pound prime rib roast
       of beef
  3 cloves garlic, minced
  1 pound sliced fresh mushrooms

Set roast in shallow ceramic dish fat-side down. Rub entire surface with garlic. Insert temperature probe into thickest portion of meat without touching bone. Place roast in oven. Plug in probe. Set recipe number 78.

Touch START. *(Oven cooks: micro/convec, 330°F, 20 minutes.)*

At Pause, turn roast onto side, being careful not to remove probe. Touch START. *(Oven cooks: micro/convec, 330°F, 5 minutes.)*

At Pause, turn roast over. Touch START. *(Oven cooks: micro/convec, 330°F, 5 minutes.)*

At Pause, stand roast on bone. Arrange mushrooms in dish around roast. Touch START. *(Oven cooks: micro/convec, 330°F, to 120°F.)* Let stand 10 minutes before serving.

4 to 6 servings

Recipe No. | 79 |

Prime Rib (medium)

Preset Cooking Time: about 50 minutes

  1 5-pound prime rib roast
       of beef
  3 cloves garlic, minced
  1 pound sliced fresh mushrooms

Set roast in shallow ceramic dish fat-side down. Rub entire surface with garlic. Insert temperature probe into thickest portion of meat without touching bone. Place roast in oven. Plug in probe. Set recipe number 79. Touch START. *(Oven cooks: micro/convec, 330°F, 20 minutes.)*

At Pause, turn roast onto side, being careful not to remove probe. Touch START. *(Oven cooks: micro/convec, 330°F, 5 minutes.)*

At Pause, turn roast over. Touch START. *(Oven cooks: micro/convec, 330°F, 5 minutes.)*

At Pause, stand roast on bone. Arrange mushrooms in dish around roast. Touch START. *(Oven cooks: micro/convec, 330°F, to 130°F.)* Let stand 10 minutes before serving.

4 to 6 servings

*Prime Rib (rare) goes great with a →
green salad*

Recipe No. [80]

Brisket of Beef

Preset Cooking Time: 2 hours

   3 large onions, sliced into rings
   1 1½- to 3-pound flat cut
      brisket of beef
   1 envelope onion soup mix
  12 large mushrooms, sliced
   4 medium-to-large potatoes,
      peeled

Arrange half of onions in 4-quart casserole. Set brisket on top, cutting in half if necessary. Sprinkle with onion soup mix. Arrange remaining onions on top. Cover. Place in oven on ceramic tray. Set recipe number 80. Touch START. *(Oven cooks: micro/convec, 320°F, 40 minutes.)*

At Pause, turn meat over. Add mushrooms and potatoes. Spoon onions and accumulated liquid over top, adding water if necessary. Cover. Place in oven. Touch START. *(Oven cooks: micro/convec, 320°F, 20 minutes.)*

At Pause, turn meat and potatoes over. Touch START. *(Oven cooks: micro/convec, 320°F, 40 minutes.)*

At Pause, transfer meat to cutting board. Keep potatoes and sauce covered. Slice meat thinly across grain. Return to dish. Place in oven. Touch START. *(Oven cooks: micro/convec, 320°F, 20 minutes.)* Serve immediately.

4 to 6 servings

Recipe No. [81] ⊞

Baked Beefy Macaroni

Preset Cooking Time: 21 minutes

   1 pound lean ground beef
   1 jar (15 ounces) spaghetti
      sauce or 2 cups Homemade
      Spaghetti Sauce (page 174)
  10 ounces elbow macaroni, cooked
  1½ cups shredded Cheddar cheese

Crumble beef into 2-quart microproof casserole. Place in oven. Set recipe number 38. Touch START. *(Oven cooks: micro, HI, 6 minutes.)* Remove from oven. Stir through meat once. Drain well.

Position wire rack in lower guides of oven. Set recipe number 81. Touch START. *(Oven preheats: convec, 350°F.)* Combine spaghetti sauce, meat, and macaroni in large bowl and blend well. Spoon into 8-inch square glass or ceramic baking dish.

At 350°F, place in oven on wire rack. Touch START. *(Oven cooks: micro/convec, 350°F, 10 minutes.)*

At Pause, sprinkle cheese over top. Place in oven. Touch START. *(Oven cooks: micro/convec, 350°F, 5 minutes.)* Serve immediately.

4 to 6 servings

Recipe No. [82]

Meatloaf

Preset Cooking Time: about 25 minutes

  1½ pounds lean ground beef
   2 eggs, beaten
   1 medium onion, finely chopped
   1 can (8 ounces) tomato sauce,
      divided
   2 slices bread, rinsed with warm
      water, squeezed dry and
      torn into pieces
   1 teaspoon Worcestershire sauce
   ½ teaspoon salt
   ¼ teaspoon pepper
   1 clove garlic, crushed
   3 hard-cooked eggs

Combine beef, beaten eggs, onion, ⅓ cup tomato sauce, bread, Worcestershire, salt, pepper, and garlic in large bowl and mix lightly to blend well. Turn half of mixture into 9×5-inch glass loaf dish, spreading evenly. Arrange hard-cooked eggs down center. Cover with remaining meat mixture, smoothing top.

Position wire rack in lower guides of oven. Insert temperature probe into center of loaf. Place in oven on wire rack. Plug in probe. Set recipe number 82. Touch START. *(Oven preheats: convec, 400°F.)*

At 400°F, brush remaining tomato sauce over meat using care not to dislodge or unplug temperature probe. Touch START. *(Oven cooks: micro/convec, 400°F, to 160°F.)* Pour off accumulated liquid. Serve meatloaf immediately.

6 to 8 servings

What a surprise! Each slice of this special loaf contains a cross-section of egg.

⊞ *Recipe can be increased. See "Quantity", page 12.*

Recipe No. 83

Beef Stew

Preset Cooking Time: 1 hour 45 minutes

- 2 pounds beef stew meat, cut into 1½-inch cubes
- ½ teaspoon salt
- 1 package (1½ ounces) brown gravy mix with mushrooms
- 1½ cups water
- 3 celery stalks, cut into 1-inch slices
- 4 medium carrots, peeled and cut into chunks
- 4 medium potatoes, peeled and halved
- 1 large onion, cut into rings

Arrange meat in 3-quart microproof casserole and sprinkle with salt. Blend gravy mix with water in small bowl. Pour over meat. Cover. Place in oven. Set recipe number 83. Touch START. *(Oven cooks: micro, 70, 30 minutes.)*

At Pause, stir in vegetables, coating evenly with sauce. Cover. Place in oven. Touch START. *(Oven cooks: micro, 50, 30 minutes.)*

At Pause, stir. Touch START. *(Oven cooks: micro, 50, 30 minutes; stands: 0, 15 minutes.)* Serve immediately.

4 to 6 servings

Recipe No. 84

Beef Stroganoff

Preset Cooking Time: 27 minutes

- 2 tablespoons butter
- 1 medium onion, sliced
- 1 round steak, boneless (1 pound), cut into thin strips
- 2 cloves garlic, minced
- ¼ teaspoon salt
- ¼ teaspoon pepper
- ⅓ cup red wine
- 1 cup sliced mushrooms
- 2 tablespoons chopped parsley
- 1 cup dairy sour cream

Combine butter, onion, meat, garlic, salt, and pepper in 2-quart microproof casserole. Cover. Place in oven on ceramic tray. Set recipe number 84. Touch START. *(Oven cooks: micro, HI, 5 minutes.)*

At Pause, add wine and stir. Cover. Touch START. *(Oven cooks: micro, 50, 10 minutes.)*

At Pause, add mushrooms and stir. Cover. Touch START. *(Oven cooks: micro, 50, 10 minutes.)*

At Pause, add parsley and stir in sour cream. Leave uncovered. Touch START. *(Oven cooks: micro, 50, 2 minutes.)*

Serve hot over freshly cooked rice or noodles.

4 servings

Recipe No. 85

Rolled Vegetable Meatloaf

Preset Cooking Time: 30 minutes

- 1¾ pounds lean ground beef
- 2 eggs, lightly beaten
- 2 tablespoons catsup
- ¼ cup dry breadcrumbs
- 1 teaspoon salt
- ¼ teaspoon pepper

Filling:

- ¾ cup chopped onions
- ½ cup chopped green pepper
- ½ cup chopped celery
- 1 jar (2 ounces) pimiento, drained
- ½ teaspoon garlic powder

Position wire rack in lower guides of oven. Set recipe number 85. Touch START. *(Oven preheats: convec, 400°F.)* Meanwhile, combine beef, eggs, catsup, breadcrumbs, salt, and pepper and mix lightly. Turn mixture out onto waxed paper and shape into 8×10-inch rectangle. Mix remaining ingredients in medium bowl. Spread evenly over meat, leaving 1-inch border on all sides. Carefully roll meat up from short end, pressing edges together to seal. Arrange roll seam-side down in 9×5-inch glass loaf dish.

At 400°F, place in oven on wire rack. Touch START. *(Oven cooks: micro/convec, 400°F, 25 minutes; stands: 0, 5 minutes.)* Serve immediately.

4 to 6 servings

Recipe No. [86]

All-American Meatballs

Preset Cooking Time: 20 minutes

- 1 pound lean ground beef
- 1 medium potato, peeled and coarsely grated
- 2 tablespoons onion soup mix
- 1 tablespoon parsley flakes
- 1 large egg, lightly beaten
- 2 cups beef broth
- 1 tablespoon Worcestershire sauce
- 2 tablespoons cornstarch
- 2 tablespoons water

Combine beef, potato, soup mix, parsley, and egg; blend well. Shape into twelve 1½-inch balls. Combine broth and Worcester-shire in 2-quart microproof casserole. Add meatballs. Cover and place in oven. Set recipe number 86. Touch START. *(Oven cooks: micro, 70, 10 minutes.)*

At Pause, dissolve cornstarch in water. Stir into casserole. Cover. Touch START. *(Oven cooks: micro, 70, 3 minutes.)*

At Pause, stir. Cover. Touch START. *(Oven cooks: micro, 70, 2 minutes; stands: 0, 5 minutes.)*

4 servings

Recipe No. [87]

Chili con Carne

Preset Cooking Time: 20 minutes

- 1 pound lean ground beef
- ½ cup minced onion
- ½ cup chopped green pepper
- 1 clove garlic, minced
- 1 can (16 ounces) whole tomatoes, broken up
- 1 can (16 ounces) kidney beans
- 1 to 2 tablespoons chili powder, to taste
- 1 teaspoon salt

Crumble beef into 2-quart microproof casserole. Add onion, green pepper, and garlic. Place in oven. Set recipe number 87. Touch START. *(Oven cooks: micro, HI, 2 minutes.)*

← *One-Step Lasagna*

At Pause, stir. Touch START. *(Oven cooks: micro, HI, 2 minutes.)*

At Pause, remove from oven; drain. Add remaining ingredients; blend well. Cover and place in oven. Touch START. *(Oven cooks: micro, 70, 9 minutes.)*

At Pause, stir. Cover. Touch START. *(Oven cooks: micro, 70, 7 minutes.)*

Let stand 5 minutes before serving.

4 servings

Recipe No. [88]

One-Step Lasagna

Preset Cooking Time: 37 minutes

- 1 pound lean ground beef
- 1 jar (15 ounces) spaghetti sauce
- ½ cup water
- 1 teaspoon salt
- 1 package (8 ounces) lasagna noodles
- 2 cups ricotta cheese, drained, divided
- 3 cups (12 ounces) shredded mozzarella cheese, divided
- ½ cup grated Parmesan cheese Chopped parsley

Crumble beef into 2-quart microproof casserole. Place in oven. Set recipe number 88. Touch START. *(Oven cooks: micro, HI, 3 minutes.)*

At Pause, stir to break up beef. Touch START. *(Oven cooks: micro, HI, 2 minutes.)*

At Pause, remove from oven. Stir; drain. Stir in spaghetti sauce, water, and salt. Spread one third of the beef mixture in 11 × 7-inch microproof baking dish. Arrange half of the noodles over sauce. Spread with 1 cup ricotta cheese. Sprinkle with 1 cup mozzarella cheese. Repeat layers once. Top with remaining beef mixture. Sprinkle with Parmesan cheese. Double wrap with plastic wrap, and place in oven. Touch START. *(Oven cooks: micro, 50, 30 minutes.)*

At Pause, sprinkle with remaining 1 cup mozzarella cheese. Do not cover. Touch START. *(Oven cooks: micro, 50, 2 minutes.)*

Sprinkle with parsley, and serve with additional Parmesan cheese, if desired.

6 servings

Stuffed Cabbage

Preset Cooking Time: 36 minutes

- 1 head (about 1½ pounds) cabbage, cored, blemished leaves discarded
- ¼ cup water
- 1 pound lean ground beef
- ½ pound ground pork
- ¾ cup cooked rice
- 1 large egg, lightly beaten
- 1 tablespoon chopped parsley
- 1 clove garlic, minced
- 1 teaspoon salt
- ½ teaspoon thyme
- ¼ teaspoon pepper
- ¼ cup butter or margarine
- 2 cans (8 ounces each) tomato sauce

Place cabbage and water in 3-quart microproof casserole. Cover and place in oven. Set recipe number 89. Touch START. *(Oven cooks: micro, HI, 6 minutes.)*

At Pause, remove from oven; drain. Let stand to cool slightly. Separate 6 to 8 large outside leaves, discarding tough centers; set aside. Combine beef, pork, rice, egg, parsley, garlic, salt, thyme, and pepper; blend well. Divide mixture evenly among large outside cabbage leaves, wrapping leaves tightly around mixture. Line bottom of 13 × 9-inch microproof baking dish with some of the remaining cabbage leaves. Top with stuffed cabbage rolls. Cover with remaining leaves. Dot with butter. Cover with tomato sauce. Cover with plastic wrap and place in oven. Touch START. *(Oven cooks: micro, 80, 15 minutes.)*

At Pause, baste with pan juices. Touch START. *(Oven cooks: micro, 80, 10 minutes; 10, 5 minutes.)*

Discard top leaves before serving.

4 servings

Beef Shanghai

Preset Cooking Time: 9 minutes

- 2 tablespoons vegetable oil
- 1 top round or sirloin steak, boneless (1 pound), cut into thin strips
- 1 can (16 ounces) whole tomatoes, broken up
- 1 medium onion, finely chopped
- 1 clove garlic, minced
- 1 teaspoon salt
- ⅛ teaspoon pepper
- 2 large green peppers, seeded and cut into thin strips
- 2 teaspoons cornstarch
- 2 tablespoons soy sauce

Pour oil into 3-quart microproof casserole. Add beef; stir to coat. Add tomatoes, onion, garlic, salt, and pepper. Cover and place in oven. Set recipe number 90. Touch START. *(Oven cooks: micro, HI, 2 minutes.)*

At Pause, stir. Cover. Touch START. *(Oven cooks: micro, HI, 2 minutes.)*

At Pause, add green peppers. Dissolve cornstarch in soy sauce; stir into beef mixture. Cover. Touch START. *(Oven cooks: micro, HI, 5 minutes.)*

Serve over hot rice and sprinkle with chow mein noodles.

4 servings

Barbecued Beef, Chili, Stew, Hash, Meatballs

Preset Cooking Time: about 4 minutes

- 1 can (16 ounces) barbecued beef, chili, stew, hash, or meatballs

Pour beef mixture into microproof casserole. Place in oven. Insert temperature probe into beef mixture, and cover. Set recipe number 91. Touch START. *(Oven cooks: micro, 80, to 110°F.)*

At Pause, stir. Cover. Touch START. *(Oven cooks: micro, 80, to 150°F; holds warm: 1.)*

1 to 2 servings

Recipe No. 92

Oriental Beef

Preset Cooking Time: 14 minutes

- ½ cup soy sauce
- ½ cup dry sherry
- ½ cup water
- 1 tablespoon sugar
- 1 clove garlic, minced
- 2 thin slices fresh ginger, minced
- 1 sirloin steak, boneless (1½ to 2 pounds), cut into thin strips
- ½ medium bunch broccoli
- ½ pound bean sprouts
- 6 green onions, cut into 2-inch pieces
- 1 can (5 ounces) sliced water chestnuts, drained

Combine soy sauce, sherry, water, sugar, garlic, and ginger in 2-quart microproof casserole. Add steak; stir to coat. Cover and let stand at room temperature 2 hours, stirring occasionally.

Cut broccoli stems diagonally into thin slices; break florets into individual pieces. Rinse bean sprouts in cold water, drain. Combine broccoli, bean sprouts, onions, and water chestnuts. Push marinated steak to center of casserole. Arrange vegetables around steak. Cover and place in oven. Set recipe number 92. Touch START. *(Oven cooks: micro, HI, 11 minutes.)*

At Pause, stir. Touch START. *(Oven cooks: micro, HI, 3 minutes.)* Serve with rice.

4 to 6 servings

You can substitute 1 package (10 ounces) frozen broccoli spears, thawed, for fresh broccoli. If fresh bean sprouts are unavailable, substitute 2 cups drained canned bean sprouts.

Recipe No. 93

Stuffed Green Peppers

Preset Cooking Time: 14 minutes

- 4 large green peppers
- 1 pound lean ground beef
- 1 medium onion, finely chopped
- 1 clove garlic, minced
- 2 tablespoons minced celery
- 1 egg
- 1 cup tomato sauce, divided
- ½ cup cooked rice
- 3 tablespoons minced fresh parsley
- 1 tablespoon Worcestershire sauce
- ½ teaspoon salt
- ¼ teaspoon pepper

Wash peppers; remove tops, seeds, and membranes. Set upside down to drain. Place beef, onion, garlic, and celery in 2-quart microproof bowl. Place in oven. Set recipe number 93. Touch START. *(Oven cooks: micro, HI, 3 minutes.)*

At Pause, stir to crumble beef. Touch START. *(Oven cooks: micro, HI, 2 minutes.)*

At Pause, stir in remaining ingredients, except 4 tablespoons tomato sauce. Fill green peppers with beef mixture, mounding on top. Arrange peppers in circle in round or oval microproof baking dish or casserole just large enough to hold peppers upright. Place in oven. Touch START. *(Oven cooks: micro, 70, 10 minutes.)* Rotate dish one-half turn during cooking if peppers are cooking unevenly.

Spread 1 tablespoon tomato sauce on top of each pepper. Serve with crusty garlic bread, if desired.

4 servings

Recipe No. ☐ 94 ☐ ⊞

Tomato Swiss Steak

Preset Cooking Time: 1 hour 3 minutes

- ¼ cup all-purpose flour
- 1 teaspoon salt
- ¼ teaspoon pepper
- 1 round steak (1 pound),
   ½ inch thick
- 1 large onion, sliced
- ½ green pepper, seeded and cut
   into strips
- 1 can (6 ounces) tomato paste
- 1 cup beef broth, or 1 cup water
   plus 1 beef bouillon cube

Combine flour, salt, and pepper. Place steak on cutting board; pound half of the flour mixture into both sides of steak with meat mallet. Cut steak in half; place in 8-inch round or oval microproof casserole. Sprinkle with remaining flour mixture. Spread onion, green pepper, and tomato paste over steak. Add broth to cover ingredients. Cover. Place in oven. Set recipe number 94. Touch START. *(Oven cooks: micro, HI, 3 minutes; 30, 20 minutes; 30, 20 minutes.)*

At Pause, turn meat over. Cover. Touch START. *(Oven cooks: micro, 30, 20 minutes.)*

2 servings

Recipe No. ☐ 95 ☐

Hungarian Goulash

Preset Cooking Time: 1 hour 25 minutes

- 2 pounds beef for stew, cut
   into 1-inch cubes
- 4 large tomatoes, peeled and cut
   into chunks
- 1 medium onion, coarsely chopped
- 1½ tablespoons paprika
- 1 teaspoon salt
- ½ teaspoon pepper
- 1 container (8 ounces) dairy
   sour cream

Combine beef, tomatoes, onion, paprika, salt, and pepper in 3-quart microproof casserole. Place in oven. Set recipe number 95. Touch START. *(Oven cooks: micro, 50, 25 minutes.)*

At Pause, stir. Touch START. *(Oven cooks: micro, 50, 30 minutes.)*

At Pause, stir. Touch START. *(Oven cooks: micro, 50, 25 minutes; 20, 5 minutes.)*

Blend in sour cream. Serve hot over freshly cooked noodles.

4 to 6 servings

Recipe No. ☐ 96 ☐

Enchilada Casserole

Preset Cooking Time: 15 minutes

- 1¾ pounds lean ground beef
- 1 large onion, chopped
- 2 cloves garlic, minced
- 1 can (16 ounces) tomato purée
- 1 envelope (1⅝ ounces) taco
   seasoning mix
- 6 corn tortillas
- 3 cups (12 ounces) shredded Cheddar
   cheese, divided

Crumble beef into 2-quart glass measure. Add onion and garlic; mix lightly. Place in oven. Set recipe number 96. Touch START. *(Oven cooks: micro, HI, 3 minutes.)*

At Pause, stir through several times. Touch START. *(Oven cooks: micro, HI, 2 minutes.)*

At Pause, stir in purée and seasoning mix. Touch START. *(Oven cooks: micro, HI, 3 minutes.)*

At Pause, remove from oven. Layer tortillas, beef mixture, and 2½ cups cheese in 2-quart round microproof casserole. Cover and place in oven. Touch START. *(Oven cooks: micro, HI, 7 minutes.)*

Sprinkle with remaining ½ cup cheese. Cut into wedges and serve.

4 to 6 servings

⊞ *Recipe can be increased. See "Quantity", page 12.*

Stuffed Green Peppers (page 93) with → Spaghetti Squash (Guide, page 148)

Recipe No. 97

Veal Parmigiana

Preset Cooking Time: 17 minutes

- 4 veal cutlets (1 pound)
- ½ cup cracker meal or dry breadcrumbs
- ½ cup grated Parmesan cheese
- 1 egg, beaten with ¼ teaspoon salt
- ½ cup chopped onions
- 1 can (8 ounces) tomato sauce
- 3 tablespoons tomato paste
- ½ teaspoon sugar
- ⅛ teaspoon oregano
- ⅛ teaspoon pepper
- 4 slices mozzarella cheese
- 2 tablespoons grated Parmesan cheese
- 2 tablespoons chopped fresh parsley

Pound veal slightly to even thickness. Mix cracker meal and ½ cup Parmesan cheese in shallow dish. Dip veal in egg, then roll in crumb mixture, coating completely. Sprinkle onions in bottom of glass or ceramic baking dish. Arrange veal in single layer over onions.

Position wire rack in lower guides of oven. Set recipe number 97. Touch START. *(Oven preheats: convec, 300°F.)*

At Pause, place dish on rack. Touch START. *(Oven cooks: micro/convec, 300°F, 12 minutes.)*

Meanwhile, blend tomato sauce, tomato paste, sugar, oregano, and pepper.

At Pause, spoon tomato mixture over veal. Top with mozzarella cheese. Touch START. *(Oven cooks: micro/convec, 300°F, 5 minutes.)* Sprinkle veal with remaining Parmesan cheese, and parsley. Serve immediately.

4 servings

Recipe No. 98 ⊞

Veal Cordon Bleu

Preset Cooking Time: 10 minutes

- 6 slices prosciutto ham
- 6 slices mozzarella cheese
- 6 slices veal (about 1 to 1¼ pounds), pounded thin
- ¼ cup seasoned breadcrumbs
- ¼ teaspoon salt
- ⅛ teaspoon pepper
- 1 egg, beaten
- 3 tablespoons vegetable oil
- 2 tablespoons chopped parsley

Position wire rack in lower guides of oven. Set recipe number 98. Touch START. *(Oven preheats: convec, 350°F.)* Place slice of ham and cheese on each veal slice. Roll up and secure with toothpick. Blend breadcrumbs, salt, and pepper. Coat each veal roll with breadcrumbs, dip in beaten egg, and coat again with breadcrumbs, covering completely. Pour half of oil into bottom of glass baking dish. Arrange veal rolls in dish and drizzle with remaining oil.

At 350°F, place in oven. Touch START. *(Oven cooks: micro/convec, 350°F, 10 minutes.)* Spoon any cheese from bottom of dish over veal. Sprinkle with parsley and serve immediately.

4 to 6 servings

⊞ *Recipe can be increased. See "Quantity", page 12.*

Ratatouille (page 158), →
Medallions of Veal (page 98)

Recipe No. 99

Veal Shoulder in Pastry Dough

Preset Cooking Time: about 1 hour

- ½ cup shredded carrot
- ½ cup finely chopped onion
- 2 small celery stalks, finely chopped
- 2 tablespoons butter
- 1 2½-pound veal shoulder roast
- 2 tablespoons dry white wine
- 2 tablespoons fresh lemon juice
- ¼ teaspoon freshly ground white pepper
- 1 package (17¼ ounces) frozen puff pastry dough, thawed
- 1 egg, beaten

Combine carrot, onion, celery, and butter in 2-cup microproof bowl. Place in oven. Set recipe number 15. Touch START. *(Oven cooks: micro, HI, 4 minutes.)*

Remove vegetable mixture from oven; stir. Set aside.

Set roast in microproof casserole. Insert temperature probe into thickest portion of meat. Place roast in oven. Plug in probe. Set recipe number 99. Touch START. *(Oven preheats: convec, 330°F.)*

At 330°F, blend wine, lemon juice, and pepper and sprinkle over meat, using care not to dislodge or unplug temperature probe. Touch START. *(Oven cooks: micro/convec, 330°F, to 90°F.)*

At Pause, turn roast over and baste with drippings. Touch START. *(Oven cooks: micro/convec, 330°F, to 155°F.)*

At Pause, remove roast from oven. Remove probe; let roast cool to room temperature. Spread vegetable mixture in center of puff pastry dough. Set roast on vegetables. Fold pastry over meat, enclosing completely. Brush seams with egg to seal. (Dough scraps can be used to decorate top if desired; brush decoration with egg.)

Return roast to oven. Touch START. *(Oven cooks: convec, 350°F, 30 minutes.)*

4 to 6 servings

Recipe No. 100

Medallions of Veal

Preset Cooking Time: 10 minutes

- ¼ cup all-purpose flour
   Salt and pepper to taste
- 8 slices veal (about ¾ pound), pounded thin
- 3 tablespoons vegetable oil
- 2 tablespoons finely minced shallots
- ½ pound fresh mushrooms, thinly sliced
- ¼ cup dry white wine

Position wire rack in upper guides of oven. Set recipe number 100. Touch START. *(Oven preheats: convec, 450°F.)* Meanwhile, combine flour, salt, and pepper in shallow dish. Coat veal on both sides with flour mixture, covering completely. Mix oil and shallots in shallow glass or ceramic baking dish.

At 450°F, place shallot mixture in oven. Touch START. *(Oven cooks: convec, 450°F, 2 minutes.)*

At Pause, add veal to dish. Place in oven. Touch START. *(Oven cooks: convec, 450°F, 4 minutes.)*

At Pause, turn veal over. Add mushrooms and wine. Touch START. *(Oven cooks: convec, 450°F, 4 minutes.)* Serve immediately.

2 to 3 servings

Recipe No. 101

Leg of Lamb

Preset Cooking Time: about 45 minutes

- 1 5- to 7-pound leg of lamb
- 2 medium cloves garlic, finely minced
- 1 teaspoon freshly ground pepper
   Juice of ½ lemon

Rub lamb with garlic, pepper, and lemon juice. Place in microproof and heatproof casserole. Insert temperature probe into thickest portion of meat without touching bone. Place roast in oven. Plug in probe. Set recipe number 101. Touch START. *(Oven preheats: convec, 330°F.)*

At 330°F, turn meat over, using care not to dislodge or unplug probe. Touch START. *(Oven cooks: micro/convec, 330°F, to 90°F.)*

At Pause, baste lamb with pan juices. Turn meat over and baste again. Touch START. *(Oven cooks: micro/convec, 330°F, to 155°F.)* Let stand 10 minutes before carving.

6 to 8 servings

Recipe No. | 102 |

Lamb Shanks for Two

Preset Cooking Time: 20 minutes

- 2 lamb shanks (about 1½ pounds)
- 1 teaspoon fresh lemon juice
- 1 clove garlic, finely minced or
  - ½ teaspoon garlic powder
  - Pepper to taste

Position wire rack in upper guides of oven. Set recipe number 102. Touch START. *(Oven preheats: convec, 450°F.)* Sprinkle lamb with lemon juice, garlic, and pepper. Arrange in glass or ceramic baking dish.

At 450°F, place in oven. Touch START. *(Oven cooks: micro/convec, 450°F, 15 minutes.)*

At Pause, turn shanks over. Touch START. *(Oven cooks: micro/convec, 450°F, 5 minutes.)* Serve immediately.

2 servings

Recipe No. | 103 |

Shish Kabobs

Preset Cooking Time: 18 minutes

- 1 cup prepared chili sauce
- ½ cup catsup
- 1 tablespoon honey
- 1 tablespoon prepared red horseradish
- 1 tablespoon chopped chutney
- 1 pound lamb, cut into 12 equal cubes
- 1 green pepper, cut into 12 pieces
- 1 large onion, cut into 12 chunks
- 12 small mushrooms
- 4 12-inch bamboo skewers

Mix chili sauce, catsup, honey, horseradish, and chutney in 1-quart glass measure. Cover. Place in oven. Set recipe number 15. Touch START. *(Oven cooks: micro, HI, 4 minutes.)* Set sauce aside.

Position wire rack in upper guides of oven. Set recipe number 103. Touch START. *(Oven preheats: convec, 350°F.)* Alternate lamb, green pepper, onion, and mushrooms on wooden skewers. Set skewers in 9×13-inch glass baking dish. Brush generously with sauce.

At 350°F, place baking dish in oven.

Touch START. *(Oven cooks: micro/convec, 350°F, 7 minutes.)*

At Pause, turn kabobs over and baste with sauce. Touch START. *(Oven cooks: micro/convec, 350°F, 7 minutes.)* Serve hot.

4 servings

This is one of several recipes that use the preset functions of another recipe for part of the cooking sequence. Set recipe number 15 first. At the end of that sequence, set recipe number 103.

Recipe No. | 104 |

Broiled Lamb Chops with Mint Glaze

Preset Cooking Time: 19½ minutes

- ¼ cup mint jelly
- 2 tablespoons wine vinegar
- 1 tablespoon brown sugar
- 2 teaspoons fresh lemon juice
- 1 teaspoon grated lemon peel
- ¼ teaspoon dry mustard
- 4 lamb chops, ¾-inch thick
- 1 teaspoon arrowroot or cornstarch
- 1 tablespoon cold water
  - Salt and pepper to taste

Combine jelly, vinegar, brown sugar, lemon juice, lemon peel, and mustard in small bowl. Whisk until smooth.

Arrange chops in 8-inch square baking dish. Pour marinade over top. Marinate 1½ to 2 hours, turning chops several times.

Drain marinade into 1-quart glass measure. Stir arrowroot and water in small cup until arrowroot is dissolved. Add to marinade. Place in oven. Set recipe number 31. *(Oven cooks: micro, HI, 2 minutes.)*

At Pause; stir. *(Oven cooks: micro, HI, 1½ minutes.)* Remove from oven; set aside.

Position wire rack in upper guides of oven. Set recipe number 104. Touch START. *(Oven preheats: convec, 450°F.)* Meanwhile, transfer chops to aluminum foil broiler pan and brush with marinade.

At 450°F, place in oven. Touch START. *(Oven cooks: convec, 450°F, 8 minutes.)*

At Pause, turn chops over. Touch START. *(Oven cooks: convec, 450°F, 8 minutes.)* Season with salt and pepper. Serve any remaining marinade on the side.

2 servings

Recipe No. 105

Lamb Ragout

Preset Cooking Time: 40 minutes

- 1 pound lamb for stew, cut into
      1-inch cubes
- 1 envelope (⅝ ounce) brown gravy
      mix
- 3 medium carrots, cut into chunks
- 2 medium stalks celery, cut into
      chunks
- 2 medium potatoes, peeled and cut
      into cubes
- 1 cup water
- ¼ cup dry red wine
- 2 tablespoons all-purpose flour
- 1 teaspoon salt
- ½ teaspoon Worcestershire sauce
- ⅛ teaspoon pepper
- 1 clove garlic, minced

Combine lamb and gravy mix in 3-quart microproof casserole. Place in oven. Set recipe number 105. Touch START. *(Oven cooks: micro, 50, 5 minutes.)*

At Pause, stir. Touch START. *(Oven cooks: micro, 50, 5 minutes.)*

At Pause, add remaining ingredients; blend well. Cover. Touch START. *(Oven cooks: micro, 50, 15 minutes.)*

At Pause, stir. Cover. Touch START. *(Oven cooks: micro, 50, 15 minutes.)*

Let stand 3 to 4 minutes before serving.

4 servings

Recipe No. 106

Pork Loin Roast

Preset Cooking Time: about 55 minutes

- 1 4- to 5-pound pork loin roast
- 2 tablespoons honey
- 1 tablespoon Worcestershire sauce
- 6 unpeeled, medium potatoes,
      halved lengthwise
- 2 medium onions, quartered

Set pork, fat side up, in 9 × 13-inch glass or ceramic baking dish. Mix honey and Worcestershire in small bowl. Brush on roast. Insert temperature probe into thickest portion of meat. Place in oven. Plug in probe. Set recipe number 106. Touch START. *(Oven cooks: micro/convec, 320°F, 25 minutes.)*

At Pause, arrange potatoes, cut-side down, and onions around roast. Touch START. *(Oven cooks: micro/convec, 320°F, to 130°F.)*

At Pause, rotate dish one-quarter turn. Touch START. *(Oven cooks: micro/convec, 320°F, to 165°F; stands: 0, 10 minutes.)*

6 to 8 servings

Orange-Glazed Pork Roast (page 104) →

Recipe No. 107

Pork Ribs

Preset Cooking Time: 50 minutes

    4 pounds country-style pork ribs
    7 cups water
    1 jar (24 ounces) sauerkraut,
          drained and rinsed
    1 jar (16 ounces) sweet-sour red
          cabbage
    1 medium onion, chopped
       Salt and pepper to taste

Arrange ribs in 4-quart microproof casserole. Add water. Cover. Place in oven. Set recipe number 275. (Oven cooks: micro, HI, 10 minutes.)

At Pause, stir. Cover. (Oven cooks: micro, HI, 10 minutes.) Drain ribs well and set aside.

Position wire rack in lower guides of oven. Set recipe number 107. Touch START. (Oven preheats: convec, 300°F.) Meanwhile, mix sauerkraut and red cabbage in 9×13-inch glass or ceramic baking dish. Arrange ribs over top. Sprinkle with onion and season with salt and pepper.

At 300°F, place in oven. Touch START. (Oven cooks: micro/convec, 300°F, 15 minutes.)

At Pause, rotate dish one-quarter turn. Touch START. (Oven cooks: micro/convec, 300°F, 15 minutes.) Serve hot.

6 servings

Recipe No. 108

Stuffed Pork Chops

Preset Cooking Time: 18 minutes

    1 cup course dry breadcrumbs
    ¾ cup chopped peeled apples
    3 tablespoons chopped raisins
    2 tablespoons sugar
    2 tablespoons minced onion
    2 tablespoons butter or
          margarine, melted
    ½ teaspoon salt
    ¼ teaspoon pepper
       Pinch of sage
    ¼ cup hot water
    8 rib or loin pork chops

Position wire rack in lower guides of oven. Set recipe number 108. Touch START. (Oven preheats: convec, 320°F.) Combine all ingredients except pork chops in large bowl and blend well. Arrange 4 chops in 8-inch round glass or ceramic dish. Divide stuffing evenly on top of chops and cover with 4 remaining chops, pressing together tightly.

At 320°F, place in oven. Touch START. (Oven cooks: micro/convec, 320°F, 18 minutes.) Serve immediately.

4 servings

Recipe No. 109

Sweet and Sour Pork

Preset Cooking Time: 46 minutes

    4 medium carrots, thinly sliced
    ¼ cup vegetable oil
    2 pounds lean pork, cut into
          ½-inch cubes
    1 medium onion, sliced
    2 green peppers, seeded and sliced
    1 can (16 ounces) pineapple chunks
    ¼ cup cornstarch
    ½ cup soy sauce
    ½ cup firmly-packed light
          brown sugar
    ¼ cup vinegar
    1 tablespoon Worcestershire sauce
    ¼ teaspoon hot pepper sauce
    ½ teaspoon pepper

Combine carrots and oil in 3-quart glass or ceramic casserole. Cover. Place in oven. Set recipe number 109. (Oven cooks: micro, HI, 6 minutes.)

At Pause, add pork, onion, and green peppers to casserole. Cover. Place in oven. Touch START. (Oven cooks: micro, HI, 5 minutes.)

At Pause, drain pineapple chunks, reserving ½ cup syrup. Transfer syrup to bowl. Stir in cornstarch. Blend in remaining ingredients. Add to pork with pineapple chunks, mixing thoroughly. Cover. Place in oven on ceramic tray. Touch START. (Oven cooks: micro/convec, 350°F, 15 minutes.)

At Pause, stir through several times. Touch START. (Oven cooks: micro/convec, 350°F, 20 minutes.) Serve over chow mein noodles or cooked rice.

4 to 6 servings

Recipe No. 110

Country Style Ribs

Preset Cooking Time: 1 hour 5 minutes

- 3 pounds meaty country-style pork ribs
- ½ cup barbecue sauce
- 3 tablespoons olive oil
- 1 tablespoon wine vinegar
- 1 tablespoon chopped onion
- 1 teaspoon chopped parsley
- ½ teaspoon salt
- ⅛ teaspoon pepper
- 1 clove garlic, minced

Cut a 1-inch strip from open end of cooking bag. Arrange ribs in bag in large microproof baking dish; tie bag with removed strip. Place in oven. Set recipe number 110. Touch START. *(Oven cooks: micro, 50, 35 minutes.)*

At Pause, remove from oven. Open bag; turn ribs over; drain. Combine remaining ingredients; blend well. Pour over ribs in bag. Close bag. Place in oven. Touch START. *(Oven cooks: micro, 50, 25 minutes; 20, 5 minutes.)*

4 to 6 servings

You can substitute ½ cup Barbecue Sauce (page 173) for ready-made sauce, if desired.

Recipe No. 111

Orange Ginger Pork Chops

Preset Cooking Time: 22 minutes

- 6 lean pork loin chops (1½ pounds), trimmed
- ¼ cup orange juice
- 2 teaspoons ginger
- ½ teaspoon salt
- ½ teaspoon garlic powder
- 6 strips orange peel
- ½ cup dairy sour cream

Place pork chops in rectangular micro-proof baking dish. Pour juice over chops. Place in oven. Cover with waxed paper. Set recipe number 111. Touch START. 2(Oven cooks: micro, 70, 6 *minutes.)*

At Pause, turn over. Cover. Touch START. *(Oven cooks: micro, 70, 6 minutes.)*

At Pause, sprinkle with ginger, salt, and garlic powder. Place 1 strip orange peel on each chop. Cover. Touch START. *(Oven cooks: micro, HI, 10 minutes.)*

Discard orange peel. Top each chop with dollop of sour cream. Let stand, covered, 5 minutes before serving.

6 servings

Recipe No. [112]

Orange-Glazed Pork Roast

Preset Cooking Time: 36 minutes

- ¼ cup orange marmalade
- 2 tablespoons orange juice
- 1 teaspoon cornstarch
- ¾ teaspoon cinnamon
- 1 pork loin roast, boneless (3 pounds)

Combine marmalade, juice, cornstarch, and cinnamon in 2-cup glass measure. Stir until cornstarch is dissolved. Place in oven. Set recipe number 112. Touch START. *(Oven cooks: micro, HI, 1 minute.)*

At Pause, remove from oven; set aside. Place roast, fat-side down, on microwave roasting rack in shallow microproof baking dish. Cover with plastic wrap and place in oven. Touch START. *(Oven cooks: micro, 50, 17 minutes.)*

At Pause, turn over. Cover. Touch START. *(Oven cooks: micro, 50, 17 minutes.)*

At Pause, brush on half of the orange glaze. Do not cover. Touch START. *(Oven cooks: micro, HI, 1 minute.)*

Brush on remaining glaze. Let stand 10 minutes before serving.

6 to 8 servings

Recipe No. [113]

Precooked Ham

Preset Cooking Time: about 35 minutes

- 1 precooked ham (3 to 5 pounds)

Place ham on microwave roasting rack in 12 × 7-inch microproof baking dish. Place in oven. Insert temperature probe horizontally into center of ham. Cover lightly with waxed paper. Set recipe number 113. Touch START. *(Oven cooks: micro, 70, to 90°F.)*

At Pause, turn over. Cover. Touch START. *(Oven cooks: micro, 70, to 120°F; stands: 0, 5 minutes.)*

6 to 10 servings

Recipe No. [114]

Baked Ham with Pineapple

Preset Cooking Time: about 28 minutes

- 1 5-pound canned ham
  Whole cloves
- 1 can (8 ounces) crushed pineapple, undrained
- ½ cup firmly-packed brown sugar
- 1 tablespoon fresh lemon juice
- 1 tablespoon cornstarch
- 2 teaspoons dry mustard

Set ham, fat side up, in ceramic or glass baking dish. Score top in checkerboard pattern and stud with cloves. Insert probe into ham. Place in oven on ceramic tray. Plug in probe. Set recipe number 114. Touch START. *(Oven cooks: micro/convec, 320°F, to 100°F.)*

At Pause, drain excess liquid and set ham aside (do not remove probe). Mix remaining ingredients in small microproof bowl. Place in oven. Touch START. *(Oven cooks: micro, HI, 2 minutes.)*

At Pause, stir. Touch START. *(Oven cooks: micro, HI, 2 minutes.)*

At Pause, spoon mixture over ham, keeping pineapple on top. Place ham in oven. Plug in probe. Touch START. *(Oven cooks: micro/convec, 320°F, to 120°F.)* Let stand 10 minutes before serving.

8 to 10 servings

Recipe No. | 115 |

Scalloped Ham and Potatoes

Preset Cooking Time: 31½ minutes

    2 large onions, thinly sliced
    4 tablespoons butter or margarine,
         divided
    4 medium potatoes (about 2 pounds),
         peeled and thinly sliced, divided
 1½ to 2 cups cubed cooked ham,
         divided
    3 tablespoons all-purpose flour
    ½ teaspoon salt
    ½ teaspoon pepper
 1½ cups (6 ounces) shredded sharp
         Cheddar cheese, divided
         Paprika
    1 cup milk

Combine onions and 2 tablespoons butter in 2-quart microproof casserole. Cover. Place in oven. Set recipe number 115. Touch START. (Oven cooks: micro, HI, 5 minutes.)

At Pause, stir. Touch START. (Oven cooks: micro, HI, 5 minutes.)

At Pause, remove onions from dish and set aside. Layer half of potatoes and half of ham in bottom of same dish. Combine flour, salt, and pepper in small bowl. Sprinkle half of mixture over ham. Top with half of onion and half of cheese. Sprinkle with paprika. Repeat layering. Pour milk into glass measure. Place in oven. Touch START. (Oven cooks: micro, HI, 1½ minutes.)

At Pause, pour milk over ham mixture. Cover casserole. Place in oven. Touch START. (Oven cooks: micro, HI, 20 minutes.) Serve immediately.

4 to 6 servings

Recipe No. | 116 |

Ham Slice

Preset Cooking Time: 12 minutes

    ¼ cup apricot nectar
    1 teaspoon firmly-packed brown
         sugar
    1 teaspoon fresh lemon juice
    ½ teaspoon cornstarch
    1 center cut ham slice
         (about 1 pound)

Combine all ingredients except ham in small bowl and stir until cornstarch is completely dissolved. Place ham in glass or ceramic baking dish just large enough to contain it. Brush with some of the apricot glaze.

Position wire rack in lower guides of oven. Set recipe number 116. Touch START. (Oven preheats: convec, 450°F.)

At Pause, place dish in oven. Touch START. (Oven cooks: convec, 450°F, 6 minutes.)

At Pause, turn ham over. Brush with remaining apricot glaze. Touch START. (Oven cooks: convec, 450°F, 6 minutes.) Serve immediately.

2 to 3 servings

Recipe No. | 117 | ⊞

Sausage

Preset Cooking Time: 5 minutes

    1 package (1 pound) bulk pork
         sausage

Crumble sausage into 1½-quart microproof casserole. Cover and place in oven. Set recipe number 117. Touch START. (Oven cooks: micro, HI, 3 minutes.)

At Pause, stir to break up sausage. Cover. Touch START. (Oven cooks: micro, HI, 2 minutes.)

Drain before serving.

2 servings

⊞ Recipe can be increased. See "Quantity", page 12.

Recipe No. ☐ 118 ☐   ⊞

Bacon

Preset Cooking Time: 4½ minutes

> 4 slices bacon

Place bacon on paper towel on microproof plate. Place in oven. Cover with paper towel. Set recipe number 118. Touch START. *(Oven cooks: micro, HI, 4½ minutes.)*

1 serving

Recipe No. ☐ 119

Liver, Bacon, and Onions

Preset Cooking Time: 20 minutes

> 4 slices bacon
> 1 large onion, sliced in rings
> 1 pound liver, about ½- to
> ¾-inch thick

Arrange bacon on microproof rack set over shallow dish. Place in oven. Set recipe number 200. Touch START. *(Oven cooks: micro, HI, 5 minutes.)*

At Pause, set rack and bacon aside. Add onion slices to bacon drippings, stirring to coat. Place in oven. Touch START. *(Oven cooks: micro, HI, 5 minutes.)* Set onion mixture aside.

Position wire rack in lower guides of oven. Set recipe number 119. Touch START. *(Oven preheats: convec, 320°F.)* Set liver in shallow glass or ceramic dish. Surround with onion.

At 320°F, place in oven on wire rack. Touch START. *(Oven cooks: micro/convec, 320°F, 5 minutes.)*

At Pause, turn liver over. Place in oven. Touch START. *(Oven cooks: micro/convec, 320°F, 5 minutes.)* Sprinkle with crumbled bacon and serve.

2 to 3 servings

This is one of several recipes that use the preset functions of another recipe for part of the cooking sequence. Set recipe number 200 first. At the end of that sequence, set recipe number 119.

Recipe No. ☐ 120 ☐   ⊞

Franks and Beans

Preset Cooking Time: 23 minutes

> ½ pound bacon, chopped
> ½ cup chopped onion
> 1 can (28 ounces) baked beans
> ¼ cup firmly-packed brown sugar
> 1 teaspoon Worcestershire sauce
> 1 pound frankfurters

Place bacon in 2-quart microproof casserole. Place in oven. Set recipe number 120. Touch START. *(Oven cooks: micro, HI, 5 minutes.)*

At Pause, add onion. Cover. Place in oven. Touch START. *(Oven cooks: micro, HI, 3 minutes.)*

At Pause, stir in beans, sugar, and Worcestershire. Set aside.

Cut franks in half lengthwise; score to prevent curling. Arrange half in single layer in 8-inch square casserole. Spread half of bean mixture over top. Repeat layering. Place in oven on ceramic tray. Touch START. *(Oven cooks: micro/convec, 350°F, 15 minutes.)*

4 servings

⊞ *Recipe can be increased. See "Quantity", page 12.*

The Best from the Barnyard

Poultry turns out crisper, browner, and juicier than you ever believed possible, thanks to the micro/convection cooking method. If you've never tried your hand at a duck or goose, now's the time. Roast Duck with Orange Sauce (page 120) and Roast Goose (page 122) are so easy to prepare in this oven that you'll want to serve them often. Don't neglect that budget-wise friend, chicken, of course. Chicken Café (page 112) is a marvel, and Oven Fried Chicken (page 114) has that finger-lickin' quality we all love. And there are new twists for turkey, too. Breast of Turkey Jardiniere (page 119) is a microwave method treat, as are many recipes that combine poultry with sauce or vegetables, such as Chicken Sukiyaki (page 116) and Chicken Noodle Casserole (page 118).

When using the microwave or micro/convection methods, keep in mind that arrangement of the food is important. Drumsticks, for example, are arranged in a circle (above left). Oven Fried Chicken (page 114) should be turned over with tongs. Hot pads or mitts are essential (above). Breast of Turkey Jardiniere (page 119) is cooked by the microwave method and may be covered with waxed paper (left).

Converting Your Recipes

Poultry recipes for which you select the micro/convection method will not need ingredient changes in preparing them for this oven. For the microwave method, compare using a similar recipe in this chapter and review the conversion explanation on page 33.

However, for a crisper texture, cook by the convection method using the upper guides and if you want an extra-crisp, well-browned skin (on your duck or turkey, for example) cook for additional time using the convection method. Some additional tips:

☐ Placing turkey or large chickens breast-side down for the final cooking sequence may reduce crispness in that area but is suggested because it will result in juicy white meat and is a natural basting process.

☐ To obtain uniform doneness and flavor, cook poultry weighing no more than 14 pounds in the oven. Poultry over 14 pounds should be cooked conventionally.

☐ Butter- or oil-injected turkeys often have uneven concentrations of fat and thus cook unevenly. For best results, use uninjected turkeys.

☐ Conventional pop-up indicators for doneness do not work correctly with the microwave or micro/convection methods.

☐ The temperature probe may be used in cooking whole poultry. Insert the probe in the fleshy part of the inside thigh muscle without touching the bone.

☐ Standing time is essential to complete cooking. Allow up to 15 minutes standing time for whole poultry depending upon size. The internal temperature will rise approximately 15°F during 15 minutes standing time. Chicken pieces and casseroles need only 5 minutes standing time.

Using the Defrosting Guide

1. Use the microwave method.
2. Poultry can begin defrosting within the original paper or plastic wrapping. Remove all metal rings, wire twist ties, and any aluminum foil. Since it is difficult to remove metal clamps from legs of frozen turkey, the clamps need not be removed until after defrosting. Be careful, of course, that the metal is at least 1 inch from the oven walls.
3. Remove wrappings as soon as possible and place poultry in microproof dish while defrosting.
4. Defrost only as long as necessary. Poultry should be cool in the center when removed from the oven.
5. To speed defrosting during standing time, poultry may be placed in a cold-water bath.
6. Separate cut-up chicken pieces as soon as partially thawed.
7. Wing and leg tips and area near breast bone may begin cooking before the center is thoroughly defrosted. As soon as these areas appear thawed, cover them with small strips of aluminum foil; this foil should be at least 1 inch from oven walls.

DEFROSTING GUIDE — POULTRY

Food	Amount	Minutes (per pound)	Micro Control	Standing Time (in minutes)	Special Notes
Capon	6 - 8 lbs.	2	70 (roast)	60	Turn over once. Immerse in cold water for standing time.
Chicken, cut up	2 - 3 lbs.	5 - 6	30 (defrost)	10 - 15	Turn every 5 minutes. Separate pieces when partially thawed.
Chicken, whole	2 - 3 lbs.	6 - 8	30 (defrost)	25 - 30	Turn over once. Immerse in cold water for standing time.
Cornish hens	1, 1 - 1½ lbs. 2, 1 - 1½ lbs. ea.	12 - 13 20 - 21	30 (defrost) 30 (defrost)	20 20	Turn over once.
Duckling	4 - 5 lbs.	4	70 (roast)	30 - 40	Turn over once. Immerse in cold water for standing time.
Turkey	Under 8 lbs. Over 8 lbs.	3 - 5 3 - 5	30 (defrost) 70 (roast)	60 60	Turn over once. Immerse in cold water for standing time.
Turkey breast	Under 4 lbs. Over 4 lbs.	3 - 5 1 2	30 (defrost) 70 (roast) 50 (simmer)	20 20	Turn over once. Start at 70 (roast), turn over, continue on 50 (simmer).
Turkey drumsticks	1 - 1½ lbs.	5 - 6	30 (defrost)	15 - 20	Turn every 5 minutes. Separate pieces when partially thawed.
Turkey roast, boneless	2 - 4 lbs.	3 - 4	30 (defrost)	10	Remove from foil pan. Cover with waxed paper.

Using the Cooking Guides

1. Defrost frozen poultry completely before cooking.
2. Remove the giblets, rinse poultry in cool water, and pat dry.
3. When cooking whole birds, place on a roasting rack set in a baking dish that is safe for the cooking method planned. Rack and dish must be microproof for the microwave method; microproof and heatproof for the micro/convection method; heatproof for convection.
4. Turn over, as directed in Guide, halfway through cooking time (between First Stage and Second Stage).
5. Toward end of cooking time, small pieces of aluminum foil may be used for shielding to cover legs, wing tips, or breast bone area to prevent overcooking. Foil should be at least 1 inch from oven walls when microwave or micro/convection method is used.
6. Cover poultry pieces, if you wish, with waxed paper when cooking by the microwave method. Use microproof and/or heatproof lids for other methods.
7. Use the Probe Method for the most accurate cooking of whole poultry. Insert the temperature probe in the thickest part of the flesh, as near horizontal as possible, between breast and thigh muscle without touching the bone.
8. Standing time completes the cooking of poultry. Cooked whole birds may be covered with aluminum foil during standing time.

COOKING GUIDE — POULTRY

Food	Programming Method	Setting	First Stage	Second Stage	Probe Method	Special Notes
Chicken, whole, 3½ - 4 lbs.	micro/convec	400°	5 - 6 min. per lb. breast down, turn over	6 min. per lb.	180°	On ceramic tray. Glass o ceramic baking dish with trivet.
Chicken pieces, 3½ - 4 lbs.	micro/convec	350°	6 min. skin down turn over	4 - 5 min. per lb.	170°	Lower guides. Preheat. Glass or ceramic baking dish.
Cornish hens, 1 - 1½ lbs.	micro/convec	350°	10 - 12 min. breast down turn over	10 - 12 min.	180°	Lower guides. Preheat. Glass or ceramic baking dish.
Duckling, 4 - 5 lbs.	micro/convec	400°	5 - 6 min. breast down turn over	6 min. per lb.	170°	On ceramic tray. For additional browning, cook (convec) at 400°.
Turkey, whole 10 - 12 lbs.	micro/convec	330°	5 - 6 min. per lb. breast up turn over	6 min. per lb.	170°	On ceramic tray. Glass or ceramic baking dish with trivet.
Turkey breast, 3 - 4 lbs.	micro/convec	350°	4 min. per lb. skin down turn over	3½ - 4½ min. per lb.	170°	Lower guides. Preheat. Glass or ceramic baking dish.
Turkey roast, boneless, 2 - 4 lbs.	micro/convec	400°	6 min. per lb. turn over	6 - 8 min. per lb.	170°	On ceramic tray. Glass or ceramic baking dish with trivet.
Turkey parts, 3 lbs.	micro/convec	350°	3½ - 4½ min. per lb.	3½ - 4½ min. per lb.		Lower guides. Preheat. Glass or ceramic baking dish. Start skin down.

Recipe No. | 121 |

Chicken with Old-Fashioned Dressing

Preset Cooking Time: 36 minutes

- ¼ cup diced onion
- ¼ cup diced celery
- 1 tablespoon butter or margarine
- 1 cup diced fresh mushrooms
- ⅔ cup chicken stock
- 1½ cups cornbread stuffing mix
- 2 tablespoons minced parsley
- 1 3- to 4-pound chicken
- 1 slice white bread
  Vegetable oil
  Garlic powder
  Paprika

Combine onion, celery, and butter in 1-quart microproof bowl. Cover with plastic wrap. Place in oven. Set recipe number 09. Touch START. (Oven cooks: micro, HI, 2 minutes.)

Position wire rack in lower guides of oven. Set recipe number 121. Touch START. (Oven preheats: convec, 400°F.) Stir in mushrooms and stock. Add stuffing mix and parsley and blend lightly. Spoon into cavity and neck of chicken. Tuck bread inside cavity to seal opening. Brush chicken with oil. Sprinkle with garlic powder and paprika. Set chicken, breast-side down, on roasting rack. Place rack in shallow glass or ceramic baking dish.

At 400°F, place in oven. Touch START. (Oven cooks: micro/convec, 400°F, 15 minutes.)

At Pause, turn chicken over. Baste with drippings and sprinkle with additional paprika. Place in oven. Touch START. (Oven cooks: micro/convec, 400°F, 19 minutes.)

4 to 6 servings

This is one of several recipes that use the preset functions of another recipe for part of the cooking sequence. Set recipe number 09 first. At the end of that sequence, set recipe number 121.

Recipe No. ☐ 122 ☐

Easy Baked Chicken

Preset Cooking Time: 34 minutes

- 1 broiler-fryer chicken
  (3½ pounds), giblets removed
  Salt and pepper
- 2 medium stalks celery, cut into
  1-inch chunks
- 1 small onion, cut into quarters
- 2 tablespoons butter or margarine,
  softened
- ⅛ teaspoon thyme

Set recipe number 122. Touch START. *(Oven preheats: convec, 400°F.)* Meanwhile, rinse chicken in cool water and pat dry. Sprinkle cavity with salt and pepper. Place celery and onion inside cavity. Tie legs together with string; tie wings to body. Place chicken, breast-side up, on microproof roasting rack in 12 × 7-inch microproof baking dish. Spread with butter and sprinkle with thyme.

At 400°F, place in oven. Touch START. *(Oven cooks: micro/convec, 400°F, 15 minutes.)*

At Pause, turn chicken over. Baste with pan juices. Place in oven. Touch START. *(Oven cooks: micro/convec, 400°F, 19 minutes.)* Serve immediately.

4 servings

Recipe No. ☐ 123 ☐

Soy Sherry Chicken

Preset Cooking Time: about 37 minutes

- 1 broiler-fryer chicken (3 pounds),
  giblets removed
- ¼ cup soy sauce
- ¼ cup dry sherry
- 1 small onion, sliced
- 3 slices fresh ginger (⅛ inch
  thick)

Cut off a 1-inch strip from open end of cooking bag. Rinse chicken in cool water and pat dry. Brush generously with soy sauce. Place chicken, breast-side up, in cooking bag in microproof baking dish. Add sherry, any remaining soy sauce, onion, and

ginger. Place in oven. Insert temperature probe into thigh. Tie bag loosely with removed strip. Set recipe number 123. Touch START. *(Oven cooks: micro, 80, to 180°F; 10, 10 minutes.)*

Turn bag over to baste chicken with juices before removing from bag. Discard ginger. Serve with cooking juices and onion.

4 servings

Recipe No. ☐ 124 ☐   ⊞

Chicken Paupiettes

Preset Cooking Time: 25 minutes

- ¼ cup butter or margarine
- 2 tablespoons chopped green pepper
- 2 tablespoons chopped celery
- 1 clove garlic, minced
- 1 tablespoon chopped green onion
- ½ teaspoon salt
- ¼ teaspoon pepper
- 2 cups fresh bread crumbs
- 4 whole boneless chicken breasts,
  pounded thin
  Paprika
  Basic White Sauce (page 173)
- 1 tablespoon chopped parsley

Combine butter, green pepper, celery, garlic, onion, salt, and pepper in 2-quart glass measure or microproof bowl. Cover with plastic wrap. Place in oven. Set recipe number 32. Touch START. *(Oven cooks: micro, HI, 2 minutes.)* Remove from oven and stir. Set aside.

Position wire rack in lower guides of oven. Set recipe number 124. Touch START. *(Oven preheats: convec, 350°F.)* Meanwhile, add bread crumbs to vegetable mixture and fold in lightly. Place one-fourth of mixture in center of each chicken breast and roll up. Arrange seam side down in small baking dish. Sprinkle lightly with paprika.

At 350°F, place in oven on wire rack. Touch START. *(Oven cooks: micro/convec, 350°F, 13 minutes; convec, 350°F, 10 minutes.)* Top with hot Basic White Sauce. Sprinkle with parsley and serve.

4 servings

⊞ *Recipe can be increased. See "Quantity", page 12.*

Recipe No. ☐ 125 ☐

Chicken and Vegetables

Preset Cooking Time: 23 minutes

        2 medium carrots
        2 medium stalks celery
        2 small parsnips, peeled
        2 small potatoes, peeled
        1 medium onion
        2 tablespoons butter or margarine
        2 tablespoons minced parsley
      ½ teaspoon salt
      ⅛ teaspoon paprika
          Dash pepper
        2 whole chicken breasts (1 pound
              each), split, skinned,
              and boned

Cut all vegetables into 1½ × ¼-inch strips (about 4 cups total). Place in shallow round or oval microproof baking dish. Dot with butter. Season with parsley, salt, paprika, and pepper. Cover with plastic wrap. Place in oven. Set recipe number 208. Touch START. *(Oven cooks: micro, HI, 7 minutes.)* Remove vegetables from oven and stir. Set aside.

Position wire rack in lower guides of oven. Set recipe number 125. Touch START. *(Oven preheats: convec, 350°F.)* Arrange chicken over vegetables around outside of dish. Sprinkle with additional paprika. Cover.

At 350°F, place in oven on wire rack. Touch START. *(Oven cooks: micro/convec, 350°F, 8 minutes.)*

At Pause, rotate dish one-half turn. Touch START. *(Oven cooks: micro/convec, 350°F, 8 minutes.)* Spoon vegetables over chicken. Sprinkle with additional parsley and serve.

4 servings

This is one of several recipes that use the preset functions of another recipe for part of the cooking sequence. Set recipe number 208 first. At the end of that sequence, set recipe number 125.

Recipe No. ☐ 126 ☐

Chicken Café

Preset Cooking Time: 32 minutes

        1 4-pound frying chicken, cut up or
              4 pounds chicken parts
        1 teaspoon garlic salt
      ½ teaspoon ground ginger
        1 can (8 ounces) pineapple chunks,
              drained, syrup reserved
      ½ cup coffee-flavored liqueur
        1 tablespoon fresh lemon juice
        2 tablespoons cornstarch
        2 tablespoons coffee-flavored liqueur
        1 can (11 ounces) mandarin orange
              segments, drained
      ¼ cup thinly sliced green onions

Position wire rack in lower guides of oven. Set recipe number 126. Touch START. *(Oven preheats: convec, 400°F.)* Rinse chicken and pat dry with paper towels. Arrange skin-side down in 9 × 13-inch glass or ceramic baking dish. Sprinkle with garlic salt and ginger.

At 400°F, place in oven on wire rack. Touch START. *(Oven cooks: micro/convec, 400°F, 15 minutes.)*

At Pause, drain off liquid. Turn chicken skin side up. Combine pineapple syrup, ½ cup liqueur, and lemon juice and pour over chicken. Place in oven. Touch START. *(Oven cooks: micro/convec, 400°F, 15 minutes.)*

At Pause, transfer chicken to platter. Skim off any fat from drippings in dish. Combine cornstarch with 2 tablespoons liqueur and stir until cornstarch is completely dissolved. Blend into drippings. Place in oven. Touch START. *(Oven cooks: micro, HI, 2 minutes.)*

Stir through several times. Add orange and pineapple. Return chicken to dish, spooning sauce and fruit over top. Sprinkle with onions and serve. (If chicken has cooled, reheat: micro, HI, 2 to 3 minutes.)

4 servings

Chicken Café →

Recipe No. 127

Oven Fried Chicken

Preset Cooking Time: 30 minutes

- 2 cups cornflake crumbs
- 1 tablespoon cornstarch
- 2 teaspoons onion powder
- ¼ teaspoon salt
- ⅛ teaspoon pepper
- 1 3-pound frying chicken, cut up, rinsed and patted dry
- 1 egg, beaten

Position wire rack in lower guides of oven. Set recipe number 127. Touch START. *(Oven preheats: convec, 350°F.)* Meanwhile, combine cornflake crumbs, cornstarch, onion powder, salt, and pepper in large plastic bag. Dip each piece of chicken into egg, then add to crumb mixture, shaking to coat well and cover completely. Arrange skin-side down in 9×13-inch glass or ceramic baking dish.

At 350°F, place in oven. Touch START. *(Oven cooks: micro/convec, 350°F, 15 minutes.)*

At Pause, turn chicken pieces over. Touch START. *(Oven cooks: micro/convec, 350°F, 15 minutes.)* Serve immediately.

4 servings

Recipe No. 128

Barbecued Chicken

Preset Cooking Time: 30 minutes

- 1 3- to 4-pound chicken, cut up
- ½ cup Barbecue Sauce (page 173)

Position wire rack in lower guides of oven. Set recipe number 128. Touch START. *(Oven preheats: convec, 350°F.)* Arrange chicken, skin-side down in 9×13-inch glass or ceramic baking dish. Brush generously with sauce.

At 350°F, place in oven on wire rack. Touch START. *(Oven cooks: micro/convec, 350°F, 15 minutes.)*

At Pause, turn chicken over. Brush again with sauce. Place in oven. Touch START. *(Oven cooks: micro/convec, 350°F, 15 minutes.)* Serve immediately.

4 servings

Recipe No. 129

Chicken Marengo

Preset Cooking Time: 50 minutes

- 1 broiler-fryer chicken (3½ pounds), cut up
- ¼ cup vegetable oil
- 2 cups soft bread crumbs
- 1 package (3 ounces) spaghetti sauce mix
- 2 cups sliced mushrooms
- 1 can (16 ounces) whole tomatoes, broken up
- 1 cup dry white wine

Rinse chicken and pat dry with paper towels. Brush with oil. Mix bread crumbs and sauce mix in plastic bag. Add chicken 1 piece at a time and shake to coat well. Arrange chicken in 3-quart round or oval microproof casserole with thickest portions toward outside of casserole. Place in oven. Set recipe number 129. Touch START. *(Oven cooks: micro/convec, 350°F, 20 minutes.)*

At Pause, add remaining ingredients. Cover. Place in oven. Touch START. *(Oven cooks: micro/convec, 350°F, 30 minutes.)* Serve immediately.

4 to 6 servings

Recipe No. 130

Chicken Milano

Preset Cooking Time: 20 minutes

- ¼ cup olive oil
- 1 teaspoon salt
- ½ teaspoon pepper
- ¼ teaspoon oregano
- ¼ teaspoon basil
- 4 chicken thighs (¼ pound each)
- 1 cup dry bread crumbs
- ½ teaspoon paprika
- 2 medium potatoes, peeled and cut into quarters

Combine oil, salt, pepper, oregano, and basil in shallow dish. Add chicken, rolling to coat all sides. Cover and refrigerate 2 hours.

Position wire rack in lower guides of oven. Set recipe number 130. Touch START. *(Oven preheats: convec, 400°F.)* Meanwhile, mix bread crumbs and paprika on plate. Remove 1 piece chicken from marinade and drain. Roll in crumb mixture to coat. Repeat with remaining chicken. Set aside remaining crumb mixture and marinade. Arrange chicken skin-side down in 9-inch round casserole with thickest portions toward outside of dish. Cut ends from potatoes to make quarters even; wipe dry. Roll potatoes in remaining marinade to coat, adding more oil to marinade if necessary. Arrange potatoes around chicken.

At 400°F, place in oven on wire rack. Touch START. *(Oven cooks: micro/convec, 400°F, 10 minutes.)*

At Pause, turn chicken and potatoes over. Sprinkle with remaining crumb mixture. Touch START. *(Oven cooks: micro/convec, 400°F, 10 minutes.)* Serve immediately.

2 servings

Recipe No. 131

Tarragon Grilled Chicken

Preset Cooking Time: 30 minutes

    ¼ cup olive oil
    ¼ cup dry sherry or chicken
        broth
    1 tablespoon onion flakes
    1 clove garlic, minced
    1 teaspoon salt
    ½ teaspoon tarragon
    ⅛ teaspoon white pepper
    1 broiler-fryer chicken (3 pounds),
        quartered

Position wire rack in lower guides of oven. Set recipe number 131. Touch START. *(Oven preheats: convec, 350°F.)* Meanwhile, combine all ingredients except chicken. Set aside. Arrange chicken, skin-side down, in shallow oval microproof baking dish with thickest portions toward outside of dish. Brush with half of the oil mixture.

At 350°F, place in oven on wire rack. Touch START. *(Oven cooks: micro/convec, 350°F, 15 minutes.)*

At Pause, turn chicken over. Brush generously with remaining oil mixture. Touch START. *(Oven cooks: micro/convec, 350°F, 15 minutes.)* Serve immediately.

4 servings

Recipe No. 132

Chicken Supreme

Preset Cooking Time: 1 hour 5 minutes

    5 slices bacon
    1 can (10¾ ounces) cream of onion
        soup, undiluted
    ½ cup dry red wine or dry sherry
    ½ cup chopped onions
    1 clove garlic, minced
    1 tablespoon minced parsley
    1½ teaspoons chicken bouillon
        granules
    ½ teaspoon salt
    ¼ teaspoon pepper
    ¼ teaspoon thyme
    6 small potatoes, peeled and cut
        in half
    2 medium carrots, thinly sliced
    1 broiler-fryer chicken
        (2½ pounds), cut up
    ½ pound mushrooms, sliced

Arrange bacon on paper towel on microproof plate. Place in oven. Cover with paper towel. Set recipe number 132. Touch START. *(Oven cooks: micro, HI, 5 minutes.)*

At Pause, remove from oven; crumble bacon and set aside. Combine soup, wine, onion, garlic, parsley, bouillon, and seasonings; set aside. Place potatoes and carrots in 3-quart microproof casserole. Arrange chicken on top, skin-side down, with thickest parts toward outside of casserole. Pour soup mixture over top. Cover and place in oven. Touch START. *(Oven cooks: micro/convec, 320°F, 30 minutes.)*

At Pause, rearrange chicken, bringing bottom pieces to top, skin-side up. Sprinkle with bacon and mushrooms. Cover. Touch START. *(Oven cooks: micro/convec, 320°F, 30 minutes.)*

4 to 6 servings

Recipe No. ☐ 133 ☐   ⊞

Chicken Wings Parmesan

Preset Cooking Time: 14 minutes

- 6 chicken wings
- 10 buttery crackers
- ¼ cup grated Parmesan cheese
- 3 tablespoons minced parsley
- 1 teaspoon garlic powder
- ⅛ teaspoon pepper
- ½ teaspoon paprika
- ½ teaspoon salt
- ¼ cup butter or margarine, melted

Position wire rack in lower guides of oven. Set recipe number 133. Touch START. *(Oven preheats: convec, 350°F.)* Meanwhile, cut chicken wings in half, discarding tip. Rinse wings, pat dry with paper towels and set aside. Mix crackers in blender or food processor to fine crumbs. Pour into bowl. Add all remaining ingredients except melted butter and blend well. Dip chicken in melted butter, then roll in crumbs, coating evenly. Arrange chicken pieces, skin-side up, in spoke pattern in 9-inch round glass pie plate with largest portions of wings toward rim.

At 350°F, place in oven on wire rack. Touch START. *(Oven cooks: micro/convec, 350°F, 14 minutes.)* Serve hot.

2 to 4 servings

Recipe No. ☐ 134

Chicken Sukiyaki

Preset Cooking Time: 13 minutes

- ½ cup soy sauce
- ½ cup chicken broth
- ¼ cup dry sherry
- 2 tablespoons sugar
- 2 chicken breasts (½ pound each), skinned, boned, and cut into ½-inch slices
- 1 pound spinach, stems removed
- ½ pound bean sprouts
- ¼ pound pea pods
- ½ cup sliced celery
- 1 medium onion, thinly sliced
- 1 medium bunch green onions, cut into 3-inch strips
- 6 small mushrooms, sliced

Combine soy sauce, broth, sherry, and sugar in 2-cup glass measure; stir until sugar is dissolved. Place in oven. Set recipe number 134. Touch START. *(Oven cooks: micro, HI, 2 minutes.)*

At Pause, remove from oven. Combine remaining ingredients in 3-quart microproof casserole; toss lightly. Pour sauce mixture over chicken mixture. Cover and place in oven. Touch START. *(Oven cooks: micro, HI, 4 minutes.)*

At Pause, stir. Cover. Touch START. *(Oven cooks: micro, HI, 3 minutes.)*

At Pause, stir. Cover. Touch START. *(Oven cooks: micro, HI, 4 minutes.)*

Pass additional soy sauce at table.

4 servings

Recipe No. ☐ 135 ☐   ⊞

Chicken à la King

Preset Cooking Time: 7 minutes

- ¼ cup butter or margarine
- 3 tablespoons all-purpose flour
- 1 can (10¾ ounces) cream of mushroom soup, undiluted
- ¼ cup milk
- 2 teaspoons chicken bouillon granules
  Pinch pepper
- 2 cups cubed cooked chicken or turkey
- ½ cup peas
- 4 to 6 English muffins, split and toasted

Place butter in 1-quart glass measure. Place in oven. Set recipe number 135. Touch START. *(Oven cooks: micro, HI, 1 minute.)*

At Pause, add flour, 1 tablespoon at a time, stirring constantly until smooth. Blend in soup, milk, bouillon, and pepper. Cover with plastic wrap. Place in oven. Touch START. *(Oven cooks: micro, HI, 1 minute.)*

At Pause, stir. Touch START. *(Oven cooks: micro, HI, 1 minute.)*

At Pause, add chicken and peas. Cover. Place in oven. Touch START. *(Oven cooks: micro, HI, 4 minutes.)* Spoon over English muffins and serve.

4 to 6 servings

⊞ *Recipe can be increased. See "Quantity", page 12.*

Chicken Paupiettes (page 111), →
Stuffed Tomatoes (page 155)

Recipe No. 136

Chicken Noodle Casserole

Preset Cooking Time: 13 minutes

3	cups cubed cooked chicken
1½	cups broken uncooked narrow egg noodles
1	cup chicken stock
½	cup milk
½	teaspoon salt
⅛	teaspoon pepper
1	cup (4 ounces) shredded Cheddar cheese
½	cup sliced stuffed green olives

Combine chicken, uncooked noodles, stock, milk, salt, and pepper in 2-quart microproof casserole and mix lightly. Cover. Place in oven. Set recipe number 136. Touch START. *(Oven cooks: micro, 70, 5 minutes.)*

At Pause, stir. Touch START. *(Oven cooks: micro, 70, 5 minutes.)*

At Pause, blend in cheese and olives. Cover. Place in oven. Touch START. *(Oven cooks: micro, HI, 3 minutes.)* Serve immediately.

4 to 6 servings

Recipe No. 137

Chicken Liver Chow Mein

Preset Cooking Time: 17 minutes

½	pound chicken livers, rinsed and drained
½	cup sliced celery
¼	cup chopped onion
3	tablespoons butter or margarine, divided
1	envelope (1¾ ounces) mushroom gravy mix
1	can (16 ounces) Chinese vegetables
1	can (8 ounces) sliced water chestnuts, drained
1	tablespoon soy sauce

Cut liver into bite-size pieces; discard membranes; set aside. Combine celery, onion, and 1 tablespoon butter in 3-quart microproof casserole. Cover and place in oven. Set recipe number 137. Touch START *(Oven cooks: micro, HI, 4 minutes.)*

At Pause, stir in gravy mix. Add Chinese vegetables, water chestnuts, and soy sauce; stir until gravy mix is dissolved. Cover. Touch START. *(Oven cooks: micro, HI, 7 minutes.)*

At Pause, remove from oven; set aside. Place liver and remaining 2 tablespoons butter in 4-cup glass measure. Place in oven. Cover with waxed paper. Touch START. *(Oven cooks: micro, 50, 4 minutes.)*

At Pause, remove from oven; drain. Carefully stir liver into vegetable mixture. Cover and place in oven. Touch START. *(Oven cooks: micro, HI, 2 minutes.)*

Let stand, covered, 5 minutes. Serve over hot rice and sprinkle with chow mein noodles.

4 to 6 servings

Recipe No. 138

Turkey with Cornbread Stuffing

Preset Cooking Time: about 1 hour 15 minutes

½	cup diced onions
½	cup diced celery
2	tablespoons butter or margarine
2	cups diced mushrooms
1	cup chicken stock, turkey stock, or bouillon
2	cups cornbread stuffing mix
1	10- to 12-pound turkey, cleaned, rinsed, and patted dry
	Vegetable oil
	Paprika

Prepare stuffing and turkey as recipe directs. Place turkey, breast-side up, on rack. Insert temperature probe in fleshy part of thigh. Place in oven. Plug in probe. Set recipe number 138. Touch START. *(Oven cooks: micro/convec, 330°F, 15 minutes.)*

At Pause, rotate dish one-quarter turn, using care not to unplug probe. Touch START. *(Oven cooks: micro/convec, 330°F, 15 minutes.)*

At Pause, baste turkey with drippings. Turn breast-side down. Touch START. *(Oven cooks: micro/convec, 330°F, 15 minutes.)*

At Pause, baste turkey with drippings. Touch START. *(Oven cooks: micro/convec, 330°F, to 170°F.)*

Remove from oven. Cover with aluminum foil. Let stand 10 minutes before carving.

8 to 10 servings

Recipe No. | 139 |

Turkey with Nut Stuffing

Preset Cooking Time: about 1 hour 15 minutes

- 1 turkey (12 pounds), neck and giblets removed
- 1 cup chicken broth
- ½ cup butter or margarine
- 2 medium stalks celery, thinly sliced
- 1 large onion, chopped
- 10 cups day-old bread crumbs or ½-inch cubes
- 1 cup coarsely chopped walnuts or pecans
- ¼ cup chopped parsley
- 1 teaspoon poultry seasoning
- ½ teaspoon salt

Rinse turkey in cool water and pat dry; set aside. Place broth, butter, celery, and onion in 4-cup glass measure. Place in oven. Insert temperature probe in center of measure. Plug in probe. Set recipe number 139. Touch START. *(Oven cooks: micro, HI, 5 minutes.)*

At Pause, remove measure from oven. Add bread crumbs, nuts, parsley, poultry seasoning, and salt; stir lightly. Stuff neck opening with part of stuffing. Secure neck skin with strong wooden toothpicks or skewers. Stuff cavity with remaining stuffing. Tie legs together with strong string; tie wings to body. Place turkey, breast-side up, on roasting rack in large baking dish. Insert probe in fleshy part of thigh. Place in oven. Plug in probe. Touch START. *(Oven cooks:*

micro/convec, 330°F, 30 minutes.)

At Pause, turn over; drain. Touch START. *(Oven cooks: micro/convec, 330°F, 15 minutes.)*

At Pause, baste with pan juices. Rotate pan one-quarter turn. Touch START. *(Oven cooks: micro/convec, 330°F, to 170°F.)*

Remove from oven. Cover with aluminum foil. Let stand 10 minutes before carving.

6 to 8 servings

Recipe No. | 140 |

Breast of Turkey Jardiniere

Preset Cooking Time: 25 minutes

- 1 medium carrot, cut into thin 2″ strips
- 1 celery stalk, cut into thin 2″ strips
- 1 small onion, cut into thin 2″ strips
- 1 very small potato, cut into thin 2″ strips
- 1 tablespoon minced parsley
- 2 tablespoons butter or margarine
  Salt and pepper to taste
- ½ turkey breast (3 to 4 pounds), boned and skinned (if desired)
  Paprika

Arrange carrot, celery, onion, potato, and parsley close together in microproof casserole just large enough to accommodate all ingredients. Dot with butter. Season lightly with salt and pepper. Cover. Place in oven. Set recipe number 2. Touch START. *(Oven cooks: micro, HI, 5 minutes.)* Remove dish from oven. Set aside.

Set recipe number 140. Touch START. *(Oven preheats: convec, 350°F.)* Set turkey breast on vegetables. Sprinkle with paprika. Cover.

At 350°F, place in oven. Touch START. *(Oven cooks: micro/convec, 350°F, 10 minutes.)*

At Pause, rotate dish one-half turn. Touch START. *(Oven cooks: micro/convec, 350°F, 10 minutes.)* Serve immediately.

1 to 2 servings

Recipe No. | 141 |

Glazed Turkey Legs

Preset Cooking Time: 21½ minutes

- ⅓ cup honey
- 1 teaspoon grated lemon peel
- 1 teaspoon lemon juice
- 1 teaspoon cornstarch
- ¼ teaspoon bottled brown sauce
- 2 turkey legs (2½ to 3 pounds)

Stir honey, lemon peel, lemon juice, cornstarch, and brown sauce in small microproof bowl until cornstarch is dissolved. Place in oven. Set recipe number 34. Touch START. *(Oven cooks: micro, HI, 1½ minutes.)* Remove glaze from oven. Set aside.

Position wire rack in upper guides of oven. Set recipe number 141. Touch START. *(Oven preheats: convec, 350°F.)* Place turkey legs in 10-inch round or 9-inch square casserole.

At 350°F, place in oven on wire rack. Touch START. *(Oven cooks: micro/convec, 350°F, 10 minutes.)*

At Pause, brush with glaze. Turn turkey over and brush again with glaze. Touch START. *(Oven cooks: micro/convec, 350°F, 10 minutes.)* Serve immediately.

2 to 4 servings

This is one of several recipes that use the preset functions of another recipe for part of the cooking sequence. Set recipe number 34 first. At the end of that sequence, set recipe number 141.

Recipe No. | 142 |

Roast Duck

Preset Cooking Time: about 45 minutes

- 1 4- to 5-pound duckling
- 1 teaspoon salt
- ¼ teaspoon pepper
- 1 small onion, quartered
  Leaves from 2 to 3 celery stalks
  Orange Sauce (page 178)

Rinse duck thoroughly in cool water; pat dry. Sprinkle cavity with salt and pepper. Set onion and celery leaves inside cavity. Tie legs and wings together with string. Pierce skin around leg and wing joints with fork. Arrange duck, breast-side down, on rack in glass or ceramic baking dish.

Insert temperature probe in breast close to leg. Place in oven. Plug in probe. Set recipe number 142. Touch START. *(Oven preheats. convec, 400°F.)*

At 400°F, pierce entire surface with fork, using care not to dislodge or unplug probe. Touch START. *(Oven cooks: micro/convec, 400°F, 15 minutes.)*

At Pause, pour off excess fat. Touch START. *(Oven cooks: micro/convec, 400°F, to 170°F; convec, 400°F, 20 minutes.)* Serve with Orange Sauce.

2 to 4 servings

Recipe No. | 143 |

Roast Raspberry Duckling

Preset Cooking Time: about 45 minutes

- 1 duckling (4 pounds), giblets removed
- 1 carrot, peeled and cut into chunks
- 1 medium onion, cut into quarters
- 1 jar (10 ounces) raspberry jelly
- ¼ cup raspberry liqueur
- 2 tablespoons fresh lemon juice

Rinse duckling in cool water and pat dry. Place carrot and onion pieces in body cavity. Secure neck skin with wooden toothpicks or skewers. Tie legs together with string; tie wings to body. Pierce skin all over to allow fat to drain. Place duckling, breast-side up, on microwave roasting rack in 12×7-inch microproof baking dish. Insert temperature probe in breast close to leg. Place in oven. Plug in probe. Set recipe number 143. Touch START. *(Oven preheats: convec, 400°F.)*

At 400°F, pierce entire surface with fork, using care not to dislodge or unplug probe. Touch START. *(Oven cooks: micro/convec, 400°F, 15 minutes.)*

Meanwhile, combine remaining ingredients in small bowl and stir until smooth.

At Pause, turn duck over. Touch START. *(Oven cooks: micro/convec, 400°F, to 170°F.)*

At Pause, brush duck with glaze. Touch START. *(Oven cooks: convec, 400°F, 10 minutes.)*

2 servings

Roast Duck →

Recipe No. [144]

Roast Goose

Preset Cooking Time: about 1 hour
20 minutes

- 1 8- to 9- pound goose
  Salt
- 1 large onion
- 3 celery stalks

Rinse goose thoroughly in cool water and pat dry. Sprinkle with salt. Set onion and celery inside cavity. Tie legs and wings together with string. Place goose, breast-side down, on rack in glass or ceramic baking dish. Insert temperature probe in breast close to leg. Place in oven. Plug in probe. Set recipe number 144. Touch START. *(Oven preheats: convec, 400°F.)*

At 400°F, pierce entire surface with fork, using care not to dislodge or unplug probe. Touch START. *(Oven cooks: micro/convec, 400°F, 30 minutes.)*

At Pause, drain off excess fat. Turn goose over. Sprinkle with ½ teaspoon salt. Pierce entire surface with fork. Touch START. *(Oven cooks: micro/convec, 400°F, to 170°F; stands: 0, 20 minutes.)*

6 servings

Recipe No. [145]

Heavenly Cornish Hens

Preset Cooking Time: 20 minutes

- 2 Cornish hens (1½ pounds each)
- ¼ cup melted butter
- ½ teaspoon paprika
- ½ teaspoon salt
- ⅛ teaspoon pepper
- ⅛ teaspoon garlic powder

Split hens lengthwise; remove backbones. Rinse hens in cool water and pat dry. Mix butter and remaining ingredients in small bowl. Brush over hens. Set hens, breast-side down, in round or oval glass or ceramic baking dish, with thickest portion of hens toward outside of dish.

Set recipe number 145. Touch START. *(Oven preheats: convec, 450°F.)*

At Pause, place in oven. Touch START. *(Oven cooks: micro/convec, 350°F, 10 minutes.)*

At Pause, baste hens with drippings. Turn hens over and baste again. Touch START. *(Oven cooks: micro/convec, 350°F, 10 minutes.)* Serve immediately.

4 servings

COOKING GUIDE — CONVENIENCE POULTRY*

Food	Programming Method	Setting	First Stage	Second Stage	Probe Method	Special Notes
Chicken, frozen fried, 1½ - 2 lbs.	micro/convec	350°	7 min.	7 - 8 min.		Lower guides. Preheat. 13×9 glass or ceramic baking dish.
Chicken Kiev 1 - 2 pieces	micro/convec	350°	10 min.	6 - 8 min.		Lower guides. Preheat. Glass or ceramic baking dish.
Chicken à la King, frozen, 5 oz.	micro	HI (max. power)	3 - 4 min.			Place on microproof plate.
Creamed chicken, 10½ oz. can	micro	80 (reheat)	2 - 4 min.		150°	Stir once.
Chicken chow mein, 14 - 24 oz. can	micro	80 (reheat)	4 - 6 min.			Stir halfway through cooking time.
Turkey tetrazzini, frozen, 12 oz.	micro	HI (max. power)	3 - 4 min.			Place on microproof plate.
Turkey, sliced in gravy, frozen, 5 oz.	micro	HI (max. power)	3 - 5 min.			Slit pouch. Place in microproof dish.

* Due to the tremendous variety in convenience food products available, times given here should be used only as guidelines. We suggest you cook food for the shortest recommended time and then check for doneness. Be sure to check the package for microwave and oven (convec) instructions.

At The Wharf

Poaching, broiling, oven-frying, baking — any way you prefer to cook fish or shellfish will be easy and quick with this oven. There are well-defined techniques for each cooking method: microwave for poaching or steaming; micro/convection for baking; and convection for broiling and oven-frying. No matter what the method, one thing is certain, seafood never tasted as fresh and good. Salmon Ring (page 133), Mountain Trout (page 131), Tuna-Mushroom Patties (page 134), and Scampi (page 127) will be favorites. For best results, prepare seafood just before serving. When planning a fish dinner, have all ingredients at hand before you start to cook.

Shrimp and Mountain Trout are shown arranged for cooking. Au gratin dishes are especially nice, as used for the trout, but any oval microproof and heatproof dish is fine (top left). Breaded Fish Fillets (page 133) are cooked by the convection method in a metal pan on the wire rack, upper guides (top right). Shellfish cooks so quickly that arrangement is especially important for even doneness. Correct arrangement for lobster tails and clams is illustrated (above left and above right).

Converting Your Recipes

Seafood is delicate with no muscle or connective tissue that needs tenderizing by a lengthy cooking process. Gentle cooking is required. The microwave method treats seafood with the necessary speed and gentleness that preserves moisture. Little or no evaporation occurs because no hot air is present to dry the surface. Shrimp should be cooked until it just turns pink (and no water is needed). Fish needs only enough cooking time to turn opaque and will toughen if overcooked.

For broiled or grilled fish steaks, or for fish that is coated with your favorite mix of crumbs or crackers and seasoning, use a preheated oven (450°F is best) and the convection method. Place the wire rack in the upper guides. No alterations are necessary to suit a conventional seafood recipe to this oven. Simply consult the Guides or find a similar recipe to help you determine the cooking time and be conservative! Remember how quickly seafood cooks and that there's no way to rescue overcooked food. Look to these tips for additional clues to seafood success:

☐ Seafood can be steamed in its own natural juice; little or no liquid should ever be required.
☐ Cook fish covered unless it is coated with crumbs, which seal in the juices.
☐ Fish is done when the flesh becomes opaque and barely flakes with a fork.
☐ Shellfish is done when flesh is opaque and just firm.
☐ Shellfish come in their own cooking containers which respond well to the microwave method. Clam and mussel shells open before your eyes. Shrimp, crab, and lobster shells turn pink.
☐ To remove seafood odors from the oven, combine 1 cup water with lemon juice and a few cloves in a small bowl. Set in oven and cook (micro) on HI (max. power) for several minutes.

Using the Defrosting Guide

1. Use the microwave method.
2. Remove wrapping and place fish on microproof dish.
3. To prevent the outer edges from drying out or beginning to cook, it is best to remove fish from oven before it has completely thawed.
4. Finish defrosting under cold running water, separating fillets.

Using the Cooking Guide

1. Defrost seafood fully; then cook.
2. Remove original wrapping. Rinse under cold running water.
3. Place seafood in baking dish selected to meet needs of the cooking method you plan to use. Place thick edges of fillets and steaks and thick ends of shellfish toward the outer edge of the dish.
4. Cover dish.
5. Test often during the cooking period to avoid overcooking.
6. Method and time are the same for seafood in the shell or without the shell.

DEFROSTING GUIDE — SEAFOOD

Food	Amount	Micro Control	Time (in Minutes)	Standing Time (in minutes)	Special Notes
Fish fillets	1 lb.	30 (defrost)	4 - 6	4 - 5	Carefully separate fillets under cold water. Turn once.
	2 lbs.	30 (defrost)	5 - 7	5	
Fish steaks	1 lb.	30 (defrost)	4 - 6	5	Carefully separate steaks under cold running water.
Whole fish	8 - 10 oz.	30 (defrost)	4 - 6	5	Shallow dish, shape of fish determines size. Should be icy when removed. Finish at room temperature. Cover head with aluminum foil. Turn once.
	1½ - 2 lbs.	30 (defrost)	5 - 7	5	
Lobster tails	8 oz.	30 (defrost)	5 - 7	5	Remove from package to baking dish.
Crab legs	8 - 10 oz.	30 (defrost)	5 - 7	5	Glass baking dish. Break apart and turn once.
Crab meat	6 oz.	30 (defrost)	4 - 5	5	Defrost in package on dish. Break apart. Turn once.
Shrimp	1 lb.	30 (defrost)	3 - 4	5	Remove from package to dish. Spread loosely in baking dish and rearrange during thawing as necessary.
Scallops	1 lb.	30 (defrost)	8 - 10	5	Defrost in package if in block; spread out on baking dish if in pieces. Turn over and rearrange during thawing as necessary.
Oysters	12 oz.	30 (defrost)	3 - 4	5	Remove from package to dish. Turn over and rearrange during thawing as necessary.

COOKING GUIDE — SEAFOOD AND FISH

Food	Micro Control	Time (in Minutes)	Probe Method	Standing Time (in minutes)	Special Notes
Fish fillets, 1 lb. ½ inch thick,	HI (max. power)	4 - 5	140°	4 - 5	11 × 7-inch dish, covered.
2 lbs.	HI (max. power)	7 - 8	140°	4 - 5	
Fish steaks, 1 inch thick, 1 lb.	HI (max. power)	5 - 6	140°	5 - 6	11 × 7-inch dish, covered.
Whole fish 8 - 10 oz.	HI (max. power)	3½ - 4	170°	3 - 4	Appropriate shallow dish.
1½ - 2 lbs.	HI (max. power)	5 - 7	170°	5	
Crab legs 8 - 10 oz.	HI (max. power)	3 - 4		5	Appropriate shallow dish, covered. Turn once.
16 - 20 oz.	HI (max. power)	5 - 6		5	
Shrimp, scallops 8 oz.	70 (roast)	3 - 4			Appropriate shallow dish, covered. Rearrange halfway.
1 lb.	70 (roast)	5 - 7			
Snails, clams, oysters, 12 oz.	70 (roast)	3 - 4			Shallow dish, covered. Rearrange halfway.
Lobster tails 1: 8 oz.	HI (max. power)	3 - 4		5	Shallow dish. Split shell to reduce curling.
2: 8 oz. each	HI (max. power)	5 - 6		5	
4: 8 oz. each	HI (max. power)	9 - 11		5	

For a delicious alternate for lobster tails, see Lobster Tails Supreme, page 126.

Recipe No. | 146 | ⊞

Crab Florentine

Preset Cooking Time: 30½ minutes

    1 package (10 ounces) frozen
        chopped spinach
    ½ cup chopped onions
    3 tablespoons butter or margarine
    6 eggs, beaten
    1 cup cream
    3 tablespoons dry white wine
    ¼ teaspoon salt
    ⅛ teaspoon pepper
    ⅛ teaspoon cayenne
    6 ounces chopped crabmeat, rinsed
        and drained
    ¼ cup grated Parmesan cheese

Place unopened package of spinach upright on microproof plate. Set recipe number 258. Place plate in oven on ceramic tray. Touch START. *(Oven cooks: micro, HI, 2½ minutes.)*

At Pause, turn spinach package on its side. Touch START. *(Oven cooks: micro, HI, 2 minutes.)*

At Pause, remove spinach from oven. Set aside. Combine onion and butter in 2-quart microproof bowl. Cover. Place in oven on ceramic tray. Touch START. *(Oven cooks: micro, HI, 3 minutes.)* Let cool slightly. Add eggs, cream, wine, salt, pepper, and cayenne and mix well.

Position wire rack in lower guides of oven. Set recipe number 146. Touch START. *(Oven preheats: convec, 330°F.)* Meanwhile, drain spinach well and squeeze dry. Blend into onion-eggs mixture. Stir in crab. Turn into ceramic au gratin or baking dish and sprinkle with cheese.

At 330°F, place in oven on wire rack. Touch START. *(Oven cooks: micro/convec, 330°F, 8 minutes.*)

At Pause, rotate dish one-quarter turn. Touch START. *(Oven cooks: micro/convec, 330°F, 10 minutes; stands: 0, 5 minutes.)*

6 to 8 servings

Recipe No. | 147 |

Crab Imperial

Preset Cooking Time: 12 minutes

    ½ cup chopped onions
    2 tablespoons butter or margarine
    1½ cups light cream
    1 cup sliced mushrooms
    3 tablespoons all-purpose flour
    3 tablespoons dry white wine
    ¼ teaspoon salt
    ⅛ teaspoon pepper
    2 egg yolks, lightly beaten
    1½ cups crabmeat chunks

Place onion and butter in 2-quart glass measure. Place in oven. Set recipe number 147. Touch START. *(Oven cooks: micro, HI, 3 minutes.)*

At Pause, add cream, mushrooms, flour, wine, salt, and pepper; blend well. Touch START. *(Oven cooks: micro, HI, 5 minutes.)*

At Pause, blend in egg yolks. Touch START. *(Oven cooks: micro, HI, 2 minutes.)*

At Pause, add crabmeat; blend well. Touch START. *(Oven cooks: micro, 70, 2 minutes.)*

Serve in au gratin dishes, individual custard cups, ramekins, or shells.

4 to 6 servings

Recipe No. | 148 | ⊞

Lobster Tails Supreme

Preset Cooking Time: 7½ minutes

    2 8-ounce lobster tails
    2 tablespoons butter or margarine,
        melted
      Clarified Butter (page 176)
      Lemon wedges

Position wire rack in lower guides of oven. Set recipe number 148. Touch START. *(Oven preheats: convec, 450°F.)* Split each lobster tail through top shell and carefully remove meat, leaving small end attached to shell and setting meat on top of shell. Place lobster in glass or ceramic baking dish. Brush meat with melted butter.

At 450°F, place in oven on wire rack. Touch START. *(Oven cooks: micro/convec, 450°F, 7½ minutes.)* Serve immediately with Clarified Butter and lemon wedges.

2 servings

Recipe No. 149

Scampi

Preset Cooking Time: 5 minutes

- 3 tablespoons vegetable oil
- 2 large cloves garlic, minced
- 3 tablespoons minced parsley
- 2 tablespoons dry white wine
- 1/8 teaspoon paprika
- 3/4 pound large shrimp, shelled, deveined, and butterflied, tails intact
  Juice of 1/2 medium lemon
  Salt and pepper to taste

Combine oil and garlic in oval microproof baking dish just large enough to hold all ingredients. Place in oven. Set recipe number 149. Touch START. (Oven cooks: micro, HI, 1 minute.)

At Pause, add parsley, wine, and paprika. Touch START. (Oven cooks: micro, HI, 1 minute.)

At Pause, add shrimp, lemon juice, salt, and pepper; stir to coat well. Arrange shrimp with tails toward center of dish. Cover with waxed paper. Touch START. (Oven cooks: micro, HI, 1 1/2 minutes.)

At Pause, stir. Cover. Touch START. (Oven cooks: micro, HI, 1 1/2 minutes.)

Garnish with parsley.

2 servings

Recipe No. 150

Shrimp Veracruz

Preset Cooking Time: 12 minutes

- 1 large onion, cut into chunks
- 1 large green pepper, seeded and cut into chunks
- 2 cloves garlic, crushed
- 2 tablespoons vegetable oil
- 1 can (8 ounces) tomato sauce
- 1/4 cup dry white wine
- 1/2 teaspoon oregano
- 1/2 teaspoon salt
- 1/4 teaspoon cumin
  Dash hot pepper sauce
- 1 pound jumbo shrimp, shelled and deveined

Combine onion, green pepper, garlic, and oil in shallow oval microproof baking dish. Place in oven. Set recipe number 150. Touch START. (Oven cooks: micro, HI, 3 minutes.)

At Pause, stir through several times. Add tomato sauce, wine, oregano, salt, cumin,

and hot pepper sauce. Touch START. (Oven cooks: micro, HI, 5 minutes.)

At Pause, add shrimp. Spoon sauce over shrimp. Touch START. (Oven cooks: micro, HI, 2 minutes.)

At Pause, stir. Cover. Touch START. (Oven cooks: micro, HI, 2 minutes.)

Garnish with parsley, and serve over hot rice or noodles.

4 servings

Recipe No. 151

Shrimp Chow Mein

Preset Cooking Time: 22 minutes

- 1 medium onion, chopped
- 1 cup sliced celery
- 1 green pepper, seeded and cut into thin strips
- 2 tablespoons butter or margarine
- 1 pound fresh bean sprouts, or 1 can (16 ounces) bean sprouts, drained
- 1 can (8 ounces) sliced water chestnuts, drained
- 8 to 10 ounces cooked deveined shelled shrimp
- 1/2 cup sliced mushrooms
- 2 tablespoons chopped pimiento
- 3 tablespoons cornstarch
- 3 tablespoons soy sauce
- 1 cup water
- 2 teaspoons chicken bouillon granules

Combine onion, celery, green pepper, and butter in 2-quart microproof casserole. Cover and place in oven. Set recipe number 151. Touch START. (Oven cooks: micro, HI, 10 minutes.)

At Pause, remove from oven. Add bean sprouts, water chestnuts, shrimp, mushrooms, and pimiento; set aside. Dissolve cornstarch in soy sauce in 4-cup glass measure. Add water and bouillon; blend well. Place soy sauce mixture in oven. Touch START. (Oven cooks: micro, HI, 3 minutes.)

At Pause, stir. Touch START. (Oven cooks: micro, HI, 3 minutes.)

At Pause, remove from oven. Stir sauce into shrimp mixture. Cover and place in oven. Touch START. (Oven cooks: micro, HI, 6 minutes.)

Stir through before serving over hot rice, topped with chow mein noodles.

5 to 6 servings

Recipe No. 152

Shrimp Creole

Preset Cooking Time: 15 minutes

- 4 green onions, thinly sliced
- ½ cup chopped green pepper
- ¼ cup chopped celery
- 1 clove garlic, minced
- 2 tablespoons butter or margarine
- 1 can (16 ounces) whole tomatoes, drained and chopped
- 1 can (6 ounces) tomato paste
- 2 teaspoons parsley flakes
- 1 teaspoon salt
- ¼ teaspoon cayenne
- 1 package (10 ounces) frozen cooked shrimp, thawed

Combine onions, green pepper, celery, garlic, and butter in 2-quart microproof casserole. Cover and place in oven. Set recipe number 152. Touch START. (Oven cooks: micro, HI, 3 minutes.)

At Pause, add remaining ingredients except shrimp; blend well. Cover. Touch START. (Oven cooks: micro, 80, 5 minutes.)

At Pause, add shrimp; blend well. Cover. Touch START. (Oven cooks: micro, 80, 3 minutes.)

At Pause, stir. Cover. Touch START. (Oven cooks: micro, 80, 4 minutes.)

Stir before serving over hot rice.

4 to 6 servings

Recipe No. 153

Coquilles St. Jacques

Preset Cooking Time: 17 minutes

- 2 shallots, finely minced
- 4 tablespoons butter or margarine, divided
- 1 pound scallops, rinsed and drained
- ⅓ cup dry white wine
- ¼ teaspoon salt
- ⅛ teaspoon pepper
- ½ cup cream
- 3 tablespoons all-purpose flour, divided
  Minced parsley

Combine shallots and 2 tablespoons butter in 9-inch microproof pie plate or quiche dish. Place in oven. Set recipe number 153. Touch START. (Oven cooks: micro, 90, 3 minutes.)

At Pause, add scallops, wine, salt, and pepper to dish. Place in oven. Touch START. (Oven cooks: micro, 50, 7 minutes.)

At Pause, drain scallops, reserving liquid. Transfer liquid to small microproof bowl. Blend in cream and 2 tablespoons flour. Place in oven. Touch START. (Oven cooks: micro, HI, 3 minutes.)

At Pause, stir. Touch START. (Oven cooks: micro, HI, 1½ minutes.)

Stir in remaining butter and flour. Set recipe number 227. Touch START. (Oven cooks: micro, HI, 1½ minutes.)

At Pause, stir. Touch START. (Oven cooks: micro, HI, 1 minute.)

Divide scallops among individual dishes. Spoon sauce over. Sprinkle with parsley and serve.

4 servings

Salmon Ring (page 133), →
Parsley New Potatoes (page 165),
and Broccoli (Guide, page 147)

Recipe No. 154

Mountain Trout

Preset Cooking Time: 9 minutes

- 2 8-ounce trout
- ¼ cup dehydrated onion flakes
- 2 tablespoons hot water
- 2 tablespoons dry white wine
- 2 tablespoons butter or margarine, melted, divided
- 6 mushrooms, sliced
- 2 tablespoons slivered almonds
- 2 tablespoons chopped parsley
  Salt and pepper to taste

Position wire rack in lower guides of oven. Set recipe number 154. Touch START. *(Oven preheats: convec, 400°F.)* Meanwhile, rinse trout and pat dry. Arrange in oval glass or ceramic baking dish. Combine onion and water in small bowl and set aside. Sprinkle cavity and surface of trout with wine. Pour 1 tablespoon butter inside cavity. Add mushrooms, almonds, and parsley to onion mixture and blend well. Spread remaining butter over trout. Divide half of mixture evenly between cavities, sprinkling remainder over tops. Season with salt and pepper.

At 400°F, place in oven on wire rack. Touch START. *(Oven cooks: micro/convec, 400°F, 9 minutes.)* Serve immediately.

2 servings

Recipe No. 155

Stuffed Bass

Preset Cooking Time: about 19½ minutes

- 1 bass (2 pounds)
- ¼ cup chopped onion
- 2 tablespoons butter or margarine
- ½ cup chopped mushrooms
- 2 tablespoons minced parsley
- ¾ cup dry bread crumbs
- 1 large egg, beaten
- 1 tablespoon lemon juice
- 1 teaspoon salt
- ⅛ teaspoon pepper
- 1 tablespoon bottled brown sauce
- 1 tablespoon water

Rinse bass well in cold water and pat dry; set aside. Place onion, butter, mushrooms, and parsley in 1-cup glass measure. Insert temperature probe. Place in oven. Plug in probe. Set recipe number 155. Touch START. *(Oven cooks: micro, HI, 2 minutes.)*

At Pause, remove measure from oven without unplugging the temperature probe. Place onion-mushroom mixture in large bowl. Add bread crumbs, egg, lemon juice, salt, and pepper. Blend well. Spoon stuffing into cavity of bass. Place on oval microproof platter. Combine brown sauce and water. Brush over bass.

Place in oven. Without unplugging temperature probe, insert probe into thickest part of fish, parallel to spine. Cover dish with plastic wrap. Touch START. *(Oven cooks: micro, HI, to 170°F; stands: 0, 5 minutes.)*

4 servings

Recipe No. 156

Poached Salmon

Preset Cooking Time: 12 minutes

- 2 cups water
- 1 medium stalk celery, cut into chunks
- ½ medium lemon, sliced
- ½ medium onion, sliced
- 3 tablespoons vinegar
- 2 tablespoons lemon juice
- 1½ teaspoons salt
- 6 whole cloves
- 1 bay leaf
- 4 salmon, swordfish, halibut, or other fish steaks (6 to 8 ounces each)
  Parsley sprigs

Combine all ingredients except fish and parsley in 2-quart microproof casserole. Cover and place in oven. Set recipe number 156. Touch START. *(Oven cooks: micro, HI, 7 minutes.)*

At Pause, add fish; spoon liquid over top. Cover. Touch START. *(Oven cooks: micro, HI, 5 minutes.)*

Carefully turn fish over. Let stand, covered, 5 minutes. Transfer to serving platter. Garnish with parsley. Serve hot or chilled.

4 servings

← Lobster Tails Supreme (page 126), Coquilles St. Jacques (page 128)

Recipe No. [157]

Broiled Halibut Steaks

Preset Cooking Time: 16 minutes

- 2 tablespoons dry white wine
- 1 tablespoon fresh lemon juice
- 1 tablespoon olive oil
- 1/4 teaspoon salt
- 1/8 teaspoon pepper
- 2 3/4-pound halibut steaks
  (3/4- to 1-inch thick)

Combine wine, lemon juice, olive oil, salt, and pepper in shallow dish. Add fish, turning several times to coat. Cover and marinate in refrigerator 3 hours, turning once or twice.

Position wire rack in upper guides of oven. Set recipe number 157. Touch START. *(Oven preheats: convec, 450°F.)* Set fish on aluminum foil or broiling pan; reserve marinade.

At 450°F, place in oven. Touch START. *(Oven cooks: convec, 450°F, 8 minutes.)*

At Pause, turn fish over and brush with marinade. Touch START. *(Oven cooks: convec, 450°F, 8 minutes.)*

2 servings

Recipe No. [158]

Salmon Ring

Preset Cooking Time: 12 minutes

- Paprika
- 1 can (16 ounces) red salmon, skin and bones discarded
- 1 cup soft bread crumbs
- 3/4 cup finely chopped celery
- 2 large eggs, lightly beaten
- 3 tablespoons minced green onion
- 2 tablespoons mayonnaise
- Pinch dillweed

Butter 6-cup microproof ring mold; sprinkle with paprika; set aside. Combine all ingredients except parsley; blend well. Turn into prepared mold, spreading evenly. Place in oven. Set recipe number 158. Touch START. *(Oven cooks: micro, HI, 7 minutes; 20, 5 minutes.)* Unmold · onto serving platter, and garnish with parsley.

4 to 6 servings

Recipe No. [159]

Breaded Fish Fillets

Preset Cooking Time: 12 minutes

- 1 1/2 pounds fish fillets about 1/2-inch thick
- 3/4 cup crushed corn flakes
- 2 tablespoons dried parsley
- 1/4 teaspoon salt
- 1/8 teaspoon pepper
- 1 egg, beaten

Position wire rack in lower guides of oven. Set recipe number 159. Touch START. *(Oven preheats: convec, 400°F.)* Meanwhile, rinse fillets with cold water and pat dry. Combine corn flakes, parsley, salt, and pepper. Dip each fillet in beaten egg, then roll in corn flake mixture, covering completely. Arrange in metal pan.

At 400°F, place in oven on wire rack. Touch START. *(Oven cooks: convec, 400°F, 12 minutes.)* Serve immediately.

4 servings

Recipe No. [160] ⊞

Fillet of Fish Amandine

Preset Cooking Time: 10 minutes

- 1/2 cup slivered almonds
- 1/4 cup butter or margarine
- 1 pound fish fillets
- 1 tablespoon lemon juice
- 1 teaspoon chopped parsley
- 1/2 teaspoon salt
- 1/4 teaspoon dillweed
- 1/8 teaspoon pepper

Place almonds and butter in 8-inch glass or ceramic baking dish. Position wire rack in lower guides of oven. Place dish in oven on wire rack. Set recipe number 160. Touch START. *(Oven preheats: convec, 350°F.)* Meanwhile, rinse fillets in cool water and pat dry.

At 350°F, add fillets to dish, turning to coat with butter. Roll up fillets and place on almonds. Sprinkle with lemon juice, parsley, salt, dillweed, and pepper. Place in oven on wire rack. Touch START. *(Oven cooks: micro/convec, 350°F, 10 minutes.)*

Spoon almonds and sauce on fillets and serve. Garnish with lemon wedges, parsley sprigs, or paprika.

← *Fillet of Fish Amandine*

2 to 3 servings

Recipe No. [161] ⊞

Fillet of Fish Mediterranean

Preset Cooking Time: 11 minutes

- 1 pound fish fillets
- 2 tablespoons butter or margarine
- 2 tablespoons dry white wine
- ½ teaspoon lemon juice
- 1 medium tomato, peeled and cut into cubes
- 2 green onions, thinly sliced
- ½ cup sliced mushrooms
- ½ teaspoon salt

Arrange fillets in 8-inch round or oval microproof baking dish with thickest parts toward outside of dish. Dot with butter. Combine wine and lemon juice; pour over fillets. Sprinkle with remaining ingredients. Place in oven. Cover with waxed paper. Set recipe number 161. Touch START. *(Oven cooks: micro, HI, 8 minutes; stands: 0, 3 minutes.)*

2 servings

⊞ *Recipe can be increased. See "Quantity", page 12.*

Recipe No. [162]

Tuna-Mushroom Patties

Preset Cooking Time: 9½ minutes

- 2 tablespoons milk
- 1 can (10¾ ounces) cream of celery soup, undiluted, divided
- 2 cans (6½ ounces each) tuna, drained
- ½ cup dry bread crumbs
- ½ cup chopped mushrooms
- 1 large egg, beaten
- 2 tablespoons instant minced onion
- ¼ teaspoon white pepper
- 2 tablespoons minced parsley

Combine milk and half of the soup in 2-cup glass measure; blend well; set aside. Combine remaining soup, tuna, bread crumbs, mushrooms, egg, onion, and pepper. Shape into 6 patties, using about ½ cup mixture for each. Place in shallow microproof baking dish. Place in oven. Cover with waxed paper. Set recipe number 162. Touch START. *(Oven cooks: micro, HI, 8 minutes.)*

At Pause, remove from oven. Place milk mixture in oven. Touch START. *(Oven cooks: micro, HI, 1½ minutes.)*

Stir and pour over tuna patties. Sprinkle with parsley before serving.

6 servings

COOKING GUIDE — CONVENIENCE SEAFOOD*

| Food | Programming | | First Stage | Second Stage | Special Notes |
	Method	Setting			
Fish sticks frozen, (12)	micro/convec	400°	5 min. turn over	change to convec 400° 4-5 min.	Upper guides. Preheat. Foil-lined glass baking dish.
Shrimp or crab newburg, frozen 6½ oz.	micro	HI (max. power)	4-6		Slit pouch, place on plate. Flex pouch to mix halfway through cooking time.
Scallops or fish kabobs, 7 oz.	micro/convec	400°	5 min. turn over	change to convec 400° 4-5 min.	Lower guides. Preheat. Foil-lined glass baking dish.
Tuna casserole, frozen, 16 oz.	micro	HI (max. power)	4-6		Remove from package to 1-quart casserole. Stir once during cooking.

* Due to the tremendous variety in convenience food products available, times given here should be used only as guidelines. We suggest you cook food for the shortest recommended time and then check for doneness. Be sure to check the package for microwave and oven (convec) instructions.

A Continental Flair

What is a quiche but a delicious combination of dairy products in their best form? Once you have tried the delightful recipes here — Sausage and Leek Quiche (page 138), Sherried Crab Quiche (page 137), and the "first" quiche, Quiche Lorraine (page 138), are just a few — you will soon begin to substitute your own fillings. They are so easy to make with this oven, perfect every time. The micro/convection method shines as the microwaves cook the filling and the hot air crisps the shell and browns the top. French-chef proficiency will be yours, too, with Spinach/Cheese Soufflé (page 141).

But attractive food and preparation ease, not elegance, are the true story of this chapter. The microwave method offers many traditional egg dishes, like Sunny-Side-Up Eggs (page 143), and Cheddar and Onion Egg (page 143). Plain and simple breakfast fare, including scrambled and poached eggs is also included. You can create your own omelet for breakfast or a light meal anytime. For some fun, though, try the convection method and our delicious and unusually-shaped Mushroom Omelet (page 142).

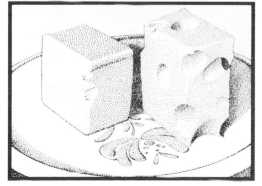

Quiches are placed on the wire rack, lower guides, and cooked the micro/convection way. Sherried Crab Quiche (page 137) can be the basis for a great, out-of-the-ordinary brunch (above left). When you see that soufflé rise, you'll wonder why it was never so easy before. Spinach/Cheese Soufflé (page 141) and other soufflés are set on the ceramic tray (above). Cold cheese can be brought to room temperature quickly, cook micro on 60 1 minute (left).

Converting Your Recipes

When eggs and cheese are the primary ingredients, the rule is that it is better to undercook than overcook. They cook so quickly that 15 seconds or less can make the difference between fluffy perfection and a rubbery disaster. Such care is exercised with all food but it is especially important here, just as it is in conventional cooking. Egg cookery is eye cookery: you simply must watch what's happening!

Soufflé recipes can be adapted easily: just follow the same format as Cheese Soufflé (page 141), using the same number of eggs and amount of liquid. Tips on other cheese and egg dishes:

☐ Undercook eggs slightly and allow standing time to complete cooking. Eggs become tough when overcooked. Always check doneness to avoid overcooking.
☐ Cover poaching or baking eggs to trap steam and assure even cooking.
☐ Eggs are usually cooked by the microwave method at 60 or 70.
☐ If you want a soft yolk, remove the egg from oven before whites are completely cooked. A brief standing time allows whites to set without overcooking yolks.
☐ Add ⅛ to ¼ teaspoon vinegar to the water when poaching eggs to help the white coagulate.
☐ Cook bacon and egg combinations micro on HI, since most of the microwaves are attracted to the bacon because of its high fat content.
☐ Omelets and scrambled eggs should be stirred at least once during cooking. Fondues and sauces profit from occasional stirring during the cooking time.
☐ Cheese melts quickly and makes an attractive topping for casseroles and sandwiches.
☐ Cook cheese dishes by microwave method on 70 or a lower setting for short periods of time to avoid separation and toughening.

COOKING GUIDE — CONVENIENCE EGGS AND CHEESE*

Food	Amount	Micro Control	Time (in minutes)	Special Notes
Omelet, frozen	10 oz.	80 (reheat)	4 - 5	Use microproof plate.
Egg substitute	8 oz.	50 (simmer)	4 - 4½	Turn carton over after 1 minute. Open carton after 1½ minutes. Stir every 30 seconds until smooth.
Soufflés: Corn, frozen	12 oz.	HI (max. power)	10 - 12	Use 1½-quart casserole, covered. Rotate casserole twice.
Cheese, frozen	12 oz.	HI (max. power)	11 - 13	Use 1½-quart casserole, covered. Rotate casserole twice.
Spinach, frozen	12 oz.	HI (max. power)	12 - 15	Use 1½-quart casserole, covered. Rotate casserole twice.
Welsh rabbit, frozen	10 oz.	70 (roast)	6 - 7	Use 1½-quart casserole, covered. Stir during cooking time.

* Due to the tremendous variety in convenience food products available, times given here should be used only as guidelines. We suggest you cook food for the shortest recommended time and then check for doneness. Be sure to check the package for microwave and oven (convec) instructions.

Recipe No. 163

Chili-Cheese Quiche
Preset Cooking Time: 27½ minutes

- 3 tablespoons butter or margarine
- 1 cup thinly sliced green onions, divided
- 1 can (4 ounces) diced green chilies
- 1 jar (2 ounces) diced pimiento
- 1 cup whipping cream or half-and-half
- ½ teaspoon salt
- ⅛ teaspoon pepper
- ⅛ teaspoon cumin
- 4 eggs, lightly beaten
- 2½ cups Monterey Jack cheese, divided
- 1 prebaked Basic Pie Crust (page 184)
- ½ cup (2 ounces) shredded Cheddar cheese
- ¼ teaspoon paprika

Place butter in 4-cup glass measure. Place in oven. Set recipe number 163. Touch START. (Oven cooks: micro, HI, 1 minute.)

At Pause, stir in half of onion. Touch START. (Oven cooks: micro, HI, 1½ minutes.) Add chilies and pimiento. Set aside to cool.

Position wire rack in lower guides of oven. Set recipe number 166. Touch START. (Oven preheats: convec, 350°F.) Meanwhile, combine cream, salt, pepper, and cumin in large bowl. Blend in eggs and 2 cups Monterey Jack cheese. Spread onion-pimiento mixture over crust. Slowly pour custard over top. Sprinkle with Cheddar cheese, paprika, remaining Monterey Jack cheese, and remaining onion.

At 350°F, place in oven on wire rack. Touch START. (Oven cooks: micro/convec, 350°F, 7½ minutes.)

At Pause, rotate dish one-half turn. Touch START. (Oven cooks: micro/convec, 350°F, 7½ minutes; stands: 0, 10 minutes.) Cut into wedges and serve

6 to 8 servings

This is one of several recipes that use the preset functions of another recipe for part of the cooking sequence. Set recipe number 163 first. At the end of that sequence, set recipe number 166.

Recipe No. 164

Sherried Crab Quiche
Preset Cooking Time: 29½ minutes

- ¼ cup butter or margarine
- ½ cup thinly sliced green onions
- 1 cup (about 6 ounces) crabmeat, diced
- 2 tablespoons dry sherry
- ¼ teaspoon pepper
- 1½ cups whipping cream
- 4 eggs, lightly beaten
- ¼ teaspoon salt
- ⅛ teaspoon ground red pepper
- 1 prebaked Basic Pie Crust (page 184)
- ½ cup (2 ounces) shredded Swiss cheese
- Paprika

Place butter in 1-quart glass measure. Place in oven. Set recipe number 164. Touch START. (Oven cooks: micro, HI, 30 seconds.)

At Pause, stir in onion. Touch START. (Oven cooks: micro, HI, 3 minutes.)

At Pause, add crab, sherry, and pepper. Touch START. (Oven cooks: micro, HI, 1 minute.) Set aside.

Position wire rack in lower guides of oven. Set recipe number 166. Touch START. (Oven preheats: convec, 350°F.) Meanwhile, combine cream, eggs, salt, and red pepper in large bowl. Add crab mixture. Slowly pour mixture into crust. Top with cheese and sprinkle with paprika.

At 350°F, place in oven on wire rack. Touch START. (Oven cooks: micro/convec, 350°F, 7½ minutes.)

At Pause, rotate dish one-half turn. Touch START. (Oven cooks: micro/convec, 350°F, 7½ minutes; stands: 0, 10 minutes.) Cut into wedges and serve.

6 to 8 servings

Recipe No. 165

Sausage and Leek Quiche

Preset Cooking Time: 38½ minutes

1½ pounds leeks, white and tender part of leaves, well rinsed, drained, and finely chopped
⅓ cup butter or margarine
½ pound bulk pork sausage
1 cup half-and-half
3 egg yolks
1 egg
½ teaspoon salt
⅛ teaspoon pepper
1 prebaked Basic Pie Crust (page 184)
Paprika

Combine leeks and butter in 2-quart microproof bowl. Cover with plastic wrap. Place in oven. Set recipe number 165. Touch START. *(Oven cooks: micro, HI, 5 minutes.)*

At Pause, stir. Cover. Touch START. *(Oven cooks: micro, HI, 5 minutes.)*

At Pause, stir. Cover and set aside. Place sausage in another 2-quart microproof bowl. Cover with plastic wrap. Place in oven. Touch START. *(Oven cooks: micro, HI, 2 minutes.)*

At Pause, stir. Cover. Touch START. *(Oven cooks: micro, HI, 1½ minutes.)* Remove sausage from bowl with slotted spoon and set aside to drain well on paper towels.

Position wire rack in lower guides of oven. Set recipe number 166. Touch START. *(Oven preheats: convec, 350°F.)* Meanwhile, beat half-and-half, egg yolks, egg, salt, and pepper in medium bowl. Stir in leeks. Spoon mixture into crust, spreading evenly. Crumble sausage over top and sprinkle with paprika.

At 350°F, place quiche in oven on wire rack. Touch START. *(Oven cooks: micro/convec, 350°F, 7½ minutes.)*

At Pause, rotate dish one-half turn. Touch START. *(Oven cooks: micro/convec, 350°F, 7½ minutes; stands: 0, 10 minutes.)*

6 to 8 servings

This is one of several recipes that use the preset functions of another recipe for part of the cooking sequence. Set recipe number 165 first. At the end of that sequence, set recipe number 166.

Recipe No. 166

Quiche Lorraine

Preset Cooking Time: 34 minutes

10 slices bacon
1½ cups (6 ounces) shredded Swiss cheese
½ cup thinly sliced green onions
1 prebaked Basic Pie Crust (page 184)
1 can (13 ounces) evaporated milk or 1½ cups skim milk
4 eggs
¼ teaspoon salt
¼ teaspoon nutmeg
Pinch ground red pepper

Arrange 5 slices bacon on paper towel - lined microproof plate. Cover with 2 sheets paper towels and arrange second layer of bacon on top. Cover with paper towel. Place in oven on ceramic tray. Set recipe number 118. Touch QUANTITY. Touch 2. Touch 5. Touch START.* *(Oven cooks: micro, HI, 9 minutes.)* Remove bacon from oven. Separate from paper towels, crumble, and set aside.

Position wire rack in lower guides of oven. Set recipe number 166. Touch START. *(Oven preheats: convec, 350°F.)* Meanwhile, sprinkle bacon, cheese, and onion over crust, reserving 1 teaspoon of each. Beat milk, eggs, salt, nutmeg, and red pepper in 1-quart bowl. Carefully pour into pie shell. Sprinkle top with reserved bacon, cheese, and onion.

At 350°F, place in oven on wire rack. Touch START. *(Oven cooks: micro/convec, 350°F, 7½ minutes.)*

At Pause, rotate dish one-half turn. Touch START. *(Oven cooks: micro/convec, 350°F, 7½ minutes; stands: 0, 10 minutes.)* Cut into wedges and serve.

6 to 8 servings

This procedure sets the oven to cook at 2½ times the original Recipe No. 118 program for 4 slices bacon. This is one of several recipes that use the preset functions of another recipe for part of the cooking sequence. Set recipe number 118 first. At the end of that sequence, set recipe number 166.

Sherried Crab Quiche (page 137), →
Sausage and Leek Quiche

Recipe No. | 167 |

Spinach Quiche

Preset Cooking Time: 25 minutes

- 1 package (10 ounces) frozen chopped spinach
- 4 eggs, beaten
- 2 cups (8 ounces) shredded Monterey Jack cheese
- ½ cup thinly sliced green onions
- 1 prebaked Basic Pie Crust (page 184)
- ½ cup grated Parmesan cheese

Set unopened package of spinach on microproof plate. Place in oven. Set recipe number 02. Touch START. (Oven cooks: micro, HI, 5 minutes.) Set aside.

Position wire rack in lower guides of oven. Set recipe number 167. Touch START. (Oven preheats: convec, 350°F.) Meanwhile, combine eggs, Monterey Jack cheese, and onion in mixing bowl. Add undrained spinach; blend well. Turn into crust. Sprinkle with Parmesan cheese.

At 350°F, place quiche in oven on wire rack. Touch START. (Oven cooks: micro/convec, 350°F, 5 minutes.)

At Pause, rotate dish one-half turn. Touch START. (Oven cooks: micro/convec, 350°F, 5 minutes; stands: 0, 10 minutes.)

6 to 8 servings

Recipe No. | 168 |

Onion Quiche

Preset Cooking Time: 46 minutes

- 2 pounds onions, chopped
- ¼ cup butter or margarine
- 1½ tablespoons all-purpose flour
- 2 eggs
- ½ cup dairy sour cream
- ¼ cup whipping cream
- 5 tablespoons shredded Swiss cheese, divided
- ½ teaspoon salt
- ½ teaspoon nutmeg
- ⅛ teaspoon pepper
- 1 prebaked Basic Pie Crust (page 184)

Combine onion and butter in 2-quart microproof casserole. Cover. Place in oven. Set recipe number 222. Touch START. (Oven cooks: micro, HI, 6 minutes.)

At Pause, stir. Touch START. (Oven cooks: micro, HI, 6 minutes.)

At Pause, stir again. Touch START. (Oven cooks: micro, HI, 6 minutes.)

At Pause, blend in flour. Place in oven. Touch START. (Oven cooks: micro, HI, 5 minutes.) Set onion mixture aside.

Position wire rack in lower guides of oven. Set recipe number 168. Touch START. (Oven preheats: convec, 350°F.) Meanwhile, beat eggs, sour cream, whipping cream, 2 tablespoons cheese, salt, nutmeg, and pepper in medium bowl. Blend into onion mixture. Spoon into crust. Sprinkle with remaining cheese and additional nutmeg, if desired.

At 350°F, place in oven on wire rack. Touch START. (Oven cooks: micro/convec, 350°F, 7 minutes.)

At Pause, rotate dish one-half turn. Touch START. (Oven cooks: micro/convec, 350°F, 6 minutes; stands: 0, 10 minutes.)

6 to 8 servings

Recipe No. | 169 |

Tomato Quiche

Preset Cooking Time: 30 minutes

- ½ pound Gruyère cheese, shredded
- 1 prebaked Basic Pie Crust (page 184)
- 3 firm small tomatoes, chopped and drained
- 3 tablespoons minced onion or green onion
- 1 teaspoon basil, crumbled Salt and pepper to taste
- 2 eggs
- ¾ cup milk
- 2 tablespoons grated Parmesan cheese
- 1 firm medium tomato, thinly sliced

Position wire rack in lower guides of oven. Set recipe number 169. Touch START. (Oven preheats: convec, 350°F.) Meanwhile, sprinkle Gruyere over crust. Arrange chopped tomato and onion over top. Sprinkle with basil, salt, and pepper. Beat eggs and milk in small bowl. Pour into pie shell. Sprinkle with Parmesan. Arrange tomato slices on top in overlapping pattern.

At 350°F, place in oven on wire rack. Touch START. (Oven cooks: micro/convec, 350°F, 25 minutes; stands: 0, 5 minutes.) Cut into wedges and serve.

6 to 8 servings

Recipe No. 170

Cheese Soufflé

Preset Cooking Time: 59 minutes

- 1 teaspoon butter
- ¼ cup grated Parmesan cheese
- ¼ cup butter or margarine
- ¼ cup all-purpose flour
- ½ teaspoon dry mustard
- ½ teaspoon salt
- ¼ teaspoon pepper
- 1 cup milk, warmed
- 1½ cups (6 ounces) shredded Cheddar cheese
- 6 eggs, separated
- ½ teaspoon cream of tartar

Coat bottom and sides of 2-quart soufflé dish with 1 teaspoon butter. Sprinkle with Parmesan cheese, rotating dish to cover evenly and letting excess cheese remain in bottom. Refrigerate.

Place ¼ cup butter in 2-quart microproof bowl. Place in oven. Set recipe number 230. Touch START. (Oven cooks: micro, HI, 1½ minutes.)

At Pause, stir in flour, mustard, salt, and pepper. Slowly stir in milk. Place in oven. Touch START. (Oven cooks: micro, HI, 1½ minutes.)

At Pause, stir through. Touch START. (Oven cooks: micro, HI, 1 minute.)

Add Cheddar cheese and stir until melted. Beat yolks until smooth and lemon-colored. Add to cheese mixture and blend thoroughly. Set aside.

Set recipe number 170. Touch START. (Oven preheats: convec, 330°F.) Meanwhile, beat egg whites in large bowl until foamy. Add cream of tartar and continue beating until stiff but not dry. Stir one-third of whites into cheese mixture. Gently fold in remaining whites. Turn into prepared soufflé dish.

At 330°F, place dish in oven on ceramic tray. Touch START. (Oven cooks: convec, 330°F, 55 minutes.) Serve immediately.

6 servings

This is one of several recipes that use the preset functions of another recipe for part of the cooking sequence. Set recipe number 230 first. At the end of that sequence, set recipe number 170.

Recipe No. 171

Spinach/Cheese Soufflé

Preset Cooking Time: 1 hour 9 minutes

- 1 package (10 ounces) frozen chopped spinach
- 1 teaspoon butter
- ¼ cup grated Parmesan cheese
- ¼ cup butter or margarine
- ¼ cup all-purpose flour
- 1 clove garlic, minced
- ½ teaspoon salt
- ¼ teaspoon dry mustard
- ¼ teaspoon pepper
- 1 cup milk
- 1½ cups shredded Cheddar cheese
- 6 eggs, separated
- ½ teaspoon cream of tartar

Set unopened package of spinach on microproof plate. Place in oven on ceramic tray. Set recipe number 209. Touch START. (Oven cooks: micro, HI, 6 minutes.) Set spinach aside.

Coat bottom and sides of 2-quart soufflé dish with 1 teaspoon butter. Sprinkle with Parmesan cheese, rotating dish to cover evenly and letting excess cheese remain on bottom. Refrigerate.

Place ¼ cup butter in 2-quart glass measure or microproof bowl. Place in oven on ceramic tray. Touch START. (Oven cooks: micro, HI, 1 minute.)

At Pause, stir in flour, garlic, salt, mustard, and pepper. Slowly blend in milk, mixing until smooth. Place in oven. Touch START. (Oven cooks: micro, HI, 1 minute.)

At Pause, stir. Touch START. (Oven cooks: micro, HI, 1 minute.) Add Cheddar cheese and stir until melted. Set aside.

Set recipe number 171. Touch START. (Oven preheats: convec, 350°F.) Meanwhile, drain spinach well and stir into cheese mixture. Beat egg yolks in small bowl until smooth and lemon-colored. Add to spinach mixture and blend well. Beat egg whites in large bowl until foamy. Add cream of tartar and continue beating until stiff peaks form. Stir one-third of whites into spinach mixture. Gently fold in remaining whites. Turn into prepared soufflé dish.

At 350°F, place dish in oven on ceramic tray. Touch START. (Oven cooks: convec, 350°F, 60 minutes.) Serve immediately.

5 servings

Recipe No. 172

Mushroom Omelet

Preset Cooking Time: 13½ minutes

- 1 cup sliced mushrooms
- ¼ cup thinly sliced green onions
- 2 tablespoons butter or margarine
- 4 eggs, beaten
- 3 tablespoons milk
- 2 tablespoons butter or margarine, melted
- ¼ teaspoon dillweed
  Salt and pepper to taste

Combine mushrooms, onions, and butter in 1-quart glass measure. Place in oven. Set recipe number 227. Touch START. *(Oven cooks: micro, HI, 1½ minutes.)*

At Pause, stir. Touch START. *(Oven cooks: micro, HI, 1 minute.)* Set dish aside.

Position wire rack in upper guides of oven. Set recipe number 172. Touch START. *(Oven preheats: convec, 450°F.)* Meanwhile, beat eggs and milk in mixing bowl. Pour melted butter into 9-inch metal pie plate. Add egg mixture.

At 450°F, place in oven on wire rack. Touch START. *(Oven cooks: convec, 450°F, 10 minutes.)* (Eggs will form a basket.)

At Pause, remove omelet and wire rack from oven. Return mushroom mixture to oven. Touch START. *(Oven cooks: micro, HI, 1 minute.)* Spoon mushrooms into egg basket. Sprinkle with dill. Season with salt and pepper. Serve immediately.

4 servings

This is one of several recipes that use the preset functions of another recipe for part of the cooking sequence. Set recipe number 277 first. At the end of that sequence, set recipe number 172.

Recipe No. 173

Poached Egg

Preset Cooking Time: 3½ minutes

- ¼ cup water
- ¼ teaspoon vinegar
  Pinch salt
- 1 large egg

Place water, vinegar, and salt in 6-ounce microproof custard cup. Place in oven. Set recipe number 173. Touch START. *(Oven cooks: micro, HI, 1½ minutes.)*

At Pause, carefully break egg into hot liquid. Carefully pierce yolk in several places with toothpick. Cover with waxed paper. Touch START. *(Oven cooks: micro, 50, 1 minute; stands: 0, 1 minute.)*

1 serving

Recipe No. 174 ⊞

Scrambled Egg

Preset Cooking Time: 2½ minutes

- 1 large egg
- 2 tablespoons low-fat milk
- 6 tablespoons (1½ ounces) shredded Monterey Jack or Cheddar cheese
  Salt and pepper to taste

Break egg into small microproof bowl. Add milk; mix well with fork. Add cheese, salt, and pepper; blend well. Place in oven. Cover with waxed paper. Set recipe number 174. Touch START. *(Oven cooks: micro, 60, 1 minute.)*

At Pause, stir. Cover. Touch START. *(Oven cooks: micro, 60, 1½ minutes.)*

Stir before serving.

1 serving

Recipe No. 176 ⊞

Cheddar and Onion Egg

Preset Cooking Time: 3 minutes

- 1 teaspoon butter or margarine
- 1 green onion, thinly sliced
- 1 large egg
- 1 heaping tablespoon shredded Cheddar cheese

Combine butter and onion in microproof custard cup. Place in oven. Set recipe number 176. Touch START. *(Oven cooks: micro, HI, 1 minute.)*

At Pause, carefully break egg into custard cup. Carefully pierce yolk in several places with toothpick. Sprinkle with cheese. Cover with waxed paper. Touch START. *(Oven cooks: micro, 60, 1 minute; stands: 0, 1 minute.)*

1 serving

Recipe No. 175

Sunny-Side-Up Eggs

Preset Cooking Time: 8 minutes

- 1 tablespoon butter or margarine
- 2 large eggs
  Salt and pepper to taste

Position wire rack in upper guides of oven. Set recipe number 175. Touch START. *(Oven preheats: convec, 450°F.)* Place butter in shallow aluminum foil baking pan.

At 450°F, place in oven on wire rack. Touch START. *(Oven cooks: convec, 450°F, 1 minute.)*

At Pause, break eggs into pan. Season with salt and pepper. Place in oven on wire rack. Touch START. *(Oven cooks: convec, 450°F, 7 minutes.)*

1 to 2 servings

⊞ *Recipe can be increased. See "Quantity", page 12.*

Vegetables and the microwave method were made for each other, or so you'll think when you sit down to dinner with a couple of these side dishes on the table. Because very little water (sometimes none at all) is used in cooking, vegetables retain their bright, fresh color, and are full of flavor. What's more, they don't lose a bit of their vitamin-filled wholesomeness. Whether it's as simple as Green Beans Italiano (page 164), as up-to-date as Ratatouille (page 158), or as unique as Potato Kugel (page 159) and Barley-Rice Casserole (page 151), you'll find the just-right answer to "I wonder what goes with...?" among these recipes. Frozen and canned vegetables are also better when reheated by the microwave method. Finally, you'll find good use for the convection method with many interesting potato recipes.

Many easy and colorful vegetable dishes provide same dish cook-and-serve elegance. Cauliflower, broccoli, and carrots are combined for cooking, micro, HI, 11 minutes (above left). Vegetable preparation, as well as arrangement, are important for best results. Arrange asparagus head-to-head for even density, slice carrots diagonally to expose more area, and slit broccoli stalks to aid even doneness (above right). When cutting vegetables for cooking, make sizes as uniform as possible (right).

*— Mushroom-Pimiento Rice (page 152),
Corn-on-the-Cob (page 162)*

Converting Your Recipes

Vegetables are best when eaten at the crisp stage, tender but resilient to the bite. However, if you prefer a softer texture, increase water and cooking time. To adapt a conventional recipe to the microwave oven, find a similar recipe in the chapter and check the vegetable cooking guides. The following tips will give you additional help in adapting or creating your own recipes:

☐ Check doneness after the shortest recommended cooking times. Add more cooking time to suit individual preferences.

☐ When using the temperature probe, a small amount of liquid should be added. Insert probe into the center of the vegetable dish and set at 150°F.

☐ If necessary, frozen vegetables may be used in recipes calling for fresh vegetables. It is not necessary to thaw frozen vegetables before cooking.

☐ Freeze small portions of your favorite vegetable dishes in boilable plastic pouches. If you use metal twist ties, be sure to replace with string or rubber band before cooking. Cut a steam vent in pouch and reheat on microproof plate.

☐ To prevent boiling over of vegetable dishes with cream sauces, use a dish large enough to allow for bubbling. Use 60 or 70.

☐ Celery, onions, green peppers, and carrots need to be partially cooked before adding to a casserole. In general, you should partially cook all vegetables before combining with already cooked meats, fish, or poultry.

☐ To cook mashed potatoes, cube potatoes. Add a small amount of water. Cook, tightly covered, until soft. Season and mash.

☐ To reheat mashed potatoes, set at 80, stirring once during cooking time.

☐ Pasta, rice, and cereals are best when added to other ingredients, as in vegetable, meat, or cheese casseroles. While the oven can cook them separately, there's no advantage. It is wise to reheat them in the oven, however. You add no water and they are like fresh cooked. Cook, micro, 80, 3 to 4 minutes for 1 cup (cooked), 5 to 6 minutes for 2 cups, etc. Cover tightly.

☐ Grits or other hot cereals are interesting side dishes for brunch, cooked in individual bowls. Cook, micro, HI, 6 to 7 minutes for $1/3$ cup grits (uncooked); 1 to 2 minutes for $1/3$ cup quick oatmeal. Follow package directions for liquid.

Using the Cooking Guide

1. All fresh or frozen vegetables are cooked and reheated on HI.
2. Choose a wide, shallow dish so vegetables can be spread out.
3. Add $1/4$ cup water for each $1/2$ to 1 pound fresh vegetables. Do not add water for washed spinach, corn on the cob, squash, baking potatoes, or eggplant.
4. Cover all vegetables tightly.
5. Stir once during cooking time.
6. Pouches of frozen vegetables require steam vents. Slit pouch and cook on microproof dish.
7. Frozen vegetables without sauces can be cooked in their cartons without water. Remove waxed paper wrapping before placing carton in oven. (Remove frozen-in-sauce vegetables if packaged in cartons rather than pouches. Place in $1\frac{1}{2}$-quart microproof casserole. Add liquid before cooking as package directs.)
8. After cooking, allow all vegetables to stand, covered, 2 to 3 minutes.

COOKING GUIDE — VEGETABLES

od	Amount	Fresh Vegetable Preparation	Time (in minutes)	Water	Standing Time (in minutes)	Special Notes
chokes " in meter	Fresh: 1 2	Wash thoroughly. Cut tops off each leaf.	7 - 8 11 - 12	¼ cup ½ cup	2 - 3 2 - 3	When done, a leaf peeled from whole comes off easily.
	Frozen: 10 oz.	Slit pouch	5 - 6			
paragus: ears and pieces	Fresh: 1 lb.	Wash thoroughly. Snap off tough base and discard.	2 - 3	¼ cup	None	Stir or rearrange once during cooking time.
	Frozen: 10 oz.		7 - 8	None	2 - 3	
ans: en, wax, ench-cut	Fresh: 1 lb.	Remove ends. Wash well. Leave whole or break in pieces.	12 - 14	¼ cup	2 - 3	Stir once or rearrange as necessary.
	Frozen: 6 oz.		7 - 8	None	None	
ets	4 medium	Scrub beets. Leave 1" of top on beet.	16 - 18	¼ cup	None	After cooking, peel. Cut or leave whole.
roccoli	Fresh, whole 1 - 2½ lbs.	Remove outer leaves. Slit stalks.	9 - 10	¼ cup	3	Stir or rearrange during cooking time.
	Frozen, whole		8 - 10	¼ cup	3	
	Fresh, chopped, 1 - 1½ lbs.		12 - 14	¼ cup	2	
	Frozen, chopped 10 oz.		8 - 9	None	2	
Brussels sprouts	Fresh: 1 lb.	Remove outside leaves if wilted. Cut off stems. Wash	8 - 9	¼ cup	2 - 3	Stir or rearrange once during cooking time.
	Frozen: 10 oz.		6 - 7	None	None	
Cabbage	½ medium head, shredded	Remove outside wilted leaves.	5 - 6	¼ cup	2 - 3	
	1 medium head, wedges		13 - 15	¼ cup	2 - 3	Rearrange wedges after 7 minutes.
Carrots	4: sliced or diced	Peel and cut off tops.	7 - 9	1 Tb.	2 - 3	Stir once during cooking time.
	6: sliced or diced	Fresh young carrots cook best.	9 - 10	2 Tbs.	2 - 3	
	8: tiny, whole		8 - 10	2 Tbs.	2 - 3	
	Frozen: 10 oz.		8 - 9	None	None	
Cauliflower	1 medium, in flowerets	Cut tough stem. Wash, remove outside leaves.	7 - 8	¼ cup	2 - 3	Stir after 5 minutes.
	1 medium, whole	Remove core.	8 - 9	½ cup	3	Turn over once.
	Frozen: 10 oz.		8 - 9	½ cup	3	Stir after 5 minutes.
Celery	2½ cups, 1" slices	Clean stalks thoroughly.	8 - 9	¼ cup	2	
Corn: kernel	Frozen: 10 oz.		5 - 6	¼ cup	2	Stir halfway through cooking time.
On the cob	1 ear 2 ears 3 ears 4 ears	Husk, wrap each in waxed paper. Place on glass tray in oven. Cook no more than 4 at a time.	3 - 4 6 - 7 9 - 10 11 - 12	None None None None	2 2 2 2	Rearrange halfway through cooking time unless cooked on microproof rack.
	Frozen, 2 ears 4 ears	Flat dish, covered.	5½ - 6 10 - 11	None None	2	Rearrange halfway through cooking time.
Eggplant	1 medium, sliced	Wash and peel. Cut into slices or cubes.	5 - 6	2 Tbs.	3	
	1 medium, whole	Pierce skin.	6 - 7			Place on micro-proof rack.
Greens: collard, kale, etc.	Fresh: 1 lb.	Wash. Remove wilted leaves or tough stem.	6 - 7	None	2	
	Frozen: 10 oz.		7 - 8	None	2	

COOKING GUIDE — VEGETABLES

Food	Amount	Fresh Vegetable Preparation	Time (in minutes)	Water	Standing Time (in minutes)	Special Note
Mushrooms	Fresh: ½ lb., sliced		2 - 4	2 Tbs.	2	Stir halfway throug cooking time.
Okra	Fresh: ½ lb.	Wash thoroughly. Leave whole or cut in thick slices.	3 - 5	¼ cup	2	
	Frozen: 10 oz.		7 - 8	None	2	
Onions	1 lb., tiny whole	Peel. Add 1 Tb. butter.	6 - 7	¼ cup	3	Stir once during cooking time.
	1 lb., medium to large	Peel and quarter. Add 1 Tb. butter.	7 - 9	¼ cup	3	
Parsnips	4 medium, quartered	Peel and cut.	8 - 9	¼ cup	2	Stir once during cooking time.
Peas: green	Fresh: 1 lb.	Shell peas. Rinse well.	7 - 8	¼ cup	2	Stir once during cooking time.
	Fresh: 2 lbs.		8 - 9	½ cup	2 - 3	
	Frozen: 6 oz.		5 - 6	None	None	
Peas and onions	Frozen: 10 oz.		6 - 8	2 Tbs.	2	
Pea pods	Frozen: 6 oz.		3 - 4	2 Tbs.	3	
Potatoes, sweet 5 - 6 oz. ea.	1	Scrub well. Pierce with fork. Place on rack or paper towel in circle, 1″ apart.	4 - 4½	None	3	
	2		6 - 7	None	3	
	4		8 - 10	None	3	
	6		10 - 11	None	3	
Potatoes, white baking 6 - 8 oz. ea.	1	Wash and scrub well. Pierce with fork. Place on rack or paper towel in circle, 1″ apart.	4 - 6	None	3	
	2		6 - 8	None	3	
	3		8 - 12	None	3	
	4		12 - 16	None	3	
	5		16 - 20	None	3	
russet, boiling	3	Peel potatoes, cut in quarters.	12 - 16	½ cup	None	Stir once during cooking time.
Rutabaga	Fresh: 1 lb.	Wash well. Remove tough stems or any wilted leaves.	6 - 7	None	2	Stir once during cooking time.
	Frozen: 10 oz.		7 - 8	None	2	
Spinach	Fresh: 1 lb.	Wash well. Remove tough stems. Drain.	6 - 7	None	2	Stir once during cooking time.
	Frozen: 10 oz.		7 - 8	None	2	
Squash, acorn or butternut	1 - 1½ lbs. whole	Scrub. Pierce with fork.	10 - 12	None		Cut and remove seeds to serve.
Spaghetti squash	2 - 3 lbs.	Scrub, pierce. Place on rack.	6 per lb.	None	5	Serve with butter, Parmesan cheese, or spaghetti sauce.
Turnips	4 cups cubed	Peel, wash.	9 - 11	¼ cup	3	Stir after 5 minutes.
Zucchini	3 cups sliced	Wash; do not peel.	7 - 8	¼ cup	2	Stir after 4 minutes.

Special Tips about Potatoes

☐ If you like your baked potatoes with a crisp skin, they can be prepared using the micro/convection method.

☐ Position wire rack in lower guides and preheat to 400°F. Cook, micro/convec, at 400°F 9 to 10 minutes for 1 or 2 potatoes, 14 to 15 minutes for 4 potatoes.

☐ For sweet potatoes, allow 11 to 12 minutes for 1. 12 to 13 minutes for 2.

* Due to the tremendous variety in convenience food products available, times given here should be used only as guidelines. We suggest you cook food for the shortest recommended time and then check for doneness. Be sure to check the package for microwave and oven (convec) instructions.

COOKING GUIDE — CONVENIENCE VEGETABLES*

Food	Programming Method	Setting	First Stage	Second Stage	Special Notes
Au gratin vegetables, frozen, 11½ oz.	micro	70 (roast)	10 - 12 min.		Glass loaf dish, covered.
Onion Rings, 9 oz.	convec	follow package directions			Upper guides. Preheat. Cookie sheet or foil tray.
Potatoes, Country-cut fries, 1 lb.	convec	follow package directions			Upper guides. Preheat. Cookie sheet or foil tray.
French fries, 1 lb.	convec	follow package directions			Upper guides. Preheat. Cookie sheet or foil tray.
Instant mashed, 4 servings	micro	HI (max. power)	5 - 6 min.		Follow package directions. Reduce liquid by 1 tablespoon.
Stuffed potatoes, 12 oz. (2)	micro/convec	400°	10 - 12 min.		Lower guides. Place in oven during preheat. Micro/heatproof container.
Tater tots, 1 lb.	convec	follow package directions			Upper guides. Preheat. Cookie sheet or foil tray.
Vegetable crêpes, 6½ oz.	micro/convec	300°	7 - 8 min.		Lower guides. Heatproof paper tray.
Vegetable soufflé, 12 oz.	micro	HI (max. power)	12 - 15 min.		Transfer to microproof paper tray.
Vegetables, frozen in pouch, 10 - 12 oz.	micro	HI (max. power)	5 - 8 min.		Slit pouch. Place on microproof plate. Flex halfway through cooking time to mix.

COOKING GUIDE — RICE

Food	Amount Uncooked	Water	Minutes to Full Boil HI (max. power)	Micro Control	Time (minutes)	Standing Time (minutes)	Special Notes
Short-grain	1 cup	2 cups	4 - 5	50 (simmer)	13 - 15	5	2-quart casserole
Long-grain	1 cup	2 cups	4 - 5	50 (simmer)	15 - 17	5	2-quart casserole
Wild rice	1 cup	3 cups	6 - 7	50 (simmer)	35 - 40	5	3-quart casserole
Brown rice	1 cup	3 cups	6 - 7	50 (simmer)	40	5	3-quart casserole
Quick-cooking	1 cup	1 cup	3 - 4	HI (max. power)	0	5	1-quart casserole

COOKING/DEFROSTING GUIDE — CONVENIENCE RICE AND PASTA*

Food	Amount	Cook Control Setting	Time (in minutes)	Special Notes
Rice, cooked refrigerated	1 cup	80 (reheat)	1½ - 2	Use covered bowl. Let stand 2 minutes, stir.
Cooked frozen	1 cup / 2 cups	80 (reheat) / 80 (reheat)	2 - 3 / 3 - 4	
Pouch, frozen	11 oz.	80 (reheat)	6 - 7	Slit pouch.
Fried rice, frozen	10 oz.	HI (max. power)	5 - 6	Use covered casserole. Stir twice. Let stand 5 minutes.
Spanish rice, canned	12 oz.	HI (max. power)	4 - 5	Use covered casserole. Stir twice. Let stand 3 minutes.
Lasagna, frozen	21 oz.	70 (roast)	19 - 20	Use covered casserole. Let stand, covered, 5 minutes.
Macaroni and beef, frozen	11 oz.	HI (max. power)	7 - 9	Use covered casserole. Stir twice.
Macaroni and cheese, frozen	10 oz.	HI (max. power)	7 - 9	Use covered casserole. Stir twice.
Spaghetti and meatballs, frozen	14 oz.	HI (max. power)	8 - 10	Use covered casserole. Stir twice.

Using the Blanching Guide

The microwave oven can be a valuable and appreciated aid in preparing fresh vegetables for the freezer. (The oven is *not* recommended for canning.) Some vegetables don't require any water at all and, of course, the less water used the better. You'll have that "fresh picked" color and flavor for your produce. Here are some tips in preparing vegetables for blanching:

☐ Choose young, tender vegetables.
☐ Clean and prepare for cooking according to Cooking Guide.
☐ Measure amounts to be blanched; place by batches, in microproof casserole.
☐ Add water according to Guide.
☐ Cover and cook on HI for time indicated in Guide.
☐ Stir vegetables halfway through cooking.
☐ Let vegetables stand, covered, 1 minute after cooking.
☐ Place vegetables in ice water at once to stop cooking. When vegetables feel cool, spread on towel to absorb excess moisture.
☐ Package in freezer containers or pouches. Seal, label, date, and freeze quickly.

BLANCHING GUIDE — VEGETABLES

Food	Amount	Water	Approximate Time (in minutes)	Casserole Size
Asparagus (cut in 1-inch pieces)	4 cups	¼ cup	4½	1½ quart
Beans, green or wax (cut in 1-inch pieces)	1 pound	½ cup	5	1½ quart
Broccoli (cut in 1-inch pieces)	1 pound	⅓ cup	6	1½ quart
Carrots (sliced)	1 pound	⅓ cup	6	1½ quart
Cauliflower (cut in florets)	1 head	⅓ cup	6	2 quart
Corn (cut from cob)	4 cups	none	4	1½ quart
Corn-on-the-cob (husked)	6 ears	none	5½	1½ quart
Onion (quartered)	4 medium	½ cup	3 - 4½	1 quart
Parsnips (cubed)	1 pound	¼ cup	2½ - 4	1½ quart
Peas (shelled)	4 cups	¼ cup	4½	1½ quart
Snow peas	4 cups	¼ cup	3½	1½ quart
Spinach (washed)	1 pound	none	4	2 quart
Turnips (cubed)	1 pound	¼ cup	3 - 4½	1½ quart
Zucchini (sliced or cubed)	1 pound	¼ cup	4	1½ quart

Recipe No. | 177 |

Spanish Rice

Preset Cooking Time: 44 minutes

- ¼ cup butter or margarine
- ½ cup chopped onions
- ¼ cup chopped green pepper
- ¼ cup chopped celery
- 1 cup long-grain rice
- 1 cup water
- 1 cup tomato sauce
- 1 can (14½ ounces) tomatoes, drained and chopped
- 1 can (4 ounces) diced green chilies (optional)

Place butter in 3-quart glass or ceramic casserole. Place in oven. Set recipe number 177. Touch START. (Oven cooks: micro, HI, 1 minute.)

At Pause, add onion, green pepper, and celery; cover. Place in oven. Touch START. (Oven cooks: micro, HI, 3 minutes.)

At Pause, stir in rice, water, tomato sauce, tomatoes, and chilies. Cover. Place in oven on ceramic tray. Touch START. (Oven cooks: micro/convec, 350°F, 30 minutes; stands: 0, 10 minutes.) Fluff rice with fork and serve immediately.

6 to 8 servings

Recipe No. | 178 |

Barley-Rice Casserole

Preset Cooking Time: 50 minutes

- ½ cup butter or margarine
- ½ pound mushrooms, sliced
- 2 celery stalks, chopped
- 1 medium onion, chopped
- 1 cup long-grain rice
- 1 cup barley
- 1 envelope onion soup mix
- 2 cans (10¾ ounces each) beef broth or beef stock
- 1 soup can water

Combine butter, mushrooms, celery, and onion in 3-quart glass or ceramic casserole; cover. Place in oven on ceramic tray. Set recipe number 178. Touch START. (Oven cooks: micro, HI, 5 minutes.)

At Pause, stir in rice and barley; cover. Place in oven. Touch START. (Oven cooks: micro, HI, 5 minutes.)

At Pause, add soup mix, broth, and water; cover. Place in oven. Touch START. (Oven cooks: micro, HI, 20 minutes.)

At Pause, stir. Place in oven. Touch START. (Oven cooks: micro/convec, 300°F, 20 minutes.) Let stand, covered, about 15 minutes, or until all remaining liquid is absorbed.

8 servings

Recipe No. | 179 |

All Seasons Rice

Preset Cooking Time: 17 minutes

- 2 cups chicken or beef broth
- 1 cup long-grain rice
- ¼ cup minced onion
- 2 tablespoons minced parsley

Combine all ingredients in 3-quart microproof casserole. Cover and place in oven. Set recipe number 179. Touch START. (Oven cooks: micro, HI, 12 minutes; stands: 0, 5 minutes.)

4 servings

Recipe No. | 180 |

Chinese Fried Rice

Preset Cooking Time: 8 minutes

- 2 tablespoons butter or margarine
- 3 cups cooked rice
- 1½ tablespoons soy sauce
- 3 large eggs
- 1 tablespoon water
- ¼ teaspoon sugar
- ¼ cup thinly sliced green onions

Place butter in 3-quart microproof casserole. Place in oven. Set recipe number 180. Touch START. (Oven cooks: micro, HI, 1 minute.)

At Pause, add rice and soy sauce; blend well. Beat eggs, water, and sugar until blended; pour into center of rice. Cover. Touch START. (Oven cooks: micro, 70, 3 minutes.)

At Pause, stir in onions. Cover. Touch START. (Oven cooks: micro, 70, 4 minutes.)

Stir before serving.

4 to 6 servings

Recipe No. 181

Mushroom-Pimiento Rice

Preset Cooking Time: 19 minutes

 12 mushrooms (about ½ pound)
  6 shallots (about 12 ounces), minced
  3 tablespoons butter or margarine
 2½ cups chicken broth
 1¼ cups long-grain rice
  1 jar (4 ounces) pimientos, drained
     and diced
     Salt and pepper to taste

Mince mushroom stems. Cut caps into ⅛-inch thick slices; set aside. Combine minced stems, shallots, and butter in 3-quart microproof casserole. Place in oven. Set recipe number 181. Touch START. *(Oven cooks: micro, 90, 2 minutes.)*
At Pause, stir. Touch START. *(Oven cooks: micro, 90, 2 minutes.)*
At Pause, stir in broth and rice. Cover. Touch START. *(Oven cooks: micro, 90, 10 minutes.)*
At Pause, add mushroom caps. Cover. Touch START. *(Oven cooks: micro, HI, 5 minutes.)*
Add pimientos; blend well. Cover and let stand until all liquid is absorbed. Season with salt and pepper before serving.

6 to 8 servings

Recipe No. 182 ⊞

Rice Pilaf

Preset Cooking Time: 23 minutes

  2 cups water
  1 cup long-grain rice
  ¼ cup chopped green pepper
  ¼ cup chopped onion
  ¼ cup instant minced onion
  2 tablespoons butter or margarine
  2 teaspoons chicken bouillon
     granules

Combine all ingredients in 2-quart microproof casserole. Cover and place in oven. Set recipe number 182. Touch START. *(Oven cooks: micro, HI, 5 minutes; 50, 13 minutes; stands: 0, 5 minutes.)*
Stir through before serving.

4 servings

Recipe No. 183

Chicken Noodles au Gratin

Preset Cooking Time: 15 minutes

 1½ cups broken uncooked thin egg
     noodles
  1 cup chicken broth
  ½ cup milk
  ½ teaspoon salt
  ⅛ teaspoon pepper
  2 to 3 cups coarsely chopped cooked
     chicken or turkey
  1 cup (4 ounces) shredded
     Cheddar cheese
  ¼ cup sliced stuffed green olives

Combine noodles, broth, milk, salt, and pepper in 2-quart microproof casserole; stir lightly. Cover and place in oven. Set recipe number 183. Touch START. *(Oven cooks: micro, 70, 5 minutes.)*
At Pause, stir in chicken, cheese, and olives. Cover. Touch START. *(Oven cooks: micro, 70, 5 minutes.)*
At Pause, stir. Cover. Touch START. *(Oven cooks: micro, 20, 5 minutes.)*

4 to 6 servings

⊞ *Recipe can be increased. See "Quantity", page 12.*

Recipe No. 184

Noodles and Cheese

Preset Cooking Time: 11 minutes

- ¼ cup butter or margarine
- ⅓ cup slivered almonds
- 2 cups (8 ounces) shredded Swiss cheese
- ½ cup milk
- 1 large egg, lightly beaten
- 1 teaspoon parsley flakes
- ¼ teaspoon pepper
- ¼ teaspoon nutmeg
- 3 cups cooked wide egg noodles

Place butter and almonds in 1½-quart microproof casserole. Place in oven. Set recipe number 184. Touch START. *(Oven cooks: micro, HI, 1 minute.)*

At Pause, add remaining ingredients except noodles; blend well. Add noodles; toss until separated and evenly coated. Cover. Touch START. *(Oven cooks: micro, HI, 4 minutes.)*

At Pause, stir. Cover. Touch START. *(Oven cooks: micro, HI, 4 minutes; stands: 0, 2 minutes.)*

4 to 6 servings

Recipe No. 185

San Francisco Dish

Preset Cooking Time: 17 minutes

- 1 tablespoon beef bouillon granules
- 2½ cups hot water
- 1 medium onion, sliced
- 2 tablespoons butter or margarine
- 1 cup long-grain rice
- ½ cup broken uncooked spaghetti (1-inch pieces)

Dissolve bouillon in hot water; set aside. Place onion and butter in 3-quart microproof casserole. Cover and place in oven. Set recipe number 185. Touch START. *(Oven cooks: micro, HI, 2 minutes.)*

At Pause, add rice, spaghetti, and bouillon; stir lightly. Cover. Touch START. *(Oven cooks: micro, HI, 15 minutes.)*

Let stand 5 minutes before serving.

5 servings

Recipe No. 186

Casserole Italiano

Preset Cooking Time: 25 minutes

- 1 pound lean ground beef
- 1½ cups spaghetti sauce
- 1½ cups water
- 1 can (16 ounces) green beans, drained
- 1 package (7 ounces) uncooked elbow macaroni
- 2 tablespoons onion flakes
- 1 tablespoon sugar
- 1 teaspoon Italian seasoning
- ½ teaspoon salt
- ⅛ teaspoon pepper
- 1 clove garlic, minced
- 1 cup (4 ounces) shredded mozzarella cheese

Crumble beef into 3-quart microproof casserole. Place in oven. Set recipe number 186. Touch START. *(Oven cooks: micro, HI, 3 minutes.)*

At Pause, remove from oven. Stir to break up beef; drain. Add remaining ingredients except cheese; blend well. Cover and place in oven. Touch START. *(Oven cooks: micro, HI, 12 minutes.)*

At Pause, stir. Cover. Touch START. *(Oven cooks: micro, 60, 10 minutes.)*

Sprinkle with cheese. Cover and let stand 10 minutes before serving.

6 to 8 servings

Recipe No. | 187 |

Stroganoff Casserole

Preset Cooking Time: 27 minutes

 1 pound lean ground beef
 ¼ cup chopped onion
 2 cloves garlic, minced
 3 cups (4 ounces) uncooked medium-
    width egg noodles
 1 cup sliced mushrooms
 1 can (13¾ ounces) beef broth
 ⅛ teaspoon pepper
 1 container (8 ounces) dairy
    sour cream
 2 tablespoons chopped parsley

Combine beef, onion, and garlic in 2-quart microproof casserole. Place in oven. Set recipe number 187. Touch START. *(Oven cooks: micro, HI, 3 minutes.)*

At Pause, stir. Touch START. *(Oven cooks: micro, HI, 2 minutes.)*

At Pause, stir in noodles, mushrooms, broth, and pepper. Cover. Touch START. *(Oven cooks: micro, 50, 11 minutes.)*

At Pause, stir. Cover. Touch START. *(Oven cooks: micro, 50, 11 minutes.)*

Let stand 2 minutes. Blend in sour cream and sprinkle with parsley before serving.

6 servings

Recipe No. | 188 |

Macaroni and Cheese Vegetable Medley

Preset Cooking Time: 25 minutes

 1½ cups hot water
  1 cup uncooked elbow macaroni
  1 package (10 ounces) frozen
     chopped broccoli
  1 package (10 ounces) frozen
     sliced carrots
  4 tablespoons butter or margarine
  ½ cup milk
  1 tablespoon cornstarch
  ½ teaspoon salt
  ¼ teaspoon pepper
  ¼ teaspoon garlic powder
  ¼ teaspoon dry mustard
  2 cups (8 ounces) shredded Cheddar
     cheese

Combine hot water, macaroni, broccoli, and carrots in 2-quart microproof casserole. Dot with butter. Cover and place in oven. Set recipe number 188. Touch START. *(Oven cooks: micro, 70, 7 minutes.)*

At Pause, stir. Cover. Touch START. *(Oven cooks: micro, 70, 8 minutes.)*

At Pause, combine milk, cornstarch, salt, pepper, garlic powder, and dry mustard. Stir until cornstarch is dissolved. Stir into macaroni mixture. Blend in cheese. Cover. Touch START. *(Oven cooks: micro, 70, 5 minutes; stands: 0, 5 minutes.)*

Let stand until all liquid is absorbed.

6 to 8 servings

Recipe No. | 189 |

Zucchini Soufflé

Preset Cooking Time: 1 hour 5 minutes

    1 teaspoon butter
  ¼ cup grated Parmesan cheese
  ½ cup butter
    1 pound young, tender zucchini,
        shredded
    3 green onions or 1 medium onion,
        finely chopped
    2 cloves garlic, minced
  ¼ cup dry white wine
    3 tablespoons minced parsley
    1 tablespoon fresh lemon juice
      Pinch nutmeg
      Salt and pepper to taste
    1 jar (2 ounces) pimientos,
        finely diced
    6 eggs, separated
    2 tablespoons grated Parmesan
        cheese
  ½ teaspoon cream of tartar

Coat bottom and sides of 2-quart soufflé dish with 1 teaspoon butter. Sprinkle with ¼ cup Parmesan cheese, rotating dish to cover evenly and letting excess cheese remain on bottom. Refrigerate.

Combine ½ cup butter, zucchini, green onions, and garlic in 2-quart microproof bowl. Place in oven. Set recipe number 214. Touch START. (Oven cooks: micro, HI, 4 minutes.)

At Pause, add wine, parsley, lemon juice, nutmeg, salt, and pepper. Place in oven. Touch START. (Oven cooks: micro, HI, 6 minutes.) Add pimientos and mix well. Set aside to cool.

Set recipe number 189. Touch START. (Oven preheats: convec, 350°F.) Meanwhile, beat egg yolks with 2 tablespoons Parmesan cheese until thick and lemon colored. Blend in zucchini mixture. Beat egg whites in large bowl until foamy. Add cream of tartar and continue beating until stiff. Stir one-third of egg whites into zucchini mixture. Gently fold in remaining whites. Turn into prepared soufflé dish.

At 350°F, place dish in oven on ceramic tray. Touch START. (Oven cooks: convec, 350°F, 55 minutes.) Serve immediately.

This is one of several recipes that use the preset functions of another recipe for part of the cooking sequence. Set recipe number 214 first. At the end of that sequence, set recipe number 189.

Recipe No. | 190 | ⊞

Stuffed Tomatoes

Preset Cooking Time: 18 minutes

    1 package (10 ounces) frozen
        chopped spinach
    4 medium-size firm tomatoes
    1 cup (4 ounces) shredded mozzarella
        cheese, divided
  ¼ cup finely minced onions
  ¼ cup grated Parmesan cheese
  ½ teaspoon salt
  ⅛ teaspoon pepper
    2 tablespoons minced parsley

Set unopened package of spinach on microproof plate. Place in oven. Set recipe number 190. Touch START. (Oven cooks: micro, HI, 5 minutes; stands: 0, 5 minutes.)

At Pause, drain spinach well; squeeze dry. Transfer to large bowl and set aside.

Slice ½-inch piece off top of each tomato. Carefully hollow out centers, discarding seeds and leaving ½-inch shell. Chop pulp finely and add to spinach. Invert shells on paper towels to drain. Add ½ cup mozzarella cheese, onion, Parmesan cheese, salt, and pepper to spinach mixture and blend well. Spoon evenly into tomato shells. Sprinkle with remaining mozzarella and parsley. Arrange in 8-inch round glass or ceramic baking dish. Position wire rack in lower guides of oven. Place dish in oven on wire rack. Touch START. (Oven cooks: micro/convec, 350°F, 8 minutes.) Serve immediately.

4 servings

⊞ *Recipe can be increased. See "Quantity", page 12.*

Recipe No. | 191 |

Asparagus Casserole

Preset Cooking Time: 10 minutes

- 20 saltine crackers, crushed
- 1 can (15 ounces) asparagus pieces
- ¾ pound Cheddar cheese, shredded, divided
- 4 hard-cooked eggs, chopped, divided
- ½ cup milk
- 1 can (10¾ ounces) cream of mushroom soup, undiluted

Position wire rack in lower guides of oven. Set recipe number 191. Touch START. *(Oven preheats: convec, 350°F.)* Meanwhile, sprinkle half of cracker crumbs into 1½-quart glass or ceramic casserole. Drain asparagus, reserving 3 tablespoons liquid. Arrange half of cheese, asparagus, and eggs over top. Repeat layering. Combine milk, soup, and reserved liquid in small bowl and blend well. Pour over top.

At 350°F, place in oven on wire rack. Touch START. *(Oven cooks: micro/convec, 350°F, 10 minutes.)* Serve hot.

6 to 8 servings

Broccoli, spinach, or zucchini can be substituted for asparagus.

Recipe No. | 192 |

Stuffed Zucchini Boats

Preset Cooking Time: 14 minutes

- 4 medium zucchini
- 1 cup (4 ounces) shredded Monterey Jack cheese
- 1 cup (4 ounces) shredded Cheddar cheese
- ¾ cup cornbread stuffing mix
- ¼ cup chopped onion
- 1 clove garlic, minced
- 2 tablespoons chopped parsley, divided
- ⅛ teaspoon pepper
- ⅛ teaspoon oregano
- 1 egg, lightly beaten
- ¼ cup grated Parmesan cheese

Position wire rack in lower guides of oven. Set recipe number 192. Touch START. *(Oven preheats: convec, 350°F.)* Meanwhile, cut zucchini in half lengthwise. Scoop out pulp, leaving ¼-inch shell. Dice pulp. Transfer to large bowl. Add Monterey Jack and Cheddar cheese, stuffing mix, onion, garlic, 1 tablespoon parsley, pepper, oregano, and egg and mix lightly. Fill zucchini shells evenly with mixture. Sprinkle with Parmesan cheese and remaining parsley. Arrange in oval glass or ceramic dish just large enough for zucchini.

At 350°F, place in oven on wire rack. Touch START. *(Oven cooks: micro/convec, 350°F, 14 minutes.)* Serve immediately.

4 to 6 servings

Dried bread crumbs can be substituted for stuffing mix. Add ¼ teaspoon salt and cook as above.

Twice Baked Potatoes (page 159), →
Delightful Yams (page 160)

Recipe No. | 193 |

Ratatouille

Preset Cooking Time: 46 minutes

  1 eggplant (about 1½ pounds),
      peeled or unpeeled
    Salt
  ½ cup olive oil
  2 medium onions, thinly sliced
  2 cloves garlic, minced
  1 green pepper, sliced into
      thin strips
  4 zucchini (about 1 pound), cut
      into ¼-inch slices
  ¼ cup chopped parsley
  ½ teaspoon pepper
  ½ teaspoon basil leaves,
      crumbled
  ½ teaspoon oregano, crumbled
  ½ pound mushrooms, sliced
  3 large tomatoes, peeled, seeded,
      and cut into wedges
  ¼ cup grated Parmesan cheese

Cut eggplant into 1-inch cubes. Transfer to colander and sprinkle with salt. Let stand 30 to 45 minutes. Rinse with cold water and drain. Combine oil, onions, garlic, and green pepper in 4-quart glass or ceramic casserole. Cover. Place in oven. Set recipe number 193. Touch START. *(Oven cooks: micro, 90, 6 minutes.)*

At Pause, stir through several times. Add eggplant, zucchini, parsley, pepper, basil, and oregano and toss lightly. Cover. Place in oven on ceramic tray. Touch START. *(Oven cooks: micro/convec, 350°F, 20 minutes.)*

At Pause, stir in mushrooms and tomatoes. Cover. Place in oven. Touch START. *(Oven cooks: micro/convec, 350°F, 10 minutes.)*

At Pause, sprinkle casserole with cheese. Place in oven, uncovered. Touch START. *(Oven cooks: convec, 350°F, 10 minutes.)* Serve hot.

6 to 8 servings

Recipe No. | 194 |

Scalloped Potatoes

Preset Cooking Time: 19 minutes

  4 medium potatoes (about 1
      pound), peeled and cut into
      ⅛-inch slices
  3 tablespoons all-purpose flour
  1 teaspoon salt
  1 teaspoon garlic powder
  ⅛ teaspoon pepper
  1 cup milk
  2 tablespoons butter or margarine
    Paprika

Arrange half of potatoes in 1½-quart microproof casserole. Combine flour, salt, garlic powder, and pepper. Sprinkle half of mixture over potatoes. Repeat layering. Pour milk into 2-cup glass measure. Place in oven. Set recipe number 194. Touch START. *(Oven cooks: micro, HI, 2 minutes.)*

At Pause, pour milk over potatoes. Dot with butter and sprinkle with paprika. Cover. Place in oven. Touch START. *(Oven cooks: micro, HI, 10 minutes.)*

At Pause, remove cover. Touch START. *(Oven cooks: micro/convec, 350°F, 7 minutes.)* Serve immediately.

4 servings

For Scalloped Potatoes au Gratin, follow above recipe and sprinkle ¾ cup shredded Cheddar cheese over each layer of potatoes.

Recipe No. | 195 | ⊞

Easy Country Fries

Preset Cooking Time: 30 minutes

  ¼ cup dehydrated onion flakes
  ⅛ teaspoon salt
  ½ teaspoon pepper
  ½ teaspoon paprika
  2 pounds potatoes
  ½ cup butter or margarine,
      divided

Position wire rack in lower guides of oven. Set recipe number 195. Touch START. *(Oven preheats: convec, 350°F.)* Mean-

⊞ *Recipe can be increased. See "Quantity", page 12.*

while, mix onion, salt, pepper, and paprika in small bowl. Rinse potatoes and pat dry (do not peel). Cut evenly into ¼-inch slices. Arrange one-third of potatoes in 8-inch square glass or ceramic baking dish. Sprinkle with one-third of onion mixture. Dot with one-third of butter. Repeat layering twice, ending with butter and onion mixture. Cover.

At 350°F, place in oven on wire rack. Touch START. *(Oven cooks: micro/convec, 350°F, 20 minutes.)*

At Pause, remove cover. Rotate dish one-half turn. Touch START. *(Oven cooks: micro/convec, 350°F, 10 minutes.)* Serve immediately.

4 to 6 servings

Recipe No. | 196

Potato Kugel

Preset Cooking Time: 55 minutes

2	medium onions, cut into eighths
3	eggs
1½	teaspoons salt
½	teaspoon baking powder
¼	teaspoon pepper
5	medium potatoes, peeled and shredded
½	cup matzo meal
2	tablespoons vegetable oil, divided

Combine onions, eggs, salt, baking powder, and pepper in 2 quart bowl. Add potatoes and mix well. Blend in matzo meal. Stir in 1 tablespoon oil.

Position wire rack in lower guides of oven. Set recipe number 196. Touch START. *(Oven preheats: convec, 350°F.)* Meanwhile, coat 8-inch square baking dish with remaining oil. Pour in potato mixture.

At 350°F, place in oven on wire rack. Touch START. *(Oven cooks: convec, 350°F, 55 minutes.)* Serve immediately.

6 servings

If you prefer, all-purpose flour can be substituted for matzo meal.

Recipe No. | 197

Twice-Baked Potatoes

Preset Cooking Time: 20 minutes

4	baking potatoes
½	cup butter or margarine, softened
½	cup dairy sour cream
½	teaspoon salt
	Pinch pepper
4	teaspoons crumbled cooked bacon (optional)

Position wire rack in lower guides of oven. Wash potatoes, pat dry, and pierce with fork several times. Arrange in circle on wire rack, spacing about 1 inch apart. Set recipe number 213. Touch START. *(Oven cooks: micro, HI, 6 minutes.)*

At Pause, turn potatoes over. Touch START. *(Oven cooks: micro, HI, 6 minutes.)* Remove potatoes from oven. Let stand several minutes.

Set recipe number 197. Touch START. *(Oven preheats: convec, 400°F.)* Meanwhile, remove ¼-inch horizontal slice from top of each potato. Carefully scoop pulp into medium bowl, keeping shells intact. Blend butter, sour cream, salt, and pepper into potato pulp and beat with electric mixer until smooth. Spoon mixture evenly into shells, mounding slightly in center (or pipe in with pastry bag). Arrange potatoes on heatproof platter.

At 400°F, place in oven on wire rack. Touch START. *(Oven cooks: convec, 400°F, 8 minutes.)* Sprinkle with bacon and serve immediately. Pass extra sour cream, if desired.

8 servings

Recipe No. | 198 |

Delightful Yams

Preset Cooking Time: 18 minutes

- 1 can (40 ounces) yams, well drained
- ¼ cup fresh orange juice
- 1 tablespoon cornstarch
- ½ cup firmly-packed brown sugar
- ¼ cup butter or margarine, melted
- 1 orange, peeled and cubed
- ½ cup coarsely chopped walnuts
- 1 tablespoon grated orange peel
- 1½ cups miniature marshmallows

Position wire rack in upper guides of oven. Set recipe number 198. Touch START. *(Oven preheats: convec, 450°F.)* Meanwhile, arrange yams in 1½-quart round glass or ceramic baking dish or quiche dish. Mix orange juice and cornstarch in medium bowl until cornstarch is completely dissolved. Blend in brown sugar and butter. Add orange, walnuts, and peel. Pour over yams.

At 450°F, place in oven. Touch START. *(Oven cooks: micro/convec, 450°F, 15 minutes.)*

At Pause, arrange about 1¼ cups marshmallows around rim of dish. Mound remaining marshmallows in center. Return dish to oven. Touch START. *(Oven cooks: convec, 450°F, 3 minutes.)* Serve immediately.

6 servings

Recipe No. | 200 |

Carrots

Preset Cooking Time: 10 minutes

- 1 pound carrots, peeled and thinly sliced
- 2 tablespoons water

Place carrots in 1-quart microproof casserole. Add water. Cover and place in oven. Set recipe number 200. Touch START. *(Oven cooks: micro, HI, 5 minutes.)*

At Pause, stir. Cover. Touch START. *(Oven cooks: micro, HI, 5 minutes.)*

Let stand 2 to 3 minutes. Drain before serving.

4 servings

Recipe No. | 199 |

Cabbage

Preset Cooking Time: 8 minutes

- ½ medium head cabbage, shredded
- ¼ cup water

Place cabbage in 1-quart microproof casserole. Add water. Cover and place in oven. Set recipe number 199. Touch START. *(Oven cooks: micro, HI, 4 minutes.)*

At Pause, stir. Cover. Touch START. *(Oven cooks: micro, HI, 2 minutes; stands: 0, 2 minutes.)*

Drain before serving.

4 servings

Recipe No. | 201 |

Canned Vegetables

Preset Cooking Time: 2½ minutes

- 1 can (8 ounces) canned vegetables, drained

Pour vegetables into 1-quart microproof casserole. Cover and place in oven. Set recipe number 201. Touch START. *(Oven cooks: micro, 80, 1 minute.)*

At Pause, stir. Cover. Touch START. *(Oven cooks: micro, 80, 1½ minutes.)*

Let stand 2 to 3 minutes before serving.

2 servings

Recipe No. 202 ⊞

Cauliflower

Preset Cooking Time: 11 minutes

1 head cauliflower (1⅓ pounds)
¼ cup water

Remove stem and outer leaves from cauliflower; discard. Rinse well. Break into florets. Place in 1½- to 2-quart microproof casserole. Add water. Cover and place in oven. Set recipe number 202. Touch START. *(Oven cooks: micro, HI, 5 minutes.)*

At Pause, stir. Cover. Touch START. *(Oven cooks: micro, HI, 3 minutes; stands: 0, 3 minutes.)*

Drain before serving.

5 to 6 servings

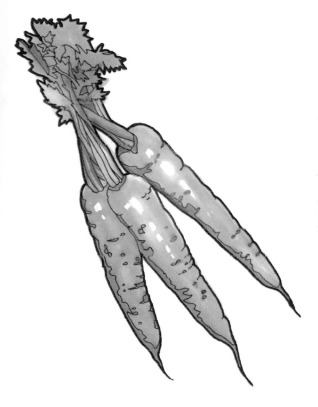

Recipe No. 203

Carrot-Broccoli Casserole

Preset Cooking Time: 15¾ minutes

1 package (10 ounces) frozen broccoli spears
1 can (10¾ ounces) cream of chicken soup, undiluted
1 cup finely shredded carrots
½ cup dairy sour cream
1 tablespoon all-purpose flour
1 tablespoon minced onion
¼ teaspoon salt
⅛ teaspoon pepper
2 tablespoons butter or margarine
¾ cup herb-seasoned stuffing cubes

Place broccoli in package on microproof plate. Place in oven. Set recipe number 203. Touch START. *(Oven cooks: micro, HI, 3 minutes.)*

At Pause, remove from oven; set aside. Combine soup, carrots, sour cream, flour, onion, salt, and pepper in 1½-quart microproof casserole. Cut broccoli into 1-inch pieces; stir into soup mixture. Cover and place in oven. Touch START. *(Oven cooks: micro, HI, 6 minutes.)*

At Pause, remove from oven. Stir; set aside. Place butter in 2-cup glass measure. Place in oven. Touch START. *(Oven cooks: micro, HI, 45 seconds.)*

At Pause, remove from oven. Add stuffing cubes to butter; blend well. Spoon over broccoli mixture. Place in oven. Touch START. *(Oven cooks: micro, HI, 6 minutes.)*

5 to 6 servings

Recipe No. 204 ⊞

Corn-on-the-Cob

Preset Cooking Time: 9 minutes

    2 unhusked ears of corn (about
         14 ounces each)
       Butter or margarine
       Salt to taste

Discard any soiled outer leaves of husks. Soak corn in cold water 5 to 10 minutes to clean and moisten. Drain well; do not dry. Place directly on microwave roasting rack. Place in oven. Set recipe number 204. Touch START. *(Oven cooks: micro, HI, 7 minutes; stands: 0, 2 minutes.)*
Serve with butter and salt.

2 servings

Corn can be husked before cooking. Wrap each ear in waxed paper or plastic wrap. Set recipe number and cook as directed above.

Recipe No. 205

Corn-Mushroom Scallop

Preset Cooking Time: 14 minutes

    1 can (17 ounces) cream-style corn
    ¼ pound mushrooms, sliced
    1 large egg, lightly beaten
    ¾ cup soda-cracker crumbs, divided
    1 tablespoon chopped chives
    ¼ teaspoon white pepper
    2 tablespoons butter or margarine

Combine corn, mushrooms, and egg in 1-quart microproof casserole; blend well. Stir in ½ cup cracker crumbs, chives, and pepper. Spread evenly in casserole. Sprinkle with remaining ¼ cup cracker crumbs. Dot with butter. Place in oven. Set recipe number 205. Touch START. *(Oven cooks: micro, HI, 9 minutes; stands: 0, 5 minutes.)*

4 servings

Recipe No. 206

Creamed Potato Mix

Preset Cooking Time: about 27 minutes

    1 package (5 ounces) creamed
         potato mix

Prepare potato mix (do not boil water) as directed on package in 3-quart round microproof casserole. Place in oven. Insert temperature probe. Cover lightly with waxed paper. Plug in probe. Set recipe number 206. Touch START. *(Oven cooks: micro, 70, to 150°F; stands: 0, 5 minutes.)*

4 servings

Recipe No. 207

Creamy Cabbage

Preset Cooking Time: 10 minutes

    1 medium head cabbage, shredded
    ¼ cup water
    1 package (3 ounces) cream cheese,
         cut into cubes
    2 tablespoons milk
    ½ teaspoon salt
    ½ teaspoon celery seeds
       Dash pepper
       Chopped parsley

Place cabbage and water in 2-quart microproof casserole. Cover and place in oven. Set recipe number 207. Touch START. *(Oven cooks: micro, HI, 5 minutes.)*
At Pause, stir. Cover. Touch START. *(Oven cooks: micro, HI, 4 minutes.)*
At Pause, add remaining ingredients except parsley. Cover. Touch START. *(Oven cooks: micro, HI, 1 minute.)*
Stir to combine cream cheese and cabbage. Sprinkle with parsley before serving.

5 to 6 servings

⊞ *Recipe can be increased. See "Quantity", page 12.*

*Twice Baked Potatoes (page 159), Green →
Beans Italiano (page 164), Cranberry Carrots
(page 169)*

Recipe No. | 208 | ⊞

Eggplant

Preset Cooking Time: 7 minutes

    1 eggplant (1 pound)

Wash eggplant and pierce skin in several places. Place on microwave roasting rack. Place in oven. Set recipe number 208. Touch START. *(Oven cooks: micro, HI, 7 minutes.)*

Let stand 3 minutes before slicing.

4 to 6 servings

Recipe No. | 209 |

Green Beans Amandine

Preset Cooking Time: 9 minutes

    ½ cup sliced almonds
    2 tablespoons butter or margarine
    1 package (10 ounces) frozen French
        cut green beans
        Salt and pepper to taste

Place almonds and butter in 1-cup glass measure; set aside. Place beans in package on microproof plate. Place in oven. Set recipe number 209. Touch START. *(Oven cooks: micro, HI, 6 minutes.)*

At Pause, remove from oven; set aside. Place almonds and butter in oven. Touch START. *(Oven cooks: micro, HI, 1 minute.)*

At Pause, stir. Touch START. *(Oven cooks: micro, HI, 1 minute.)*

At Pause, remove from oven. Transfer beans to microproof serving dish. Add almonds, salt, and pepper; toss lightly. Place in oven. Touch START. *(Oven cooks: micro, HI, 1 minute.)*

3 to 4 servings

Recipe No. | 210 |

Green Beans Italiano

Preset Cooking Time: 17½ minutes

    3 slices bacon
    2 packages (10 ounces each) frozen
        green beans
    1 small onion, thickly sliced
    ¾ cup Italian dressing

Arrange bacon on paper towel-lined microproof plate. Place in oven. Cover with paper towel. Set recipe number 210. Touch START. *(Oven cooks: micro, HI, 3½ minutes.)*

At Pause, remove from oven. Crumble bacon; set aside. Place beans in packages on microproof plate. Place in oven. Touch START. *(Oven cooks: micro, HI, 5 minutes.)*

At Pause, turn packages over. Touch START. *(Oven cooks: micro, HI, 5 minutes.)*

At Pause, remove from oven. Transfer beans to 1½-quart microproof casserole. Add onion and dressing; blend well. Cover and place in oven. Touch START. *(Oven cooks: micro, HI, 4 minutes.)*

Sprinkle with crumbled bacon before serving.

6 servings

⊞ *Recipe can be increased. See "Quantity", page 12.*

Recipe No. [211]

Harvard Beets

Preset Cooking Time: 8 minutes

> 1 can (16 ounces) diced or
>   sliced beets
> ¼ cup sugar
> ¼ cup wine vinegar
> 1 tablespoon cornstarch
> ½ teaspoon salt
> ⅛ teaspoon pepper

Drain beet liquid into 1-cup glass measure. Add water to equal 1 cup liquid; set aside. Combine sugar, vinegar, cornstarch, salt, and pepper in 1-quart microproof casserole; stir until cornstarch is dissolved. Stir in beet-water mixture. Place in oven. Set recipe number 211. Touch START. *(Oven cooks: micro, HI, 1½ minutes.)*

At Pause, stir. Touch START. *(Oven cooks: micro, HI, 1½ minutes.)*

At Pause, add beets; stir to coat. Cover. Touch START. *(Oven cooks: micro, HI, 5 minutes.)*

4 servings

Recipe No. [212]

Onions

Preset Cooking Time: 12 minutes

> 1 pound onions, peeled and cut
>   into quarters
> ¼ cup water
> 1 tablespoon butter

Place onions, water, and butter in wide shallow microproof baking dish. Cover and place in oven. Set recipe number 212. Touch START. *(Oven cooks: micro, HI, 4 minutes.)*

At Pause, stir. Cover. Touch START. *(Oven cooks: micro, HI, 5 minutes; stands: 0, 3 minutes.)*

3 to 4 servings

Recipe No. [213] ⊞

Parsley New Potatoes

Preset Cooking Time: 12 minutes

> 12 new potatoes (1 pound)
> ¼ cup water
> 2 tablespoons butter
> 1 tablespoon minced parsley
>   Dash salt and pepper

Cut ½-inch strip around middle of each potato. Place in 2-quart microproof casserole. Add water. Cover and place in oven. Set recipe number 213. Touch START. *(Oven cooks: micro, HI, 6 minutes.)*

At Pause, stir. Cover. Touch START. *(Oven cooks: micro, HI, 6 minutes.)*

Drain. Stir in butter, parsley, salt, and pepper. Serve hot.

4 servings

Recipe No. [214]

Peas Francine

Preset Cooking Time: 10 minutes

> 2 cups shelled green peas
> ¼ cup water
> 1 teaspoon sugar
> 3 or 4 large lettuce leaves
>   Dash salt and pepper

Combine peas, water, and sugar in 1½-quart microproof casserole. Cover and place in oven. Set recipe number 214. Touch START. *(Oven cooks: micro, HI, 4 minutes.)*

At Pause, stir. Cover with lettuce, overlapping leaves as necessary. Cover. Touch START. *(Oven cooks: micro, HI, 6 minutes.)*

Discard lettuce leaves. Drain peas; stir in salt and pepper. Cover and let stand 2 to 3 minutes before serving.

4 servings

⊞ *Recipe can be increased. See "Quantity", page 12.*

Recipe No. ☐ 215 ☐ ⊞

Green Peas

Preset Cooking Time: 10 minutes

> 1 pound peas in shells
> ¼ cup water

Shell peas; rinse and drain. Place peas and water in wide, shallow, microproof baking dish. Cover and place in oven. Set recipe number 215. Touch START. (Oven cooks: micro, HI, 4 minutes.)

At Pause, stir. Cover. Touch START. (Oven cooks: micro, HI, 4 minutes; stands: 0, 2 minutes.)

Drain and serve seasoned with butter and salt, if desired.

2 servings

Recipe No. ☐ 216

Baked Potatoes

Preset Cooking Time: 9 minutes

> 2 potatoes (6 ounces each)

Scrub potatoes and rinse well. Pierce at intervals with fork. Place about 1 inch apart on microwave roasting rack. Place in oven. Set recipe number 216. Touch START. (Oven cooks: micro, HI, 5 minutes.)

At Pause, turn potatoes over. Touch START. (Oven cooks: micro, HI, 4 minutes.)

Let stand 3 minutes before serving.

2 servings

Recipe No. ☐ 217

Savory Cauliflower

Preset Cooking Time: 10½ minutes

> 1 head cauliflower (1⅓ pounds)
> ¼ cup water
> ½ cup mayonnaise
> 1 tablespoon instant minced onion
> ½ teaspoon dry mustard
> ¼ teaspoon salt
> 4 slices Cheddar cheese
> Paprika

Cut cone-shaped wedge from cauliflower core. Place cauliflower, cut-side up, in 1½-quart microproof casserole. Add water. Cover and place in oven. Set recipe number 217. Touch START. (Oven cooks: micro, HI, 5 minutes.)

At Pause, turn over. Cover. Touch START. (Oven cooks: micro, HI, 4 minutes.)

At Pause, remove from oven; drain. Combine mayonnaise, onion, mustard, and salt; spoon over cauliflower. Lay cheese slices on top. Place in oven. Do not cover. Touch START. (Oven cooks: micro, 70, 1½ minutes.)

Sprinkle with paprika. Let stand 2 minutes before serving.

6 servings

Recipe No. ☐ 218

Scalloped Potato Mix

Preset Cooking Time: 19 minutes

> 1 package (7 ounces) scalloped potato mix

Prepare scalloped potatoes as directed on package in 3-quart microproof casserole. Cover and place in oven. Set recipe number 218. Touch START. (Oven cooks: micro, HI, 4 minutes; 50, 10 minutes; stands: 0, 5 minutes.)

Stir through before serving.

6 servings

⊞ Recipe can be increased. See "Quantity", page 12.

Harvard Beets (page 165) →

Recipe No. | 219 |

Spinach

Preset Cooking Time: 6 minutes

> 1 pound spinach, tough stems removed
> Salt and pepper to taste

Rinse spinach and drain. Place in wide shallow microproof baking dish. Cover and place in oven. Set recipe number 219. Touch START. *(Oven cooks: micro, HI, 6 minutes.)*

Let stand 2 minutes before draining. Season with salt and pepper before serving.

2 servings

Recipe No. | 220 |

Spinach Oriental

Preset Cooking Time: 5 minutes

> 10 ounces spinach, tough stems removed
> 1 can (8 ounces) sliced water chestnuts, drained
> 4 green onions, sliced
> 2 tablespoons vegetable oil
> 2 tablespoons wine vinegar
> 2 tablespoons soy sauce
> 1 teaspoon sugar

Rinse spinach and drain; tear into bite-size pieces. Combine spinach, water chestnuts, and onions in 2-quart microproof casserole. Cover and place in oven. Set recipe number 220. Touch START. *(Oven cooks: micro, HI, 4 minutes.)*

At Pause, remove from oven; drain. Stir, cover, and set aside. Combine oil, vinegar, soy sauce, and sugar in 1-cup glass measure; stir until sugar is dissolved. Place in oven. Touch START. *(Oven cooks: micro, HI, 1 minute.)*

Stir and pour over spinach mixture; toss lightly. Serve immediately.

4 servings

Recipe No. | 221 | ⊞

Sweet Potatoes

Preset Cooking Time: 5 minutes

> 1 sweet potato (about 5 ounces)

Scrub potato and rinse well. Pierce at intervals with fork. Place on microwave roasting rack. Place in oven. Set recipe number 221. Touch START. *(Oven cooks: micro, HI, 5 minutes.)*

Let stand 3 minutes before serving.

1 serving

Recipe No. | 222 |

Sweet-Sour Red Cabbage

Preset Cooking Time: 23 minutes

> 1 head red cabbage (1½ pounds), shredded
> 1 tart apple, peeled, cored, and diced
> 5 tablespoons wine vinegar
> 1 tablespoon butter or margarine
> 3 tablespoons sugar
> 1 teaspoon salt

Combine cabbage, apple, vinegar, and butter in 3-quart microproof casserole; blend well. Cover and place in oven. Set recipe number 222. Touch START. *(Oven cooks: micro, HI, 6 minutes.)*

At Pause, stir. Cover. Touch START. *(Oven cooks: micro, HI, 6 minutes.)*

At Pause, stir. Cover. Touch START. *(Oven cooks: micro, HI, 6 minutes.)*

At Pause, add sugar and salt; blend well. Cover. Touch START. *(Oven cooks: micro, HI, 5 minutes.)*

6 servings

⊞ *Recipe can be increased. See "Quantity", page 12.*

Recipe No. 223

Cranberry Carrots

Preset Cooking Time: 13 minutes

- 1 pound carrots, thinly sliced
- 2 tablespoons water
- ¼ cup butter or margarine
- ¼ cup jellied cranberry sauce
  Salt to taste

Place carrots and water in 1½- to 2-quart microproof casserole. Cover and place in oven. Set recipe number 223. Touch START. *(Oven cooks: micro, HI, 10 minutes.)*

At Pause, remove from oven. Remove carrots from casserole; drain water. Set carrots aside. Place butter and cranberry sauce in casserole. Cover and place in oven. Touch START. *(Oven cooks: micro, HI, 1 minute.)*

At Pause, stir in carrots. Season with salt. Touch START. *(Oven cooks: micro, HI, 2 minutes.)*

4 servings

Recipe No. 224

Corn and Pepper Pudding

Preset Cooking Time: 24 minutes

- 2 tablespoons butter or margarine
- 2 tablespoons chopped green pepper
- 2 tablespoons chopped pimiento
- 2 cans (17 ounces each)
    cream-style corn
- 2 large eggs, lightly beaten
- 3 tablespoons all-purpose flour
- 1 tablespoon instant minced onion
- 1 teaspoon salt
- ¼ teaspoon pepper

Combine butter, green pepper, and pimiento in shallow 1½-quart round or oval microproof baking dish. Place in oven. Set recipe number 224. Touch START. *(Oven cooks: micro, 90, 2 minutes.)*

At Pause, stir in remaining ingredients; blend well. Cover. Touch START. *(Oven cooks: micro, 70, 9 minutes.)*

At Pause, stir. Do not cover. Touch START. *(Oven cooks: micro, 70, 8 minutes; stands: 0, 5 minutes.)*

6 servings

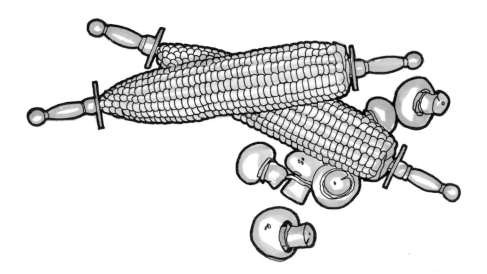

Sauce Sorcery

Sauces are a cinch in your Kenmore Auto Recipe 300 Micro/Convection Oven. They are definitely a microwave success story. For those of us who have slaved over a hot stove with whisk in hand and double boiler at full speed, those days are gone forever. Sauces simply do not stick or scorch as they do when prepared on the stove top. They heat evenly and require less time and attention. You don't have to stir constantly and can simply retire that double boiler.

Usually, just an occasional stirring is all that is required to prevent lumping. Sometimes, a quick beating after cooking can be added to make a sauce velvety-smooth. You can measure, mix, and cook all in the same cup, or in the serving pitcher itself! Choose Tarragon Sauce (page 180) or Béarnaise Sauce (page 176) to perk up meat or vegetables, others for desserts. Just try making a sauce the microwave way and you'll turn an ordinary food into an elegant treat.

Basic White Sauce (page 173) is typical of the preparation ease the microwave method provides. The simple steps are illustrated (right and above right). The addition of herbs or spices turns Basic White Sauce into something new each time you use it (above).

← *Hollandaise Sauce (page 177) on Asparagus (Guide, 147). A Raisin Brandy Sauce demonstrates the ease and speed with which elegant sauces are prepared in the microwave. Blend 3 tablespoons brown sugar and 1 tablespoon cornstarch; stir in 1 cup apple juice and 2 tablespoons lemon juice. Cook on HI, 3 minutes. Stir in 1/2 cup raisins soaked in 1/4 cup apple brandy, and 1/8 teaspoon each ground cloves and nutmeg. Cook on HI, 2 minutes. Serve warm over Center Cut Ham Slice (Guide, page 82).*

Converting Your Recipes

All those sauces generally considered too difficult for the average cook are easy in the microwave oven. When looking for a sauce recipe similar to the conventional one you want to convert, find a recipe with a similar quantity of liquid and similar main thickening ingredient such as cornstarch, flour, egg, cheese, or jelly. Read the directions carefully to determine procedure, timing, and cook control setting. Then, when you stir, notice the progress of the sauce, and remove when the right consistency or doneness is reached. Keep notes to help you the next time. The following tips will help:

☐ Use a microproof container about twice the volume of ingredients to safeguard against the sauce boiling over — so easy with milk- and cream-based sauces.

☐ Sauces and salad dressings with ingredients not sensitive to high heat should be cooked on HI (max. power). Basic White Sauce is an example.

☐ Bring flour and other starch-thickened mixtures to a boil and remove as soon as thickened. Remember, overcooking will destroy the thickening agent and sauce will be too thin.

☐ You will notice that more flour or cornstarch is required in microwave cooking than in conventional cooking to thicken sauces and gravies, since they will not be reduced by evaporation.

☐ Stirring quickly two or three times during cooking is sufficient to assure even cooking. Too many stirrings may slow cooking.

☐ To reheat sauces: Dessert sauces to 125°F with temperature probe. Main dish sauces, such as gravy or canned spaghetti sauce, to 150°F with temperature probe.

☐ When sauces require time to develop flavor or if they contain eggs, which might curdle, they should be cooked slowly, on 50 or even 30. Don't allow delicate egg yolk sauces to boil.

☐ You can make your own special sauce by flavoring Basic White Sauce (page 173) as desired. For example, add cheese, cooked mushrooms, cooked onions, your favorite spices, tomato paste, horseradish, etc.

Recipe No. ☐ 225 ☐ ⊞

Basic White Sauce

Preset Cooking Time: 7 minutes

- 1 cup milk
- 2 tablespoons butter
- 2 tablespoons all-purpose flour
  Dash white pepper
  Dash nutmeg

Pour milk into 4-cup glass measure. Place in oven. Set recipe number 225. Touch START. *(Oven cooks: micro, 70, 2 minutes.)*

At Pause, set milk aside. Place butter in 2-cup glass measure. Place in oven. Touch START. *(Oven cooks: micro, HI, 1 minute.)*

At Pause, stir flour into butter. Touch START. *(Oven cooks: micro, HI, 1 minute.)*

At Pause, slowly stir milk into flour mixture, blending until smooth. Season with pepper and nutmeg. Place in oven. Touch START. *(Oven cooks: micro, HI, 3 minutes.)* Stir through several times. Serve hot.

1 cup

Recipe No. ☐ 226 ☐

Beef Gravy

Preset Cooking Time: 11 minutes

- ½ cup beef drippings
- ½ cup all-purpose flour
- 4 cups water, heated
  Salt and pepper to taste
  Bottled brown sauce (optional)

Combine drippings and flour in 4-quart microproof casserole and blend well. Place in oven. Set recipe number 226. Touch START. *(Oven cooks: micro, HI, 30 seconds.)*

At Pause, stir. Touch START. *(Oven cooks: micro, HI, 30 seconds.)*

At Pause, blend in water. Touch START. *(Oven cooks: micro, HI, 5 minutes.)*

At Pause, stir. Touch START. *(Oven cooks: micro, HI, 5 minutes.)* Season with salt and pepper. Add several drops of brown sauce to deepen color, if desired.

1 quart

Recipe No. ☐ 227 ☐ ⊞

Lemon Sauce

Preset Cooking Time: 2½ minutes

- ⅔ cup water
- ⅓ cup sugar
- 2 tablespoons cornstarch
- 3 tablespoons fresh lemon juice
- 1 egg yolk
- 1 tablespoon butter or margarine
- 1 teaspoon grated lemon peel
  Pinch salt
  Yellow food coloring (optional)

Combine all ingredients in 1-quart glass measure and blend well. Place in oven. Set recipe number 227. Touch START. *(Oven cooks: micro, HI, 1½ minutes.)*

At Pause, stir. Touch START. *(Oven cooks: micro, HI, 1 minute.)* Stir briskly until thick and smooth. Serve over pound cake.

about 1 cup

Recipe No. ☐ 228 ☐ ⊞

Barbecue Sauce

Preset Cooking Time: 8 minutes

- ⅓ cup chopped onion
- 1 clove garlic, minced
- 1 tablespoon butter or margarine
- 1 can (8 ounces) tomato sauce
- 2 tablespoons dark brown sugar
- 2 tablespoons fresh lemon juice
- I teaspoon Worcestershire sauce
- ½ teaspoon salt
- ¼ teaspoon paprika
- ¼ teaspoon dry mustard
- ¼ teaspoon pepper
- ⅛ teaspoon ground turmeric

Combine onion, garlic, and butter in 2-quart glass measure. Place in oven. Set recipe number 228. Touch START. *(Oven cooks: micro, HI, 3 minutes.)*

At Pause, stir in remaining ingredients. Place in oven. Touch START. *(Oven cooks: micro, HI, 3 minutes.)*

At Pause, stir. Touch START. *(Oven cooks: micro, HI, 2 minutes.)*

1½ cups

⊞ *Recipe can be increased. See "Quantity", page 12.*

Recipe No. 229

Homemade Spaghetti Sauce

Preset Cooking Time: 23 minutes

- 1 medium onion, sliced
- ¼ cup sliced celery
- 6 medium mushrooms, sliced
- ½ green pepper, sliced into thin strips
- 2 cloves garlic, minced
- 1½ tablespoons vegetable oil
- ½ pound lean ground beef
- 1 can (14 ounces) whole peeled tomatoes, chopped, liquid reserved
- 1 can (6 ounces) tomato paste
- 1 tablespoon chopped parsley
- ½ teaspoon oregano, crumbled

Combine onion, celery, mushrooms, green pepper, garlic, and oil in 2-quart glass or ceramic casserole. Cover. Place in oven. Set recipe number 229. Touch START. *(Oven cooks: micro, HI, 5 minutes.)*

At Pause, stir in beef. Place in oven. Touch START. *(Oven cooks: micro, HI, 3 minutes.)*

At Pause, stir through several times. Blend in tomatoes with liquid, tomato paste, parsley, and oregano. Cover. Place in oven. Touch START. *(Oven cooks: micro/convec, 350°F, 15 minutes.)*

about 4 cups

Recipe No. 230 ⊞

Apricot Dessert Sauce

Preset Cooking Time: 4 minutes

- 1 cup apricot nectar
- ¼ cup sugar
- 1 tablespoon cornstarch
- 1 teaspoon grated lemon peel
- 3 tablespoons apricot-flavored brandy

Combine apricot nectar, sugar, cornstarch, and lemon peel in 2-cup glass measure; stir until sugar and cornstarch are dissolved. Place in oven. Set recipe number 230. Touch START. *(Oven cooks: micro, HI, 1½ minutes.)*

At Pause, stir. Cover. Touch START. *(Oven cooks: micro, HI, 1½ minutes.)*

At Pause, add brandy; blend well. Touch START. *(Oven cooks: micro, HI, 1 minute.)*

Stir through several times. Serve warm or chilled over ice cream, rice pudding, tapioca, or pound cake.

1⅓ cups

To make a Lemon Dessert Sauce, substitute ½ cup water for the 1 cup apricot nectar, lemon juice for the brandy, and add 1 egg yolk and 1 tablespoon butter.

⊞ *Recipe can be increased. See "Quantity", page 12.*

*Apricot Dessert Sauce with Fluffy Tapioca →
(page 198), Lemon Dessert Sauce variation on
pound cake*

Recipe No. 231 ⊞

Béarnaise Sauce

Preset Cooking Time: 1½ minutes

- 4 egg yolks
- 2 teaspoons tarragon vinegar
- 1 teaspoon instant minced onion
- ½ teaspoon chervil
  Dash white pepper
- ½ cup butter or margarine
- 1 teaspoon minced parsley

Combine egg yolks, vinegar, onion, chervil, and pepper in blender or food processor container; set aside. Place butter in 1-cup glass measure. Place in oven. Set recipe number 231. Touch START. *(Oven cooks: micro, HI, 1½ minutes.)*

With blender at high speed, gradually add melted butter through cover opening; process until thick and creamy. Stir in parsley. Serve warm over broiled steak, green vegetables, poached eggs, or fish.

½ cup

Recipe No. 233 ⊞

Choco-Peanut Butter Sauce

Preset Cooking Time: 3½ minutes

- ¼ cup milk
- 1 square (1 ounce) unsweetened chocolate
- 1 cup sugar
- 1 tablespoon light corn syrup
- ⅓ cup peanut butter
- ¼ teaspoon vanilla

Place milk and chocolate in 4-cup glass measure. Place in oven. Set recipe number 233. Touch START. *(Oven cooks: micro, HI, 1½ minutes.)*

At Pause, stir until chocolate is melted. Add sugar and corn syrup; blend well. Touch START. *(Oven cooks: micro, HI, 2 minutes.)*

Add peanut butter and vanilla; blend well. Serve hot or chilled over ice cream, cake, or sliced bananas.

1 cup

Recipe No. 232 ⊞

Clarified Butter

Preset Cooking Time: 2½ minutes

- 1 cup butter

Place butter in 2-cup glass measure. Place in oven. Set recipe number 232. Touch START. *(Oven cooks: micro, 20, 2½ minutes.)*

Let stand 3 to 4 minutes. Skim foam from top. Slowly pour off yellow oil. This is the clarified butter. Discard the leftover impurities. Serve as dipping sauce for steamed clams, crab legs, or shrimp.

⅓ cup

⊞ *Recipe can be increased. See "Quantity", page 12.*

Recipe No. | 234 | ⊞

Hollandaise Sauce

Preset Cooking Time: 2 minutes

- ¼ cup butter
- ¼ cup light cream
- 2 egg yolks, well beaten
- 1 tablespoon lemon juice
- ½ teaspoon dry mustard
- ¼ teaspoon salt

Place butter in 4-cup glass measure. Place in oven. Set recipe number 234. Touch START. *(Oven cooks: micro, HI, 1 minute.)*

At Pause, remove from oven. Add remaining ingredients. Beat with electric mixer or wire whisk until smooth. Place in oven. Touch START. *(Oven cooks: micro, 70, 30 seconds.)*

At Pause, beat until blended. Touch START. *(Oven cooks: micro, 70, 15 seconds.)*

At Pause, stir. Touch START. *(Oven cooks: micro, 70, 15 seconds.)*

Beat until smooth. Serve immediately over cooked asparagus or broccoli.

¾ cup

If sauce curdles, beat in 1 teaspoon hot water, and continue beating until smooth.

To reheat Hollandaise Sauce, cook on 20 for 15 to 30 seconds. Stir; let stand 1 minute. Repeat until hot.

Recipe No. | 235 | ⊞

Hot Fudge Sauce

Preset Cooking Time: 5 minutes

- 1 cup sugar
- 2 squares (1 ounce each) unsweetened chocolate
- ⅓ cup milk
- 3 tablespoons light corn syrup
- 1 large egg, well beaten
- 1 teaspoon vanilla

Combine all ingredients except vanilla in 4-cup glass measure; blend well. Place in oven. Set recipe number 235. Touch START. *(Oven cooks: micro, HI, 2 minutes.)*

At Pause, stir until blended. Touch START. *(Oven cooks: micro, 50, 1½ minutes.)*

At Pause, stir. Touch START. *(Oven cooks: micro, 50, 1½ minutes.)*

Blend in vanilla. Briskly stir with wire whisk until clear and shiny. Refrigerate until cool; sauce will thicken as it stands. Serve over ice cream, chocolate cake, fresh fruit, or as a fondue for dipping pound cake or fresh berries.

1 cup

Recipe No. | 236 | ⊞

Lemon Butter Sauce

Preset Cooking Time: 1½ minutes

- ½ cup butter
- 2 tablespoons lemon juice
- ⅛ teaspoon salt
- ⅛ teaspoon white pepper

Combine all ingredients in 2-cup glass measure. Place in oven. Set recipe number 236. Touch START. *(Oven cooks: micro, HI, 1½ minutes.)*

Stir sauce. Serve immediately with seafood, hot green vegetables, or Salmon Ring (page 133).

⅔ cup

Recipe No. ☐ 237 ☐ ⊞

Orange Sauce

Preset Cooking Time: 3 minutes

- ⅔ cup orange juice
- 3 tablespoons fat-free duckling drippings
- 2 tablespoons brown sugar
- 1 tablespoon cornstarch
- 2 teaspoons grated orange peel
- 2 tablespoons orange-flavored liqueur

Combine all ingredients except liqueur in 2-cup glass measure; stir until brown sugar and cornstarch are dissolved. Place in oven. Set recipe number 237. Touch START. *(Oven cooks: micro, HI, 1½ minutes.)*

At Pause, stir. Touch START. *(Oven cooks: micro, HI, 1½ minutes.)*

Stir in liqueur. Serve hot with Roast Duck (page 120).

1¼ cups

Not having duckling? Any poultry drippings will do. Or, simply increase orange juice by 3 tablespoons and use as a dessert sauce.

Recipe No. ☐ 238 ☐

Raspberry Sauce

Preset Cooking Time: 6 minutes

- 1 package (10 ounces) frozen raspberries
- 1 teaspoon cornstarch
- 1 tablespoon water

Place raspberries in 1½-quart microproof bowl. Place in oven. Set recipe number 238. Touch START. *(Oven cooks: micro, HI, 3 minutes.)*

At Pause, remove from oven. Break up raspberries with wooden spoon. Press through sieve, discarding seeds, if desired. Return to bowl. Dissolve cornstarch in water; stir into berries. Place in oven. Touch START. *(Oven cooks: micro, HI, 3 minutes.)*

Stir through several times. Serve over angel food cake or ice cream.

1½ cups

⊞ *Recipe can be increased. See "Quantity", page 12.*

Filet Mignon with Tarragon Sauce (page 180), →
Carrots with Clarified Butter (page 176)

Recipe No. 239 ⊞

Strawberry Sauce

Preset Cooking Time: 4 minutes

- 1 pint strawberries, hulled
- 1 cup water
- ½ cup sugar
- 2 tablespoons cornstarch
- 2 tablespoons butter
- ½ cup lemon juice

Set aside a few of the best strawberries for garnish. Force remaining strawberries through food mill, or purée with blender or food processor. Strain to remove seeds; set purée aside. Combine water, sugar, and cornstarch in 4-cup glass measure; stir until sugar and cornstarch are dissolved. Place in oven. Set recipe number 239. Touch START. *(Oven cooks: micro, HI, 2 minutes.)*

At Pause, stir. Cover. Touch START. *(Oven cooks: micro, HI, 1 minute.)*

At Pause, stir. Cover. Touch START. *(Oven cooks: micro, HI, 1 minute.)*

Add butter; stir until melted. Stir in lemon juice and strawberry purée; blend well. Serve chilled over pound cake, vanilla pudding, custard, or as a parfait sauce.

2½ cups

Recipe No. 240 ⊞

Tarragon Sauce

Preset Cooking Time: 4 minutes

- ½ cup unsalted butter
- ⅓ cup dry white wine
- 2 tablespoons minced fresh tarragon or 2 teaspoons dried tarragon
- 1 tablespoon chopped chives
- 1 tablespoon tarragon vinegar
- ½ teaspoon salt
- ¼ teaspoon pepper
- 3 egg yolks, beaten

Combine all ingredients except egg yolks in 4-cup glass measure; blend well. Place in oven. Set recipe number 240. Touch START. *(Oven cooks: micro, HI, 2 minutes.)*

At Pause, remove from oven. Stir small amount butter mixture into egg yolks; gradually stir yolk mixture into butter mixture. Place in oven. Touch START. *(Oven cooks: micro, 50, 1 minute.)*

At Pause, stir. Touch START. *(Oven cooks: micro, 50, 1 minute.)*

Beat with wire whisk until smooth. Serve immediately with poached eggs, broiled meat, cooked cauliflower, or carrots.

1½ cups

⊞ *Recipe can be increased. See "Quantity", page 12.*

How Sweet It Is!

When the recipe testing for this book began, it began here! The cakes, pies, cookies, candies, and other tempting sweets should capture your delighted interest. And they are all so much fun to make! If you thought candies were too much bother, let the microwave method change your mind: one bowl, no scorching. When you add the convenience provided by automatic, preset control of the power setting and the timing, each recipe will quickly become one of your specialities. The convection method helps you rise to any occasion with an incredible Chocolate Soufflé (page 192), or Pineapple Baked Alaska (page 193). Convection is the choice, too, to keep that cookie jar filled. Finally, the micro/convection method is the wonder that helps you create pies of all kinds. Sweet tooth ready? Go!

Pie shells (Basic Pie Crust, page 184) are prebaked, then filled. During prebaking, the dough is weighted using dried beans in aluminum foil. Pecan Pie (page 186) is just one of the final results possible (above left). Don't forget your conventional cooking knowledge! Test as usual for doneness (above right). Chocolate Chip Cookies (page 192) are baked by the convection method using a cookie sheet on the wire rack, lower guides. The convection method is the only one that permits metal utensils to be used on the wire rack (right).

Converting Your Recipes

The best route to adapting your dessert recipes is to find a recipe here that is similar to the one you want to try. Most puddings can be cooked by either the microwave or micro/convection method. They don't need a water bath and only occasional stirring. Fruit is microwave territory and needs little or no water. It retains its orchard-ripe color and just-picked flavor. Candies convert readily to the microwave method. The only caution is to compare the amount of any water, milk, or juice that might be called for to a recipe in the book. You may need to reduce such liquids a bit because evaporation is such a minimal process in microwave cooking. Some tips:

- ☐ For even cooking, select fruit of uniform size to be cooked whole.
- ☐ Remove baked custards from the oven when centers are nearly firm. They will set as they cool.
- ☐ To avoid lumping, puddings should be stirred once or twice.
- ☐ If you really like to pile on the meringue, you may want to set recipes like Pineapple Baked Alaska (page 193) on the ceramic tray. Always consider closeness to the heat source in determining what cooking level to use.
- ☐ Following the recipe for Chocolate Soufflé (page 192) as a guide, you can create your favorite flavor: strawberry, mint, etc. A few drops of food coloring is in order if, for example, you flavor with extracts instead of liqueurs.
- ☐ You can bake pie shells in metal pie plates. But be sure to carefully transfer to a glass pie plate if the recipe for the pie or quiche requires cooking (even partially) by the microwave or micro/convection method.

GUIDE TO CONVENIENCE DESSERTS*

Food	Programming Method	Setting	Time	Special Notes
Brownies, bar cookies, 12 - 13	micro	30 (defrost)	2 to 3 min.	Original ¾" foil tray, lid removed. Let stand 5 minutes.
Cookies, 16 oz.	convec	350°	10 to 12 min.	Lower guides. Preheat. Cookie sheet or foil tray.
Fruit, frozen, 10 oz.	micro	HI (max. power)	5 to 5½ min.	Slit pouch. On microproof plate. Flex pouch halfway through cooking time to mix.
Fruit turnover, 12½ oz.	convec	follow package directions		Lower guides. Preheat. Metal baking sheet.
Pudding and pie filling mix. 3¼ oz.	micro	HI (max. power)	6½ to 7 min.	Follow package directions. Stir every 3 minutes.
Cake, frozen 2- or 3-layer	micro	30 (defrost)	2½-3 min.	Remove from foil pan to plate. Watch carefully, frosting melts fast. Let stand 5 minutes.
Cheesecake, 17-19 oz.	micro	30 (defrost)	4-5 min.	Remove from foil pan to plate. Let stand 1 minute.
Coffeecake, whole frozen 10-13 oz.	micro	80 (reheat)	1½-2 min.	Place on paper plate or towel.
Cupcakes, crumb cakes, (1 or 2)	micro	30 (defrost)	½-1 min.	Place on shallow microproof plate.
Doughnuts, (4)	micro	80	35-40 sec.	Place on paper plate or towel. Add 15 seconds if frozen.
Fruit pie, 2-crust, 9", 2½-3 lbs	convec	follow package directions		Lower guides. Preheat. Original foil tray. On preheated cookie sheet.
Orange Danish, refrigerated, 11 oz.	convec	follow package directions		Lower guides. Preheat. Cookie sheet or foil tray.
Pound cake, frozen, 10¾ oz.	micro	30 (defrost)	2 min.	Remove from foil pan to plate. Rotate once. Let stand 5 minutes.

* Due to the tremendous variety in convenience food products available, times given here should be used only as guidelines. We suggest you cook food for the shortest recommended time and then check for doneness. Be sure to check the package for microwave and oven (convec) instructions.

COOKING GUIDE — PUDDING AND PIE FILLING MIX

Food	Amount	Time (minutes)	Micro Control	Special Notes
Pudding and pie filling mix	3¼ ounces 5½ ounces	6½ - 7 8 - 10	HI (max. power) HI (max. power)	Follow package directions. Stir every 3 minutes. Use 4-cup glass measure.
Egg custard	3 ounces	8 - 10	70 (roast)	Follow package directions. Stir every 3 minutes. Use 4-cup glass measure.
Tapioca	3¼ ounces	6 - 7	HI (max. power)	Follow package directions. Stir every 3 minutes. Use 4-cup glass measure.

Recipe No. | 241 |

Apple Pie

Preset Cooking Time: 35 minutes

Pastry for Basic Pie Crust
two-crust pie (right)
¾ cup sugar
¼ cup all-purpose flour
¾ teaspoon cinnamon
¼ teaspoon nutmeg
Pinch salt
8 tart medium green apples,
peeled, cored, and thinly
sliced
2 tablespoons butter or margarine
1 egg white, lightly beaten

Bake bottom pie crust according to directions for Basic Pie Crust.

Position wire rack in lower guides of oven. Set recipe number 241. Touch START. *(Oven preheats: convec, 380°F.)* Meanwhile, mix sugar, flour, cinnamon, nutmeg, and salt in large bowl. Add apples and toss until coated. Spoon apples into prebaked crust. Dot with butter. Brush rim of crust with egg white. Roll out uncooked dough to ⅛-inch thickness. Drape over fruit, then gently press edges of pastry together with fork to seal. Cut slits in top crust to allow steam to escape. Brush top with remaining egg white.

At 380°F, place in oven on wire rack. Touch START. *(Oven cooks: micro/convec, 380°F, 15 minutes.)*

At Pause, rotate dish one-half turn. Touch START. *(Oven cooks: micro/convec, 380°F, 20 minutes.)* Let cool 5 to 10 minutes before serving.

8 servings

Recipe No. | 242 |

Basic Pie Crust

Preset Cooking Time: 12 minutes

1 cup flour
½ teaspoon salt
⅓ cup shortening
2 to 3 tablespoons cold water
1 egg white, beaten with 1
teaspoon water

Position wire rack in lower guides of oven. Set recipe number 242. Touch START. *(Oven preheats: convec, 420°F.)* Meanwhile, mix flour and salt in medium bowl. Cut in shortening using pastry blender or 2 knives until mixture resembles coarse meal. Stir in water, 1 tablespoon at a time, until flour is moistened. Shape dough into ball, then flatten on lightly floured surface. Roll dough into circle about ¼-inch thick and 1½ inches larger than 9-inch glass or ceramic pie plate or quiche dish. Fit into pie plate and trim, leaving ½-inch overlap. Turn excess dough under to form rolled rim. Flute edges. Pierce crust with fork. Line with aluminum foil and fill with uncooked rice or dried beans.

At 420°F, place in oven on wire rack. Touch START. *(Oven cooks: convec, 420°F, 6 minutes.)*

At Pause, remove beans and foil. Brush crust with egg white mixture. Place in oven. Touch START. *(Oven cooks: convec, 420°F, 6 minutes.)* Let cool.

1 9-inch pie crust

For two-crust pie or 2 one-crust pie shells: Double each ingredient except egg white. Mix as directed. Divide dough in half. For two shells, prepare and cook separately as directed above. For two-crust pie, roll out one half and cook as directed above. Fill as directed in specific recipe. Roll out second half of dough and finish according to recipe directions.

If you are preparing a pie shell for a pie that is cooked by convection only, or for a pie requiring no cooking once the filling is added, you may use a metal pie plate.

Apple Pie →

Recipe No. [243]

Deep Dish Cranapple Pie

Preset Cooking Time: 35 minutes

- 1¼ cups sugar
- ½ cup all-purpose flour
- 8 to 9 tart green apples, peeled, cored, and sliced
- 2 cups fresh or frozen cranberries
- 2 tablespoons butter or margarine
  Pastry for Basic Pie Crust
  (page 184)
- 1 egg white, mixed with 1 teaspoon water (optional)

Position wire rack in lower guides of oven. Set recipe number 243. Touch START. *(Oven preheats: convec, 380°F.)* Meanwhile, mix sugar and flour in small bowl. Alternate layers of apples, cranberries, and sugar mixture in 8-inch square glass or ceramic baking dish, beginning and ending with apples. Dot with butter. Roll dough out on lightly floured surface into 9-inch square. Fold dough in half. Set over fruit and unfold. Seal to edges of dish. Cut slits in top to allow steam to escape. Brush crust with egg mixture.

At 380°F, place in oven on wire rack. Touch START. *(Oven cooks: micro/convec, 380°F, 15 minutes.)*

At Pause, rotate dish one-half turn. Touch START. *(Oven cooks: micro/convec, 380°F, 20 minutes.)* Serve warm.

8 to 10 servings

Recipe No. [244]

Fresh Pear Pie

Preset Cooking Time: 30 minutes

- Pastry for Basic Pie Crust two-crust pie (page 184)
- ½ cup sugar
- ⅓ cup all-purpose flour
- ½ teaspoon mace
- 9 medium-size firm pears, peeled, cored, and sliced
- 1 tablespoon fresh lemon juice
- 2 tablespoons butter or margarine
- 1 egg white, lightly beaten

Bake bottom pie crust according to directions for Basic Pie Crust on page 184.

Position wire rack in lower guides of oven. Set recipe number 244. Touch START. *(Oven preheats: convec, 380°F.)* Meanwhile, mix sugar, flour, and mace in large bowl. Add pears and toss until coated. Spoon pears into prebaked crust. Sprinkle with lemon juice and dot with butter. Brush rim of crust with some of the egg white. Roll out uncooked dough to thickness of ⅛ inch. Drape over fruit, then gently press edges of pastry together with fork to seal. Cut slits in top crust to allow steam to escape. Brush top with remaining egg white.

At 380°F, place in oven on wire rack. Touch START. *(Oven cooks: micro/convec, 380°F, 15 minutes.)*

At Pause, rotate dish one-half turn. Touch START. *(Oven cooks: micro/convec, 380°F, 15 minutes.)* Let cool 5 to 10 minutes before serving.

6 to 8 servings

Recipe No. [245]

Pecan Pie

Preset Cooking Time: 20 minutes

- ¼ cup butter or margarine, melted
- 3 eggs, well beaten
- 1 cup sugar
- ¾ cup light corn syrup
- 2 cups pecan halves
- 1 teaspoon vanilla
- 1 prebaked Basic Pie Crust (page 184)

Position wire rack in lower guides of oven. Set recipe number 245. Touch START. *(Oven preheats: convec, 350°F.)* Meanwhile, blend melted butter, eggs, sugar, corn syrup, pecan halves, and vanilla in large bowl. Turn mixture into crust.

At 350°F, place in oven on wire rack. Touch START. *(Oven cooks: micro/convec, 350°F, 5 minutes.)*

At Pause, rotate dish one-half turn. Touch START. *(Oven cooks: micro/convec, 350°F, 5 minutes; stands: 0, 10 minutes.)* Serve warm.

8 servings

Recipe No. 246

Perfect Lemon Meringue Pie

Preset Cooking Time: 15 minutes

    1/3 cup cornstarch
    1/2 cup cold water
    1 3/4 cups sugar, divided
    1 cup hot water
    1/4 teaspoon salt
    5 eggs, separated
    2 tablespoons butter or margarine
    1/2 cup fresh lemon juice
    2 tablespoons finely grated
        lemon peel
    1 prebaked Basic Pie Crust
        (page 184)
    1/4 teaspoon cream of tartar
    1/2 teaspoon vanilla

Dissolve cornstarch in cold water in 2-quart microproof bowl. Add 1 1/4 cups sugar, hot water, and salt and blend well. Cover. Place in oven. Set recipe number 12. Touch START. *(Oven cooks: micro, HI, 7 minutes.)*

At Pause, stir through mixture several times. Beat egg yolks in another bowl until thick. Gradually beat into cornstarch mixture. Place in oven. Touch START. *(Oven cooks: micro, HI, 2 minutes.)* Add butter and stir until melted. Blend in lemon juice and peel. Pour into crust. Set aside to cool slightly.

Position wire rack in lower guides of oven. Set recipe number 246. Touch START. *(Oven preheats: convec, 450°F.)* Meanwhile, beat egg whites with cream of tartar in large bowl until foamy. Gradually beat in remaining sugar until whites are stiff and glossy. Blend in vanilla. Spread over cooled filling, sealing to edges.

At 450°F, place in oven on wire rack. Touch START. *(Oven cooks: convec, 450°F, 6 minutes.)* Let cool to room temperature before serving.

6 to 8 servings

This is one of several recipes that use the preset functions of another recipe for part of the cooking sequence. Set recipe number 12 first. At the end of that sequence, set recipe number 246.

Recipe No. 247

Pumpkin Pie

Preset Cooking Time: 35 minutes

    1 1/2 cups canned or cooked
        pumpkin
    1 1/2 cups half-and-half
    1/2 cup firmly-packed brown sugar
    3 eggs, beaten
    1 tablespoon all-purpose flour
    1 teaspoon cinnamon
    1/4 teaspoon ginger
    1/4 teaspoon nutmeg
    1/4 teaspoon salt
    1/8 teaspoon ground cloves
    1 prebaked Basic Pie Crust
        (page 184)

Position wire rack in lower guides of oven. Set recipe number 247. Touch START. *(Oven preheats: convec, 350°F.)* Meanwhile, mix all ingredients except pie shell in large bowl. Pour into pie shell.

At 350°F, place in oven. Touch START. *(Oven cooks: micro/convec, 350°F, 30 minutes; stands: 0, 5 minutes.)*

8 servings

Recipe No. 248

Angel Food Cake

Preset Cooking Time: 30 minutes

    1 package (16 ounces) Angel
        Food Cake mix
        Raspberry Sauce (page 178)

Set recipe number 248. Touch START. *(Oven preheats: convec, 350°F.)* Meanwhile, prepare cake according to package directions. Pour batter into ungreased 10-inch metal tube pan.

At 350°F, place in oven on ceramic tray. Touch START. *(Oven cooks: convec, 350°F, 25 minutes.)*

At Pause, rotate dish one-half turn. Touch START. *(Oven cooks: micro/convec, 350°F, 5 minutes.)* Invert pan onto cooling rack (do not remove pan). Cool completely before removing from pan. Serve with Raspberry Sauce.

10 servings

Recipe No. [249]

Carrot Cake

Preset Cooking Time: 20 minutes

- 1½ cups all-purpose flour
- 2 teaspoons cinnamon
- 1½ teaspoons baking soda
- 1 teaspoon nutmeg
- ½ teaspoon salt
- 3 cups grated carrots
- 1½ cups sugar
- 1 cup vegetable oil
- 1 cup chopped walnuts
- 3 eggs, beaten

Frosting:
- 1 package (8 ounces) cream cheese, softened
- ½ cup butter or margarine, softened
- ¼ cup chopped walnuts
- 2 teaspoons vanilla
- 3 cups confectioners sugar, sifted

Position wire rack in lower guides of oven. Set recipe number 249. Touch START. *(Oven preheats: convec, 350°F.)* Meanwhile, generously grease 10-cup glass or ceramic Bundt-type pan. Sift together flour, cinnamon, baking soda, nutmeg, and salt. Combine carrots, sugar, oil, nuts, and eggs in large bowl. Add dry ingredients and mix thoroughly. Turn into prepared pan.

At 350°F, place in oven on wire rack. Touch START. *(Oven cooks: micro/convec, 350°F, 15 minutes.)*

At Pause, rotate dish one-half turn. Touch START. *(Oven cooks: micro/convec, 350°F, 5 minutes.)* Let cool in pan in oven.

Invert cake onto serving platter. Beat cream cheese and butter in large bowl. Add nuts and vanilla and blend well. Gradually beat in sugar. Frost cake. Sprinkle with additional chopped walnuts, if desired.

8 to 10 servings

Recipe No. [250]

Lemon Chiffon Cake

Preset Cooking Time: 40 minutes

- 2 cups all-purpose flour
- 1½ cups sugar
- 1 tablespoon baking powder
- ½ teaspoon salt
- ½ cup vegetable oil
- ½ cup cold water
- ¼ cup fresh lemon juice
- 6 egg yolks
- 2 tablespoons grated lemon peel, divided
- 9 egg whites
- ½ teaspoon cream of tartar
  Snow White Frosting (page 200)

Set recipe number 250. Touch START. *(Oven preheats: convec, 350°F.)* Meanwhile, mix flour, sugar, baking powder, and salt in large bowl. Make well in center. Add oil, water, lemon juice, egg yolks, and all but ½ teaspoon lemon peel to well and stir until smooth. Beat egg whites in another bowl until foamy. Add cream of tartar and continue beating until stiff peaks form. Stir ¼ of egg yolk mixture into whites. Gently fold in remaining egg yolk mixture, blending thoroughly. Turn into ungreased 10-inch metal tube pan.

At 350°F, place in oven on ceramic tray. Touch START. *(Oven cooks: convec, 350°F, 30 minutes; micro/convec, 350°F, 5 minutes; stands: 0, 5 minutes.)*

Invert cake onto rack and let cool completely. Frost with Snow White Frosting. Sprinkle with ½ teaspoon lemon peel.

8 servings

← Party Cake, variation (page 190),
Pecan Pie (page 186)

Recipe No. | 251 |

Party Cake

Preset Cooking Time: 36 minutes

 2   cups all-purpose flour
1¼ cups sugar
3½ teaspoons baking powder
 1   teaspoon salt
 ¼   cup butter or margarine,
       softened
 ¼   cup shortening
 1   cup milk
1½ teaspoons vanilla
 3   eggs

Frosting:
 ⅓   cup butter or margarine,
       softened
 3   cups confectioners sugar
 2   tablespoons milk
 1   tablespoon maraschino cherry
       juice
 1   teaspoon vanilla
 5   drops red food color
 8   maraschino cherries, drained
       and chopped

Position wire rack in lower guides of oven. Set recipe number 251. Touch START. *(Oven preheats: convec, 350°F.)* Meanwhile, grease and flour 9 × 13-inch glass or ceramic baking dish. Mix flour, sugar, baking powder, and salt in large bowl. Add all remaining ingredients except frosting and beat well. Pour into prepared dish.

At 350°F, place in oven. Touch START. *(Oven cooks: convec, 350°F, 25 minutes; micro/convec, 350°F, 6 minutes; stands: 0, 5 minutes.)* Remove from oven and let cool.

Cream butter with sugar. Add milk, cherry juice, vanilla, and food color and mix until smooth. Stir in chopped cherries. Spread frosting over top of cake. Cut into squares and serve.

16 to 20 servings

Recipe No. | 252 |

Pineapple Praline Upside-Down Cake

Preset Cooking Time: 30 minutes

 ¼   cup butter or margarine,
       melted
 ½   cup firmly-packed brown sugar
 6   slices canned pineapple,
       well drained
 ¼   cup pecan halves
 6   maraschino cherries
1¼ cups all-purpose flour
 1   cup sugar
 1   teaspoon baking powder
 ¾   cup milk
 ⅓   cup butter or margarine, melted
 1   egg, lightly beaten
 1   teaspoon vanilla

Position wire rack in lower guides of oven. Set recipe number 252. Touch START. *(Oven preheats: convec, 350°F.)* Meanwhile, pour ¼ cup melted butter into 9-inch round glass or ceramic dish. Add brown sugar, spreading evenly over bottom. Place 1 pineapple slice in center. Surround with remaining slices. Arrange pecans around pineapple, rounded side down. Put cherry in center of each pineapple slice. Set aside.

Mix dry ingredients in large bowl. Combine milk, ⅓ cup melted butter, egg, and vanilla in another bowl. Add to flour mixture, blending thoroughly. Carefully pour batter into dish.

At 350°F, place in oven on wire rack. Touch START. *(Oven cooks: convec, 350°F, 20 minutes.)*

At Pause, rotate dish one-half turn. Touch START. *(Oven cooks: micro/convec, 350°F, 10 minutes.)* Let stand in oven 5 minutes. Remove from oven and let cool. Invert onto platter. Cut into wedges and serve.

8 servings

Lemon Pineapple Creme (page 198), Baked Maple Bananas (page 195) →

Recipe No. 253

Chocolate Chip Cookies

Preset Cooking Time: 12 minutes
(repeat)

- 1 cup butter or margarine, softened
- ¾ cup sugar
- ¾ cup firmly-packed brown sugar
- 2 eggs
- 1½ teaspoon vanilla
- 2½ cups all-purpose flour
- 2 cups semi-sweet chocolate pieces
- 1 cup chopped walnuts
- 1 teaspoon baking soda
- 1 teaspoon salt

Position wire rack in lower guides of oven. Set recipe number 253. Touch START. *(Oven preheats: convec, 370°F.)* Meanwhile, beat butter, sugars, eggs, and vanilla in large bowl. Stir in remaining ingredients. Drop dough by rounded tablespoons onto ungreased baking sheet.

At 370°F, place in oven. Touch START. *(Oven cooks: convec, 370°F, 12 minutes.)* Transfer to wire rack to cool. Repeat with remaining dough, setting recipe number 253 and touching START each time. Store cookies in airtight container.

about 4 dozen

Recipe No. 254

Peanut Butter Cookies

Preset Cooking Time: 14 minutes
(repeat once)

- 1 cup natural-style crunchy peanut butter
- ½ cup butter or margarine, softened
- ½ cup firmly-packed brown sugar
- ½ cup sugar
- 1 egg, beaten
- 1 teaspoon vanilla
- 1½ cups all-purpose flour
- ¾ teaspoon baking soda
- ¼ teaspoon salt

Position wire rack in lower guides of oven. Set recipe number 254. Touch START. *(Oven preheats: convec, 350°F.)* Lightly grease aluminum or metal baking sheet.

Combine peanut butter, butter, sugars, egg, and vanilla in large bowl and beat until smooth. Blend in flour, baking soda, and salt. Shape dough into thirty 1-inch balls. Arrange 15 on prepared sheet, spacing 3 inches apart. Flatten into 2-inch rounds using fork in crisscross pattern.

At 350°F, place in oven on wire rack. Touch START. *(Oven cooks: convec, 350°F, 14 minutes.)* Transfer to wire rack to cool. Repeat with remaining dough, setting recipe number 254 and touching START again. Store cookies in airtight container.

30 cookies

Recipe No. 255

Chocolate Soufflé

Preset Cooking Time: 1 hour 14 minutes

- 2 teaspoons butter
- 3 tablespoons confectioners sugar, sifted
- 1 cup milk
- ½ cup sugar
- 2 tablespoons cornstarch
- 2 squares (1 ounce each) unsweetened chocolate
- ¼ cup semi sweet chocolate pieces
- 3 tablespoons butter or margarine
- 1 teaspoon vanilla
- 5 egg yolks
- 8 egg whites (1⅓ cups)
- 1 teaspoon cream of tartar
- 1 tablespoon confectioners sugar

Coat bottom and sides of 2-quart soufflé dish with 2 teaspoons butter. Sprinkle with 3 tablespoons confectioners sugar, rotating dish to cover evenly and letting excess sugar remain in bottom. Refrigerate.

Combine milk, sugar, cornstarch, and chocolate in microproof bowl. Place in oven. Set recipe number 230. Touch START. *(Oven cooks: micro, HI, 1½ minutes.)*

At Pause, stir. Touch START. *(Oven cooks: micro, HI, 1½ minutes.)*

At Pause, stir again. Touch START. *(Oven cooks: micro, HI, 1 minute.)* Add 3 tablespoons butter and vanilla to chocolate mixture and blend thoroughly. Beat egg yolks in another bowl until pale yellow. Gradually beat into chocolate mixture. Let cool to room temperature.

Set recipe number 255. Touch START. *(Oven preheats: convec, 450°F.)* Meanwhile, beat egg whites in separate bowl with electric mixer until foamy. Add cream of tartar and continue beating until stiff peaks form. Fold in 1 tablespoon confectioners sugar. Stir $\frac{1}{3}$ of whites into chocolate mixture. Gently fold in remaining whites. Turn into chilled dish, reaching edges, without handling inside of coated dish.

At 450°F, place in oven on ceramic tray. Touch START. *(Oven cooks: convec, 330°F, 70 minutes.)* Serve immediately.

6 to 8 servings

This is one of several recipes that use the preset functions of another recipe for part of the cooking sequence. Set recipe number 230 first. At the end of that sequence, set recipe number 255.

Recipe No. 256

Pineapple Baked Alaska

Preset Cooking Time: 5 minutes

- 1 small-to-medium pineapple
- 4 scoops ice cream
- 8 maraschino cherries
- $\frac{1}{2}$ cup chopped nuts
- 4 egg whites
- $\frac{1}{3}$ cup sugar
- $\frac{1}{4}$ teaspoon cream of tartar

Cut pineapple in half lengthwise. Carefully hollow out pulp, leaving thick shell. Pour off juice. Cut pulp into bite-size chunks. Fill shell with ice cream, pineapple chunks, cherries, and nuts. Freeze until solid.

Just before serving, position wire rack in lower guides of oven. Set recipe number 256. Touch START *(Oven preheats: convec, 430°F.)* Meanwhile, beat egg whites until soft peaks form. Gradually add sugar and cream of tartar, beating constantly until whites are stiff and glossy. Spread over pineapple filling, covering completely and sealing meringue to edges. Set shell on heatproof plate or oval baking dish.

At 430°F, place in oven on wire rack. Touch START. *(Oven cooks: convec, 430°F, 5 minutes.)* Serve immediately.

4 to 6 servings

Recipe No. 257 ⊞

Creme Caramel

Preset Cooking Time: 17 minutes

- $\frac{2}{3}$ cup sugar, divided
- 2 tablespoons water
- 2 cups milk
- 3 eggs
- 3 egg yolks
- 1 teaspoon vanilla

Mix $\frac{1}{3}$ cup sugar and water in $1\frac{1}{2}$-quart glass or ceramic brioche dish or fluted dish. Place in oven. Set recipe number 273. Touch START. *(Oven cooks: micro, HI, 4 minutes.)*

At Pause, carefully tilt dish to coat bottom and sides evenly. Set aside. Place milk in 1-quart glass measure. Place in oven. Touch START. *(Oven cooks: micro, HI, 3 minutes.)* Meanwhile, beat eggs, egg yolks, remaining sugar, and vanilla in 2-quart bowl. Remove milk from oven and slowly pour into egg mixture, beating constantly until smooth. Pour into caramelized dish. Set aside.

Position wire rack in lower guides of oven. Set recipe number 257. Touch START. *(Oven preheats: convec, 350°F.)*

At 350°F, place in oven on wire rack. Touch START. *(Oven cooks: micro/convec, 350°F, 10 minutes.)* Remove from oven and let cool completely. To serve, run knife along edge of custard, then invert onto small platter to unmold.

6 to 8 servings

This is one of several recipes that use the preset functions of another recipe for part of the cooking sequence. Set recipe number 273 first. At the end of that sequence, set recipe number 257.

⊞ *Recipe can be increased. See "Quantity", page 12.*

Recipe No. 258 ⊞

Almond Bark

Preset Cooking Time: 7½ minutes

- 1 cup whole blanched almonds
- 1 teaspoon butter or margarine
- 1 pound white chocolate

Line large baking sheet with waxed paper; set aside. Place almonds and butter in 9-inch glass pie plate. Place in oven. Set recipe number 258. Touch START. *(Oven cooks: micro, HI, 2½ minutes.)*

At Pause, stir. Touch START. *(Oven cooks: micro, HI, 2 minutes.)*

At Pause, remove from oven; set aside. Place chocolate in large microproof bowl. Place in oven. Touch START. *(Oven cooks: micro, HI, 3 minutes.)*

Stir almonds into chocolate. Pour onto prepared baking sheet. Spread to desired thickness. Refrigerate until set. Break into pieces, and store in airtight container.

1½ pounds

Recipe No. 260 ⊞

Baked Apples

Preset Cooking Time: 8 minutes

- 2 baking apples (1 pound)
  Lemon juice
- 2 teaspoons slivered almonds
- 2 teaspoons raisins
- 2 teaspoons brown sugar
- ¼ teaspoon cinnamon
- 4 tablespoons water
- 2 teaspoons butter or margarine

Core apples, starting from tops, without cutting all the way through. Remove a thin circle of peel around tops. Sprinkle with lemon juice. Combine almonds, raisins, brown sugar, and cinnamon; mix lightly. Fill apples with mixture. Place each apple in microproof custard cup. Add 2 tablespoons water to each cup. Dot each apple with 1 teaspoon butter. Place in oven. Cover with waxed paper. Set recipe number 260. Touch START. *(Oven cooks: micro, HI, 5 minutes; stands: 0, 3 minutes.)*

2 servings

Recipe No. 259

Applesauce

Preset Cooking Time: 12 minutes

- 6 cups sliced peeled cooking apples
- ½ cup water
- 1 tablespoon lemon juice
- ¼ cup sugar
- ½ teaspoon cinnamon or nutmeg

Place apples, water, and lemon juice in 2-quart microproof casserole. Cover and place in oven. Set recipe number 259. Touch START. *(Oven cooks: micro, HI, 6 minutes.)*

At Pause, stir. Touch START. *(Oven cooks: micro, HI, 6 minutes.)*

Stir in sugar and cinnamon. Serve warm or chilled with pork or as a light dessert.

4 to 6 servings

⊞ *Recipe can be increased. See "Quantity", page 12.*

Recipe No. 261

Baked Maple Bananas

Preset Cooking Time: 4½ minutes

- 2 tablespoons butter or margarine
- 3 tablespoons maple syrup
- 4 bananas, cut in half crosswise
  and then lengthwise
- 1 tablespoon lemon juice
- ¼ teaspoon cinnamon (optional)

Place butter in shallow microproof baking dish. Place in oven. Set recipe number 261. Touch START. *(Oven cooks: micro, HI, 1 minute.)*

At Pause, add maple syrup; blend well. Add bananas. Spoon butter mixture over bananas. Touch START. *(Oven cooks: micro, HI, 1½ minutes.)*

At Pause, turn bananas over. Touch START. *(Oven cooks: micro, HI, 2 minutes.)*

Sprinkle with lemon juice and cinnamon. Serve warm.

4 servings

You can also cook whole bananas and cut into serving portions at the table.

Recipe No. 262

Brownie Mix

Preset Cooking Time: 17 minutes

- 1 package (16 ounces) brownie mix
- 1 tablespoon confectioners sugar

Position wire rack in lower guides of oven. Set recipe number 262. Touch START. *(Oven preheats: convec, 380°F.)* Meanwhile, butter 8-inch glass pie plate and set aside. Prepare brownie mix according to package directions. Pour into prepared pie plate.

At 380°F, place in oven on wire rack. Touch START. *(Oven cooks: convec, 380°F, 15 minutes.)*

At Pause, rotate pie plate one-half turn. Touch START. *(Oven cooks: micro/convec, 380°F, 2 minutes.)*

Dust with confectioners sugar, cut into squares, and serve.

16 brownies

Recipe No. 263

Cake Mix

Preset Cooking Time: 23 minutes

- 1 package (9 ounces) single-layer
  cake mix
  Confectioners sugar

Position wire rack in lower guides of oven. Set recipe number 263. Touch START. *(Oven preheats: convec, 380°F.)* Meanwhile, line bottom of 9-inch round microproof baking dish with waxed paper; set aside. Prepare cake mix according to package directions. Pour into prepared dish.

At 380°F, place in oven on wire rack. Touch START. *(Oven cooks: convec, 380°F, 20 minutes.)*

At Pause, rotate dish one-half turn. Touch START. *(Oven cooks: micro/convec, 380°F, 3 minutes.)*

Let cool in pan 3 to 5 minutes. Invert cake onto platter. Remove waxed paper. Dust cake with confectioners sugar before serving.

1 layer

Recipe No. 264

Chocolate Fudge Frosting

Preset Cooking Time: 3 minutes

- 1 square (1 ounce) unsweetened
  chocolate
- 1 cup sugar
- ⅓ cup milk
- ¼ cup butter or margarine
- ⅛ teaspoon salt
- 1 teaspoon vanilla
- ¼ cup chopped nuts

Combine chocolate, sugar, milk, butter, and salt in 4-cup glass measure. Place in oven. Set recipe number 264. Touch START. *(Oven cooks: micro, HI, 1½ minutes.)*

At Pause, stir. Touch START. *(Oven cooks: micro, HI, 1½ minutes.)*

Add vanilla; beat with electric mixer until almost cool. Add nuts; beat until mixture is spreading consistency.

1 cup

Recipe No. | 265 |

Chocolate Cherry Bundt Cake

Preset Cooking Time: 23 minutes

    1 tablespoon sugar
    1 package (18 ounces)
        chocolate cake mix
        with pudding
    1 cup cherry pie filling
    3 eggs
    ¾ cup water
    ¼ cup vegetable oil
    1 teaspoon almond extract

Generously grease 12-cup microproof Bundt-type pan; chill. Sprinkle pan with 1 tablespoon sugar and shake well to coat. Mix remaining ingredients. Carefully pour into prepared pan. Place in oven. Set recipe number 265. Touch START. *(Oven cooks: micro, 70, 7 minutes.)*

At Pause, rotate pan one-half turn. Touch START. *(Oven cooks: micro, 70, 6 minutes; stands: 0, 10 minutes.)* Invert onto serving platter and let cool completely.

10 to 12 servings

Recipe No. | 266 |

Cranapple Jelly

Preset Cooking Time: 24 minutes

    4 cups cranapple juice
    1 package (1¾ ounces) powdered
        fruit pectin
    4 cups sugar

Combine juice and pectin in 4-quart microproof casserole. Cover and place in oven. Set recipe number 266. Touch START. *(Oven cooks: micro, HI, 7 minutes.)*

At Pause, stir. Cover. Touch START. *(Oven cooks: micro, HI, 5 minutes.)*

At Pause, add sugar; blend well. Do not cover. Touch START. *(Oven cooks: micro, HI, 12 minutes.)*

Skim foam with metal spoon. Pour into hot sterilized jars, and seal.

6 cups

Recipe No. | 267 |

Blueberry Pie

Preset Cooking Time: 15 minutes

    4 to 4½ cups frozen blueberries,
        defrosted and drained
    1 teaspoon grated lemon peel
    ¾ cup sugar
    3 tablespoons cornstarch
    1 prebaked Basic Pie Crust
        (page 184), for single
        crust pie
    1 tablespoon lemon juice

Toss blueberries with grated lemon peel. Mix sugar and cornstarch. Sprinkle over blueberries and toss thoroughly. Spoon mixture into crust. Sprinkle with lemon juice.

Set recipe number 267. Touch START. *(Oven preheats: convec, 350°F.)*

At Pause, place pie in oven. Touch START. *(Oven cooks: micro/convec, 350°F, 10 minutes.)*

At Pause, rotate dish one-half turn. Touch START. *(Oven cooks: micro/convec, 350°F, 5 minutes.)*

Remove pie from oven. Let cool 15 minutes before serving.

8 servings

Frozen pie crusts can be used. Timing will be the same.

If using fresh blueberries, reduce cornstarch to 2 tablespoons.

Chocolate Cherry Bundt Cake →

Recipe No. | 268 |

Fluffy Tapioca

Preset Cooking Time: 16 minutes

- 2 cups milk
- 3 tablespoons quick-cooking tapioca
- 5 tablespoons sugar, divided
- 1 large egg, separated
- ⅛ teaspoon salt
- 1 teaspoon vanilla
     Apricot Dessert Sauce (page 174)

Combine milk, tapioca, 3 tablespoons sugar, egg yolk, and salt in 2-quart micro-proof casserole; blend well. Place in oven. Set recipe number 268. Touch START. *(Oven stands: 0, 5 minutes; cooks: micro, HI, 6 minutes.)*
    At Pause, beat with wire whisk until well blended. Touch START. *(Oven cooks: micro, 70, 5 minutes.)*
    Meanwhile, beat egg white in small mixing bowl with electric mixer until foamy. Gradually beat in remaining 2 tablespoons sugar until soft peaks form.
    Stir vanilla into tapioca. Fold egg whites into tapioca a little at a time until just blended. Serve topped with Apricot Dessert Sauce.

5 servings

Recipe No. | 269 |

Golden Apple Chunks

Preset Cooking Time: 8 minutes

- 4 medium cooking apples, peeled, cored, and cut into quarters
- ¼ cup firmly-packed brown sugar
- 1 teaspoon cinnamon
- 2 tablespoons butter or margarine

Place apples in 1-quart microproof casserole. Combine brown sugar and cinnamon; sprinkle over apples. Dot with butter. Cover and place in oven. Set recipe number 269. Touch START. *(Oven cooks: micro, HI, 4 minutes.)*
    At Pause, stir. Touch START. *(Oven cooks: micro, HI, 4 minutes.)*

4 servings

⊞ *Recipe can be increased. See "Quantity", page 12.*

Recipe No. | 270 |

Lemon Pineapple Crème

Preset Cooking Time: 6 minutes

- 1 can (8 ounces) crushed pineapple
- ¾ cup sugar, divided
- ⅔ cup water
- 3 tablespoons cornstarch
- 2 large eggs, separated
- 1 package (3 ounces) cream cheese, cut into cubes
- 2 tablespoons lemon juice
- 1 teaspoon grated lemon peel

Combine pineapple, ½ cup sugar, water, and cornstarch in 4-cup glass measure; stir until cornstarch is dissolved. Place in oven. Set recipe number 270. Touch START. *(Oven cooks: micro, HI, 2½ minutes.)*
    At Pause, stir. Touch START. *(Oven cooks: micro, HI, 2½ minutes.)*
    At Pause, beat egg yolks in small mixing bowl with electric mixer until lemon-colored. Stir into pineapple mixture; stir in cream cheese, lemon juice, and lemon peel. Touch START. *(Oven cooks: micro, 80, 1 minute.)*
    Beat with electric mixer until blended. Let stand until cool. Beat egg whites in small bowl until frothy. Gradually beat in remaining ¼ cup sugar until soft peaks form. Fold into pudding. Spoon into individual dessert dishes, and chill before serving.

5 to 6 servings

Recipe No. | 271 |

Peanut Brittle

Preset Cooking Time: 10 minutes

- 1 cup sugar
- ½ cup corn syrup
- 1¾ to 2 cups unsalted dry-roasted peanuts
- 1 teaspoon butter or margarine
- 1 teaspoon vanilla
- 1 teaspoon baking soda

Generously grease large baking sheet; set aside. Combine sugar and corn syrup in 2-quart glass measure. Place in oven. Set recipe number 271. Touch START. *(Oven cooks: micro, HI, 4 minutes.)*
    At Pause, stir in peanuts with wooden spoon. Touch START. *(Oven cooks: micro, HI, 4 minutes.)*

At Pause, stir in butter and vanilla. Touch START. *(Oven cooks: micro, HI, 2 minutes.)*

Add baking soda; stir until light and foamy. Pour onto prepared baking sheet; spread quickly to edges using back of wooden spoon. As candy cools, stretch into thin sheet using palms of hands. Cool completely before breaking into pieces. Store in airtight container in cool place.

1 pound

Recipe No. 272

Peanut Crispy Bars

Preset Cooking Time: 3½ minutes

- ¼ cup butter or margarine
- 5 cups miniature or 40 regular marshmallows
- ⅓ cup peanut butter
- 5 cups crispy rice cereal
- 1 cup unsalted dry-roasted peanuts, chopped

Lightly grease 12 × 7-inch baking dish; set aside. Place butter in 3-quart microproof bowl. Place in oven. Set recipe number 272. Touch START. *(Oven cooks: micro, HI, 1 minute.)*

At Pause, add marshmallows. Cover. Touch START. *(Oven cooks: micro, HI, 2½ minutes.)*

Add peanut butter; stir until smooth. Stir in cereal and peanuts. Press warm mixture into prepared baking dish. Cool before cutting into bars.

36 bars

Recipe No. 273 ⊞

Pudding Mix

Preset Cooking Time: 7 minutes

- 1 package (3¼ ounces) pudding and pie filling mix
- 2 cups milk

Place pudding mix in 2-quart microproof bowl. Stir in milk. Place in oven. Set recipe number 273. Touch START. *(Oven cooks: micro, HI, 4 minutes.)*

At Pause, stir. Touch START. *(Oven cooks: micro, HI, 3 minutes.)*

Pour into individual dessert dishes, and chill before serving.

4 servings

Recipe No. 274

Raisin Bread Pudding

Preset Cooking Time: 20½ minutes

- 4 slices raisin bread, cut into cubes (about 4 cups)
- ¼ cup raisins
- 3 large eggs
- ½ cup firmly-packed brown sugar
- 1 teaspoon vanilla
    Dash salt
- 2 cups milk
- 2 tablespoons butter or margarine
    Cinnamon or nutmeg

Combine bread and raisins in 2-quart round microproof baking dish; set aside. Combine eggs, brown sugar, vanilla, and salt; beat until well blended; set aside. Combine milk and butter in 2-quart glass measure. Place in oven. Set recipe number 274. Touch START. *(Oven cooks: micro, HI, 4½ minutes.)*

At Pause, remove from oven. Gradually stir egg mixture into milk mixture. Pour over bread and raisins. Sprinkle with cinnamon. Place in oven. Cover with waxed paper. Touch START. *(Oven cooks: micro, 50, 16 minutes.)*

Center may be slightly soft but will set as pudding cools. Serve warm or chilled.

6 servings

Recipe No. 275

Rich Chocolate Fudge

Preset Cooking Time: 20 minutes

- 4 cups sugar
- 1 can (13 ounces) evaporated milk, undiluted
- 1 cup butter or margarine
- 1 package (12 ounces) semisweet chocolate pieces
- 1 jar (7 ounces) marshmallow creme
- 1 cup chopped nuts
- 1 teaspoon vanilla

Butter 9-inch square or 12×7-inch baking dish; set aside. Combine sugar, milk, and butter in 4-quart microproof bowl. Place in oven. Set recipe number 275. Touch START. *(Oven cooks: micro, HI, 10 minutes.)*

At Pause, stir. Touch START. *(Oven cooks: micro, HI, 10 minutes.)*

Stir in chocolate and marshmallow creme; blend well. Stir in nuts and vanilla. Pour into prepared dish. Cool before cutting into squares.

48 squares

Recipe No. 276

Rocky Road Candy

Preset Cooking Time: 5 minutes

- 1 package (12 ounces) semisweet chocolate pieces
- 1 package (12 ounces) butterscotch pieces
- ½ cup butter
- 1 package (10½ ounces) miniature marshmallows
- 1 cup chopped nuts

Butter 13×9-inch baking dish; set aside. Combine chocolate, butterscotch, and ½ cup butter in 4-quart microproof bowl. Place in oven. Set recipe number 276. Touch START. *(Oven cooks: micro, 70, 5 minutes.)*

Stir until blended. Stir in marshmallows and nuts. Pour into prepared dish and spread evenly. Refrigerate 2 hours, or until set before cutting into squares.

45 squares

Recipe No. 277

Snow White Frosting

Preset Cooking Time: about 5 minutes

- 1 cup sugar
- ½ cup water
- ¼ teaspoon cream of tartar
  Dash salt
- 2 egg whites
- 1 teaspoon vanilla

Combine sugar, water, cream of tartar, and salt in 2-cup glass measure. Place in oven. Insert temperature probe and plug probe in. Set recipe number 277. Touch START. *(Oven cooks: micro, 70, to 200°F; holds warm: 1.)*

Beat egg whites in small mixing bowl with electric mixer until soft peaks form. Gradually beat hot syrup into egg whites. Beat in vanilla. Beat 5 minutes, or until thick and fluffy.

1½ to 2 cups

Recipe No. 278

Rhubarb Cobbler

Preset Cooking Time: 18 minutes

- 1 can (16 ounces) rhubarb in extra heavy syrup
- 1 tablespoon cornstarch
- 2 cups yellow cake mix
- ½ cup coarsely chopped walnuts or pecans
- ¼ cup butter, melted
- 1 teaspoon cinnamon
- 1 container (9 ounces) frozen whipped topping

Set recipe number 278. Touch START. *(Oven preheats: convec, 350°F.)* Meanwhile, mix ¼ cup rhubarb syrup with cornstarch in large bowl, stirring until cornstarch is completely dissolved. Add rhubarb and remaining syrup and blend well. Pour into 9-inch glass or ceramic pie plate. Set aside.

Combine cake mix, nuts, butter, and cinnamon in another bowl. Sprinkle evenly over rhubarb mixture.

At Pause, place in oven. Touch START. *(Oven cooks: micro/convec, 350°F, 13 minutes.)*

At Pause, rotate dish one-half turn. Touch START. *(Oven cooks: micro/convec, 350°F, 5 minutes.)* Let stand 10 minutes. Remove from oven and let cool. Garnish with whipped topping and serve.

6 servings

From Freezer to Table — Fast!

One of the great attractions of the microwave method is its ability to defrost raw food or heat frozen cooked food. Detailed Defrosting Guides are provided at the beginning of the recipe chapters, in general, to aid your preparation of the food included in those recipes. Here, as a special convenience, many common and frequently used items that have been included among the 300 preset recipes are presented for you. We've also included some basic information about microwave defrosting. You'll also want to spend more time studying the special Programmed Defrost method and instructions on using the temperature probe spacer in your Use & Care Manual. Many of the same principles and techniques that apply to microwave cooking also apply to microwave defrosting and heating. Microwaves are attracted to water or moisture molecules. As soon as microwaves have thawed a portion of the item, they are more attracted to the thawed portion. The frozen portion continues to thaw, but

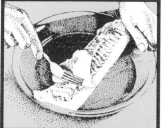

Large items, such as turkey, are turned over to promote even defrosting (above left). Thawed portions of ground beef (above) are removed from the oven so cooking does not start. Fish fillets (far left) are separated as soon as possible. Most food is defrosted in its original frozen package (left).

this is due to the warmth produced in the thawed portion. Special techniques, such as shielding and rotating, are helpful to be sure the thawed portion does not cook before the rest defrosts. It is often necessary to turn, stir, and separate to assist the defrosting process. Defrosting requires standing time to complete. Because food differs in size, weight, and density, recommended defrosting times can only be approximate. Additional standing time may be necessary to defrost completely. Read the Defrosting Guides throughout the book for times, temperature, and special instructions about defrosting specific foods. Here are some tips to aid you toward fast and easy defrosting.

☐ Poultry, seafood, fish, meat, and most vegetables may begin defrosting in their original closed packages. Remove wrappings as soon as possible and place food on microproof plate. You may leave metal clips in poultry during defrosting, but you should remove them as soon as possible before cooking.

☐ Plastic-wrapped packages from the supermarket meat department may not be wrapped with a plastic wrap recommended for microwave use. If in doubt, unwrap package and place food on a microproof plate.

☐ Poultry wings, legs, and the small or bony ends of meat or fish may need to be covered with pieces of aluminum foil for part of the thawing time to prevent cooking while the remainder thaws.

☐ Large items should be turned and rotated halfway through defrosting time to provide more even thawing.

☐ Food textures influence thawing time. Because of air space, porous foods like cake and bread defrost more quickly than a solid mass, such as a sauce, or roast.

☐ Do not thaw food wrapped in aluminum or in foil dishes except as approved, page 17.

☐ The edges will begin cooking if meat, fish, and seafood are completely thawed in the microwave oven. Therefore, food should still be icy in the center when removed from oven. It will finish thawing while standing.

☐ Remove portions of ground meat as soon as thawed, returning frozen portions to the oven.

☐ To thaw half of a frozen vegetable package, wrap half the package with aluminum foil. When unwrapped side is thawed, separate and return balance to freezer.

☐ Thin or sliced items, such as fish fillets, meat patties, etc., should be separated as soon as possible. Remove thawed pieces and allow others to continue thawing.

☐ Casseroles, saucy foods, vegetables, and soups should be stirred once or twice during defrosting to redistribute heat.

☐ Frozen fried foods may be defrosted but will not be crisp when heated in the microwave oven.

☐ Freezing tips: It is helpful to freeze in small quantities rather than in one large piece. When freezing casseroles, it's a good idea to insert an empty paper cup in the center so no food is present there. This speeds thawing. Depressing the center of ground meat when freezing also hastens thawing later. Take care to wrap and package food well to retain its original quality. The wrapped food should be air-free, with air-tight seals. Store at 0°F. or less for no longer than the times recommended for freezing.

Recipe No. [279]

Ground Beef

Preset Defrost Time: 12 minutes

1 pound frozen lean ground
beef

Remove any metal rings, wire twist ties, or foil wrapping from package. Place beef in package in microproof baking dish. Place in oven. Set recipe number 279. Touch START. *(Oven defrosts: micro, 30, 3 minutes.)*

At Pause, turn meat over. Remove thawed portions from oven. Touch START. *(Oven defrosts: micro, 30, 4 minutes; stands: 0, 5 minutes.)*

Recipe No. [280] ⊞

Rolled Rib Roast

Preset Defrost Time: 28 minutes

1 frozen rolled rib roast
(3 pounds)

Remove any metal rings, wire twist ties, or foil wrapping from package. Place roast in package in microproof baking dish. Place in oven. Set recipe number 280. Touch START. *(Oven defrosts: micro, 30, 10 minutes.)*

At Pause, turn over. Touch START. *(Oven defrosts: micro, 30, 8 minutes; stands: 0, 10 minutes.)*

It may be necessary to let roast stand additional time if still slightly frozen in center.

Recipe No. [281] ⊞

Steaks

Preset Defrost Time: 18 minutes

1 frozen steak (2 pounds)

Remove any metal rings, wire twist ties, or foil wrapping from package. Place steak in package in microproof baking dish. Place in oven. Set recipe number 281. Touch START. *(Oven defrosts: micro, 30, 4 minutes.)*

At Pause, turn over. Touch START. *(Oven defrosts: micro, 30, 4 minutes; stands: 0, 10 minutes.)*

Recipe No. [282] ⊞

Stew Beef

Preset Defrost Time: 20 minutes

2 pounds frozen beef for stew

Remove any metal rings, wire twist ties, or foil wrapping from package. Place beef in package in microproof baking dish. Place in oven. Set recipe number 282. Touch START. *(Oven defrosts: micro, 30, 5 minutes.)*

At Pause, turn beef over and separate into pieces. Touch START. *(Oven defrosts: micro, 30, 5 minutes; stands: 0, 10 minutes.)*

Recipe No. [283]

Pork Chops

Preset Defrost Time: 15 minutes

2 pounds frozen pork chops,
½ inch thick

Remove any metal rings, wire twist ties, or foil wrapping from package. Place chops in package in microproof baking dish. Place in oven. Set recipe number 283. Touch START. *(Oven defrosts: micro, 30, 2 minutes.)*

At Pause, turn chops over and separate. Touch START. *(Oven defrosts: micro, 30, 3 minutes; stands: 0, 10 minutes.)*

⊞ *Recipe can be increased. See "Quantity", page 12.*

Recipe No. | 284 |

Cut-Up Chicken

Preset Defrost Time: 22 minutes

2 pounds frozen chicken parts

Remove any metal rings, wire twist ties, or foil wrapping from package. Place chicken in package in microproof baking dish. Place in oven. Set recipe number 284. Touch START. *(Oven defrosts: micro, 30, 7 minutes.)*

At Pause, turn parts over and separate. If wing and leg tips begin to cook before centers are thoroughly defrosted, cover with small strips of aluminum foil, keeping foil at least 1 inch away from oven walls. Touch START. *(Oven defrosts: micro, 30, 5 minutes; stands: 0, 10 minutes.)*

⊞ Recipe can be increased. See "Quantity", page 12.

Recipe No. | 285 |

Whole Chicken

Preset Defrost Time: 28 minutes

1 frozen whole chicken
(3 pounds)

Remove any metal rings, wire twist ties, or foil wrapping from package. Place chicken in package in microproof baking dish. Place in oven. Set recipe number 285. Touch START. *(Oven defrosts: micro, 30, 9 minutes.)*

At Pause, turn chicken over. Touch START. *(Oven defrosts: micro, 30, 9 minutes; stands: 0, 10 minutes.)*

Recipe No. | 286 | ⊞

Fish Fillets

Preset Defrost Time: 11 minutes

1 pound frozen fish fillets

Remove any metal rings, wire twist ties, or foil wrapping from package. Place fillets in package in microproof baking dish. Place in oven. Set recipe number 286. Touch START. *(Oven defrosts: micro, 30, 4 minutes.)*

At Pause, turn fillets over and separate. Touch START. *(Oven defrosts: micro, 30, 2 minutes; stands: 0, 5 minutes.)*

Recipe No. | 287 | ⊞

Whole Fish

Preset Defrost Time: 11 minutes

1 frozen fish (10 ounces)

Remove any metal rings, wire twist ties, or foil wrapping from package. Place fish in package in shallow microproof baking dish. Place in oven. Cover head with aluminum foil. Set recipe number 287. Touch START. *(Oven defrosts: micro, 30, 4 minutes.)*

At Pause, turn over. Touch START. *(Oven defrosts: micro, 30, 2 minutes; stands: 0, 5 minutes.)*

*Frozen vegetables (page 207) can be thawed and cooked right in the package. Many →
other frozen foods can be placed right on a serving plate and thawed and cooked.*

Recipe No. 288 ⊞

Crab Meat

Preset Defrost Time: 7 minutes

1 package (6 ounces) frozen
  crabmeat

Remove any metal rings, wire twist ties, or foil wrapping from package. Place crab meat in package in microproof baking dish. Place in oven. Set recipe number 288. Touch START. *(Oven defrosts: micro, 30, 1 minute.)*

At Pause, turn crab meat over and separate. Touch START. *(Oven defrosts: micro, 30, 1 minute; stands: 0, 5 minutes.)*

Recipe No. 290 ⊞

Bread, Rolls

Preset Defrost Time: 2 minutes

1 loaf (1 pound) frozen bread,
  or 1 pound frozen rolls

Remove any metal rings, wire twist ties, or foil wrapping from package. Place bread in package in oven. Set recipe number 290. Touch START. *(Oven defrosts: micro, 30, 1 minute.)*

At Pause, turn over. Touch START. *(Oven defrosts: micro, 30, 1 minute.)*

Recipe No. 289 ⊞

Shrimp

Preset Defrost Time: 9 minutes

1 package (1 pound) frozen
  shrimp

Remove shrimp from package and spread in shallow microproof baking dish. Place in oven. Set recipe number 289. Touch START. *(Oven defrosts: micro, 30, 2 minutes.)*

At Pause, rearrange shrimp. Touch START. *(Oven defrosts: micro, 30, 2 minutes; stands: 0, 5 minutes.)*

Recipe No. 291 ⊞

Vegetables in Sauce

Preset Defrost/Cooking Time: 10 minutes

1 package (10 ounces) frozen vegetables
  in sauce

Slit pouch and place on microproof plate. Place in oven. Set recipe number 291. Touch START. *(Oven defrosts: micro, 70, 5 minutes.)*

At Pause, turn over. Touch START. *(Oven cooks: micro, 70, 5 minutes.)*

Pour into serving bowl, and stir before serving.

⊞ *Recipe can be increased. See "Quantity", page 12.*

Recipe No. ☐ 292 ☐ ⊞

Broccoli, Carrots, Cauliflower

Preset Defrost/Cooking Time: 8 minutes

1 package (10 ounces) frozen broccoli, carrots, or cauliflower

Place vegetables in package on microproof plate. Place in oven. Set recipe number 292. Touch START. *(Oven defrosts/cooks: micro, HI, 8 minutes.)*

Pour into serving bowl, and stir before serving.

Recipe No. ☐ 293 ☐ ⊞

Green Peas

Preset Defrost/Cooking Time: 6 minutes

1 package (10 ounces) frozen green peas

Place peas in package on microproof plate. Place in oven. Set recipe number 293. Touch START. *(Oven defrosts/cooks: micro, HI, 6 minutes.)*

Pour into serving bowl, and stir before serving.

Recipe No. ☐ 294 ☐ ⊞

Spinach

Preset Defrost/Cooking Time: 7 minutes

1 package (10 ounces) frozen spinach

Place spinach in package on microproof plate. Place in oven. Set recipe number 294. Touch START. *(Oven defrosts/cooks: micro, HI, 7 minutes.)*

Let stand 2 minutes before serving.

Recipe No. ☐ 295 ☐ ⊞

Brownies and other frozen bar cookies

Preset Defrost/Cooking Time: 2 minutes

1 package (12 ounces) frozen brownies or other bar cookies

Remove lid from tray and place in oven. Set recipe number 295. Touch START. *(Oven defrosts: micro, 30, 2 minutes.)*

Let stand 5 minutes before serving.

⊞ *Recipe can be increased. See "Quantity", page 12.*

REMINDER

Additional defrosting information is provided in the Use & Care Manual and in the following Guides:

Dinner's in the Oven!

Dinner's in the oven! Who doesn't look forward to hearing this familiar saying as mealtime approaches? You'll find that just as in conventional cooking you can prepare a whole two- or three-dish meal at the same time in your microwave oven. For the most successful whole meal, it is important to consider the placement of dishes in the oven, the size and shape of the microproof containers, the kinds of food you select, the timing, and the sequence of cooking. This chapter provides you with all the necessary information and step-by-step instructions for organizing your own whole meals. Start by reading the following basic tips on how to approach whole meal planning:

☐ Since microwaves enter from the top of the oven, they are primarily attracted to food placed on the wire rack; a smaller amount reaches the ceramic tray. It is logical then to place delicate, quick-cooking food on the ceramic tray and longer cooking food on the wire rack.

☐ Whenever the wire rack is not being used, remove it from oven.

☐ An ideal procedure for whole-meal cooking is to place two foods with similar cooking times on the wire rack and one shorter-cooking food on the ceramic tray.

☐ If all foods require the same cooking time, reverse the location of dishes in the oven halfway through cooking period.

☐ While the wire rack can be used in two positions, the upper position is generally best. Use the lower position whenever greater capacity on the top is needed. This does limit the usable space below.

☐ Check your cooking dishes to be sure they will fit together on a shelf before filling with food.

☐ Often covers with knobs are too high to fit easily when the wire rack is used. Use plastic wrap instead of casserole lids when necessary.

☐ All whole-meal cooking is done on HI.

IMPORTANT GUIDELINES FOR TIMING AND PLANNING

☐ If all foods take less than 15 minutes individually, add cooking times together and program the menu for the total time.

☐ If all foods take 15 to 35 minutes individually, add cooking times together and subtract about 5 minutes.

☐ If any one food takes over 35 minutes, all the food can be cooked in the time suggested for food taking the longest time.

← *Seasoned Pork Chops, Parsley Potatoes and Mixed Vegetables cooked all at once in the oven.*

The following chart presents six main dishes appearing in the recipe chapters and 12 complementary dishes. There's no need to keep with the particular combinations we've provided. Simply choose any dish from column "A" and complete the menu with any "B" and any "C".

1. Choose a menu from the chart.
2. Review the individual recipe. You may find that an ingredient should be prepared ahead. (Onion is often sautéed as a separate step, for example).
3. Check the dishes to be sure they fit in the oven together. Change the size and type of dish as required. *Be sure you are always thinking microproof.*
4. Place dishes in oven with food from column "A" on the wire rack (it is the most dense and needs to receive the most microwave energy); "B" and "C" are placed on the ceramic tray.
5. Apply the rules in "Important Guidelines for Timing." The approximate cooking time for each recipe follows the recipe title in the menu chart.
6. Most recipes in whole-meal cooking are best stirred or rearranged halfway through cooking time.

A	B	C
One-Step Lasagna (37) (page 91)	Brussels Sprouts (9) (page 147)	Parsley New Potatoes (12) (page 165)
Beef Shanghai (9) (page 92)	Green Beans Amandine (9) (page 164)	Pudding Mix (7) (page 199)
All-American Meatballs (20) (page 91)	Cauliflower (11) (page 161)	All-Seasons Rice (17) (page 151)
Salmon Ring (12) (page 133)	Stuffed Tomatoes (18) (page 155)	Golden Apple Chunks (8) (page 198)
Shrimp Veracruz (12) (page 127)	Carrots (10) (page 160)	Fluffy Tapioca (16) (page 198)

Now let's take a step-by-step look at the All-American menu:

(A) All-American Meatballs
     (page 91) .... 20 minutes
(B) Cauliflower
     (page 161) ..... 11 minutes
(C) Golden Apple Chunks
     (page 198) ..... 8 minutes

Note that one recipe takes longer than 15 minutes. Using the "Guidelines" (page 209), this meal will cook in 34 minutes.

1. Refer to the photograph as a guide to selection of the dishes.

2. Prepare the All-American Meatballs according to the recipe; omit the cornstarch and water at this time. Cover and set aside.

3. Prepare Cauliflower, adding one tomato, cut in quarters.
4. Prepare Golden Apple Chunks, adding 2 peach halves and 4 whole maraschino cherries.
5. Place wire rack in oven. Place meatballs on rack. Place cauliflower dish and fruit dish on ceramic tray. Cook, micro, HI 34 minutes. After 10 minutes stir cornstarch and water into meatballs and cover.
6. Remove dishes from oven and let stand, covered, on heat-resistant surface for 5 minutes.

Special Techniques

This special method uses microwave, HI, for approximately half of the cooking time and micro/convection for the balance. Microwave speed gets it started; micro/convection provides texture and browning. The menu:

Barbecued Chicken
    (page 114) ..... 30 minutes
Baked Potatoes, 4 medium,
    (Guide, page 148) 14 minutes
Broccoli, 1 pound,
    (Guide, page 147) 11 minutes

1. Timing for this menu has been tested and programmed for you.
2. Note dish selection and placement in the photograph.
3. Prepare chicken according to directions in the recipe.
4. Scrub and pierce potatoes. Set aside. Clean broccoli, split stems, arrange in 1½-quart casserole. Cover with plastic wrap.
5. Place chicken, potatoes and broccoli in oven. Cook, micro, on HI, 25 minutes.

6. Remove chicken and broccoli from oven. Let broccoli stand, covered. Remove wire rack. Rearrange potatoes, placing two at extreme left and two at extreme right. Preheat oven to 330°F.
7. Turn chicken over (skin-side-up). Brush liberally with Barbecue Sauce. Return to preheated 330°F oven, placing chicken dish between potatoes. Cook, micro/convec, at 330°F, 20 to 25 minutes or until chicken is done.
8. Remove chicken from oven; let stand. Check potatoes for doneness; they may need a few additional minutes of cooking, on micro, HI.
9. Discard plastic wrap from broccoli. Return to oven and cook, micro, on HI 1 to 1½ minutes or until hot. Serve.

Have you ever been truly frustrated because there's a gorgeous steak in the freezer but you got home late and don't have time to thaw it? The next page presents a whole meal using micro/convection from start to finish that can erase a traffic jam in a hurry.

2   small potatoes (9 ounces), peeled
    and quartered
1   tablespoon butter or margarine
1   package (10 ounces) frozen peas
1½ pounds sirloin steak, frozen
    (T-bone or Porterhouse may be
    substituted)

1. Place potatoes and butter in 1-
    quart flat glass or ceramic cas-
    serole. Cover; set on ceramic
    tray. Remove peas from carton
    and place in separate 1-quart
    glass or ceramic casserole.
    Cover; set on ceramic tray.
    Position wire rack in upper guides

and preheat to 450°F. (Potatoes
and peas remain in oven during
preheating.)

2. Trim excess fat from frozen steak,
    using sharp knife. Place steak in
    shallow glass or ceramic baking
    dish just large enough to accom-
    modate meat.

3. Place steak on wire rack and
    cook (micro/convec) at 450°F 5
    minutes for rare, 7 minutes for
    medium, or 9 minutes for well
    done.

4. Serve steak, potatoes, and peas.
    Steak drippings are a fine gravy
    for the potatoes if fat has been
    well-trimmed.

As you continue to enjoy
micro/convection cook-
ing, you'll discover many
time-saving whole meal
techniques on your own.
Simply remember that
the convection method
is similar to your conventional oven, that the mi-
cro/convection method
gives convection bene-
fits with microwave
energy, and that the
microwave method uses
the "Guidelines" on
page 186. Now, here are
our seven preset Whole
Meals for extra conven-
ience.

← *Barbecued Chicken Dinner,
Whole Meal Directions (page
211)*

Recipe No. | 296 |

Scrambled Eggs, Bacon, and Sweet Rolls

Preset Cooking Time: 11½ minutes

6	large eggs
⅓	cup milk
2	tablespoons butter, melted
6	slices bacon
6	sweet rolls

Position wire rack in upper guides of oven. Combine eggs, milk, and butter in 1-quart microproof casserole; beat with fork until blended. Cover; set aside. Arrange bacon on paper towel-lined microproof plate. Cover with paper towel; set aside. Arrange rolls on microproof plate; set aside. Arrange egg mixture and bacon in oven as shown in "A." Set recipe number 296. Touch START. *(Oven cooks: micro, HI, 4 minutes.)*

At Pause, stir eggs. Cover. Touch START. *(Oven cooks: micro, HI, 3½ minutes.)*

At Pause, remove eggs from oven. Stir. Cover. Set aside. Add rolls as shown in "B." Touch START. *(Oven cooks: micro, HI, 1 minute; stands: 0, 3 minutes.)*

4 to 6 servings

Recipe No. | 297 |

Beef Stew, Garlic Bread, and Pudding

Preset Cooking Time: 13 minutes

1	can (24 ounces) beef stew
¼	cup butter, melted
½	teaspoon garlic powder
½	pound French bread, cut into 1-inch thick slices
1	package (3¼ ounces) pudding mix
2	cups milk

Position wire rack in upper guides of oven. Pour stew into 1-quart microproof casserole. Cover; set aside. Combine butter and garlic powder. Brush both sides of bread slices with butter mixture. Reshape into loaf and wrap in paper towels. Place on microproof plate; set aside. Place pudding mix in 1-quart microproof casserole. Stir in milk; set aside. Arrange stew and pudding mixture in oven as shown in "A." Set recipe number 297. Touch START. *(Oven cooks: micro, HI, 5 minutes.)*

At Pause, stir stew and pudding. Cover stew. Touch START. *(Oven cooks: micro, HI, 3½ minutes.)*

At Pause, stir pudding. Place bread in oven as shown in "B." Touch START. *(Oven cooks: micro, HI, 4½ minutes.)*

3 servings

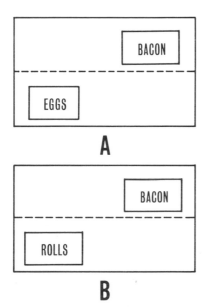

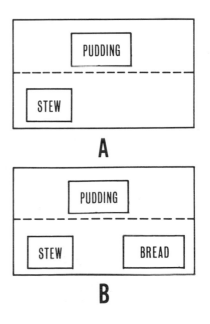

Recipe No. | 297 | Alternate

Chili, Corn Muffins, and Apple Crisp

Preset Cooking Time: 13 minutes

- 1 can (24 ounces) chili
- 3 corn muffins
- 1 recipe Apple Crisp (below)

Position wire rack in upper guides of oven. Pour chili into 1½-quart microproof casserole. Cover; set aside. Wrap corn muffins in paper towels; set aside. Prepare Apple Crisp as directed below. Cover with waxed paper. Arrange chili and Apple Crisp in oven as shown in "A." Set recipe number 297. Touch START. *(Oven cooks: micro, HI, 5 minutes.)*

At Pause, stir chili. Cover. Change position of dishes as shown in "B." Touch START. *(Oven cooks: micro, HI, 3½ minutes.)*

At Pause, stir chili. Cover. Place muffins in oven as shown in "C." Touch START. *(Oven cooks: micro, HI, 4½ minutes.)*

Let Apple Crisp stand 3 minutes before serving.

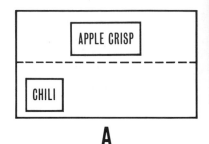

A

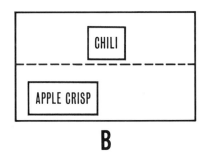

B

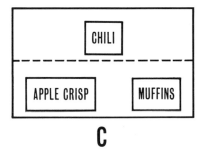

C

Apple Crisp

- 4 cups sliced tart apples
- ½ cup rolled oats
- ¼ cup butter or margarine
- ¼ cup all-purpose flour
- ¼ cup firmly-packed brown sugar
- 1 teaspoon lemon juice
- ½ teaspoon cinnamon
- ⅛ teaspoon nutmeg

Arrange apple slices in 8-inch square microproof baking dish. Combine remaining ingredients; blend well. Crumble over apples.

Recipe No. 298

Baked Chicken, Rice, and Asparagus

Preset Cooking Time: 26 minutes

- ¾ cup corn-flake crumbs
- ⅓ cup grated Parmesan cheese
- 1 broiler-fryer chicken (2½ to 3 pounds), quartered
- ¼ cup butter, melted
- 1 package (11 ounces) frozen rice in pouch
- 2 cans (14½ ounces each) asparagus spears, drained

Position wire rack in upper guides of oven. Combine corn-flake crumbs and Parmesan cheese. Brush chicken lightly with butter; coat with crumb mixture. Arrange chicken in large microproof baking dish, skin-side up, with thickest parts toward outside of dish. Cover with waxed paper; set aside. Place rice in pouch on small microproof plate; slit pouch; set aside. Place asparagus in 8 × 4-inch microproof loaf pan. Cover lightly with plastic wrap. Arrange all 3 dishes in oven as shown in "A." Set recipe number 298. Touch START. *(Oven cooks: micro, HI, 10 minutes.)*

At Pause, rotate chicken dish one-half turn. Touch START. *(Oven cooks: micro, HI, 10 minutes.)*

At Pause, rotate rice one-quarter turn. Touch START. *(Oven cooks: micro, HI, 4 minutes.)*

At Pause, remove chicken and asparagus from oven. Rotate rice as shown in "B." Touch START. *(Oven cooks: micro, HI, 2 minutes.)*

3 to 4 servings

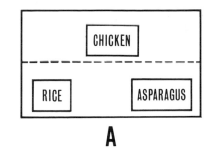

A

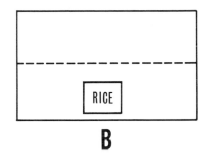

B

Recipe No. | 298 | Alternate

Seasoned Pork Chops, Parsley Potatoes, and Mixed Vegetables

Preset Cooking Time: 26 minutes

- 1 envelope (2¼ ounces) seasoned coating mix for pork
- 4 pork chops (1¼ pounds)
- 3 potatoes (5 ounces each), peeled and cut into ¾-inch cubes
- ¼ cup water
- 1 can (16 ounces) mixed vegetables, drained
    Butter or margarine
- 1 tablespoon chopped parsley

Position wire rack in upper guides of oven. Empty coating mix into plastic bag. Shake pork chops, one at a time, in coating mix. Place chops in 12×7-inch microproof baking dish. Cover with waxed paper; set aside. Place potatoes and water in 8×4-inch microproof loaf pan. Cover with plastic wrap; set aside. Place mixed vegetables in 1-quart microproof casserole. Arrange all 3 dishes in oven as shown in "A." Set recipe number 298. Touch START. *(Oven cooks: micro, HI, 10 minutes.)*

At Pause, rotate pork dish one-half turn. Touch START. *(Oven cooks: micro, HI, 10 minutes.)*

At Pause, stir potatoes. Cover. Touch START. *(Oven cooks: micro, HI, 4 minutes.)*

At Pause, check pork chops. If done, remove from oven. Touch START. *(Oven cooks: micro, HI, 2 minutes.)*

Remove all dishes from oven. Stir vegetables. Dot potatoes with butter, and sprinkle with parsley before serving.

3 to 4 servings

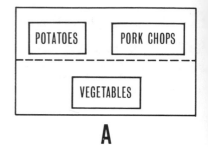

A

Recipe No. 299

Beef & Spaghetti Casserole, Green Peas,and Baked Apple Chunks

Preset Cooking Time: 30 minutes

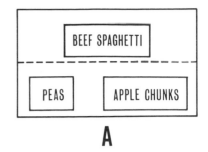

A

- 1 package (7½ ounces) spaghetti meat-noodle main dish mix
- 1 pound lean ground beef
- 4 cups hot water
- 1 package (10 ounces) frozen green peas
- 1 recipe Baked Apple Chunks (below)

Position wire rack in upper guides of oven. Prepare meat-noodle mix, adding beef and hot water as directed on package. Place in 2-quart microproof casserole. Cover; set aside. Place peas in 1-quart microproof casserole. Cover; set aside. Prepare Baked Apple Chunks as directed below. Arrange dishes in oven as shown in "A." Set recipe number 299. Touch START. *(Oven cooks: micro, HI, 20 minutes.)*

At Pause, stir beef mixture and Baked Apple Chunks. Cover both casseroles. Touch START. *(Oven cooks: micro, HI, 5 minutes; stands: 0, 5 minutes.)*

4 servings

Baked Apple Chunks

- 4 medium-size tart cooking apples, peeled, cored, and cut into quarters
- ¼ cup firmly-packed brown sugar
- 1 teaspoon cinnamon
- 2 tablespoons butter or margarine

Place apples in 8 × 4-inch microproof loaf pan. Combine brown sugar and cinnamon; blend well. Crumble over apples. Dot with butter.

Recipe No. ☐ 300 ☐

Meatloaf, Yellow Squash, and Chocolate Fudge Layer Cake

Preset Cooking Time: 23 minutes

- 1 recipe Meatloaf (below)
- 1 recipe Chocolate Fudge Layer Cake (below)
- 1 medium yellow squash, peeled and thinly sliced
- 1 tablespoon butter
- ¼ teaspoon salt
  Whipped cream

Position wire rack in upper guides of oven. Prepare Meatloaf and Chocolate Fudge Layer Cake as directed below; set aside. Place squash in 8 × 4-inch microproof loaf pan. Cover with plastic wrap. Arrange all 3 dishes in oven as shown in "A." Set recipe number 300. Touch START. *(Oven cooks: micro, HI, 15 minutes.)*

At Pause, rotate meatloaf and cake dishes one-half turn. Stir squash; cover. Touch START. *(Oven cooks: micro, HI, 7 minutes.)*

At Pause, insert toothpick into cake. If toothpick comes out clean, remove cake from oven. Touch START. *(Oven cooks: micro, HI, 1 minute.)*

Stir butter and salt into squash. Let cake stand 3 to 5 minutes. Gently twist glass to remove. Invert cake onto serving plate. Remove waxed paper. Slice and serve topped with whipped cream.

6 servings

Meatloaf

- 1½ pounds lean ground beef
- 2 cups soft bread crumbs
- 1 can (8 ounces) tomato sauce, divided
- ½ cup finely chopped onions
- ¼ cup finely chopped green pepper
- 1 large egg
- 1½ teaspoons salt

Combine beef, bread crumbs, ½ cup tomato sauce, onion, green pepper, egg, and salt; blend well. Pack into 8-inch round microproof baking dish. Insert straight-sided, 2-inch diameter glass, open end up, into center of dish. Pour remaining sauce over beef mixture.

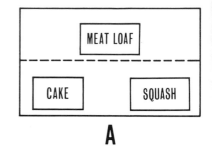

A

Chocolate Fudge Layer Cake

- 1 package (15 ounces) snacking chocolate fudge cake mix

Prepare cake batter as directed on package. Line bottom of 9-inch round microproof baking dish with waxed paper. Place straight-sided, 2-inch diameter glass, open end up, in center of dish. Pour batter into dish.

A 6-cup microproof Bundt-type pan or ring mold can be substituted for baking dish with glass.

INDEX